Writers & Thinkers

Writers & Thinkers

Selected Literary Criticism

Daniel Fuchs

Transaction Publishers
New Brunswick (U.S.A.) and London (U.K.)

This book is printed on acid-free paper that meets the American National Standard for Permanence of Paper for Printed Library Materials.

Library of Congress Catalog Number: 2015008390
ISBN: 978-1-4128-5691-1 (cloth); 978-1-4128-6266-0 (paper)
eBook: 978-1-4128-5658-4
Printed in the United States of America

Library of Congress Cataloging-in-Publication Data

Fuchs, Daniel, 1934-
    Writers and thinkers : selected literary criticism / Daniel Fuchs.
    pages cm
    Includes bibliographical references.
    ISBN 978-1-4128-5691-1 (acid-free paper) 1. Criticism. 2. Literature--
Philosophy. 3. Literature--History and criticism--Theory, etc. I. Title.
    PN85.F83 2016
    801'.95--dc23
                                                                    2015008390

To Andrew, Natasha, Susannah

Contents

Preface

Literary critics are sometimes asked to explain the kind of criticism they write. This is one such occasion. Though I have never been particularly concerned with methodology, my interest is in the character of the writer, in the illumination of the salient details of what he wrote, and in related problems of cultural definition. These essays are written in a Morningside Heights style.

This kind of criticism has had two tendencies, public and scholarly, with some of the critics in between or, as the case may be, moving with relative ease from one to another. The New York intellectuals in their heyday of the forties, fifties, and first half of the sixties were later thought of as public intellectuals, meaning, for one thing, that they addressed public issues that came within their intellectual purview. (I use this term neutrally and not as an honorific of left politics). This tag is somewhat exaggerated since many of them could be quite scholarly in their writing. Broadly speaking, these two tendencies in the critic can be traced back to Matthew Arnold. Lionel Trilling, the leading literary figure of this group, if it was a group, was a public intellectual in some of his writing, but one could argue that his two best books (as a critic he wrote only three books as such, plus, of course, the influential collections of essays) were the biographical *Matthew Arnold* and *Sincerity and Authenticity*. These two books were addressed to an academic audience. *The Liberal Imagination* is often taken to be typical of the public intellectual and certainly is in the essay on *The Kinsey Report* about a current issue, a current event, as it were. But "The Meaning of a Literary Idea," which shows what the consequences are when writers cannot "think," is directed toward an aesthetic problem more deeply anchored in time and consequently to a learned audience. This essay too is "public" in that it addresses an exigent literary problem from a general perspective in an accessible style, but it is public in a different sense. In any case, how public can literary criticism get? There will never be a statue to a critic—certainly not in America.

The dual aspect of Trilling's criticism is reflected in two of his prominent students, Norman Podhoretz and Steven Marcus. Podhoretz's criticism has the urgency of a bulletin, as Richard Poirier has said, whereas Marcus's has the scholarly depth more often associated with Trilling. The essays in this book, with the exception of the journalistic account of the Bellow/Grass Confrontation, are in the second line of development, essays in scholarly criticism, overlapping at points into cultural history in the sense of intellectual history. In the introduction to my recent book, *The Limits of Ferocity: Sexual Aggression and Modern Literary Rebellion*,[1] I wrote that "this study is directed to an informed audience, though I do not wish to reach only the happy few who can spell Krafft-Ebing" (a line which somehow fell through the minor editorial cracks and did not appear in the book). The essays in *Writers and Thinkers* are also directed to an informed audience. It includes, therefore, not only "litry chaps" (critics, professors, students of literature, reviewers, editors) but philosophers, historians, social scientists, psychoanalysts, cultivated lawyers and others with a literary bent.

Criticism like this has its historical origins in what M.H. Abrams considers expressive theory. That is, the romantic switch in cultural icons toward the end of the eighteenth century from the mirror to the lamp, from literature as an imitation of nature to literature as an expression of subjectivity, is the beginning. The depth of the writer's feeling, his conscious, and in the modern period, his unconscious intentions, the unique quality of his imagination become the focus of criticism. In dealing with language as cultural and psychological analysis, the New York or, as the case often was, the Columbia style of criticism was extrinsic and ran in a contrary direction to formalist or intrinsic criticism, most notably the New Criticism of the postwar period. The aim was to get at the essence of the writer by defining the point where motivation and inspiration met. The idea was to get at the writer's heart and mind, to capture the moment when thought and feeling became one.

There were various formalisms. I can recall a conversation in Trilling's office at Columbia in the late fifties where he was inveighing against the then popular reader's guides, which he called "absurd." (His book on E.M. Forster, though, might qualify). Though he did not name him, he had in mind a critic like William York Tindall, who was thriving on such guides. Trilling's assumption was that cultural criticism was an in-depth experience and that reader's guides were obvious. Aware of this sort of judgment, Tindall, a Yeats as well as a Joyce scholar, had a comeback: "That's what you see the fellows at *Partisan Review* doing, 'studying monuments of their own magnificence.'" So went the battle between intrinsic and extrinsic, Columbia style. A related instance occurred during a conversation with Wayne Booth after an English Institute session at Columbia. Booth had taken it upon himself to defend Chicago Aristotelianism (which he did not have to do since his own criticism goes beyond it). His presentation drew considerable flack. When I stood up for New York criticism at lunch, he stuck to his guns: "Criticism isn't brilliant conversation that dissipates once the meal is done." Criticism had to have a solidity based on formal considerations.

The essays in this book, though primarily extrinsic, give due attention to artistic particularity. They are detailed but not formalist, focusing rather on how the particulars illustrate cultural and psychological realities. They are, in this sense, thematic. They are cultural criticism with no political program (the latter being cultural criticism in the English sense, since Raymond Williams—Frank Kermode is the most notable exception). I do think image, symbol, setting, character, narrative voice, selectively considered, are indispensible to the essential patterning of a work and that the critic should not forget this patterning. *Writers and Thinkers* is a collection of essays, but given the alternative space of a book on a single subject, I think that establishing the detailed relation of significant pattern to the primary ground of personal and cultural motive is even more important. D.J. Enright, in a *Times Literary Supplement* review of my Bellow book, said that my only fault as a critic was that I explained too much. Though I side with cultural criticism, I have often observed in it a shortcoming, a sort of condescension in actually referring to the particulars of an art work, or even to the work at all. To me, the critic is somewhat analogous to the conductor of an orchestra: the reader often responds to the critic's ability to illuminate detail, to generate the drama of particulars. To this extent I am sympathetic to the close reading or practical criticism enterprise.

I am not sympathetic to the deconstructionists, to the tendency, reinforced by the Foucauldians, to present criticism as power struggle, literature as social construct. The intrusion of power relations as the primary critical desideratum negates the autonomy of the writer, which, for all our modern awareness of influences cultural and psychological, still exists. This intrusion necessarily reverses the trajectory—not to say progress—of criticism since Hazlitt as well. The essays in this book assume that the writer is the primary authority in his work and that what motivates or inspires him, together with the resultant art work, is the primary task of the critic to elucidate. The so-called death of the writer derives from a political determinism. No humanist could believe it. Philip Roth has remarked about a conference on his work he attended in France. A sophisticated observer and especially knowledgeable on the subject, Roth could not understand a word that was spoken. One can well imagine what power-defining abstractions were being substituted for the heart—and mind—of the matter. This incident stands as an indictment of a criticism separated from the writer. Writers write about what matters deeply, personally, difficult though this may be to express. The struggle to articulate is another name for thought—not logic to be sure, but thought nonetheless.

The writer thinks of himself as a unified subject, which, say, to the parlor Marxist (Irving Howe's expression) was an illusory class-specific notion, a bourgeois notion, waiting for the desiccation of deconstruction. This is the "subject" both are trying to decenter, the merely social "product" of a higher materialistic determinism. All of which will establish a collective radical culture. Narrative may be radically redefined as fragmentary, spectacular. Sade is canonized. Autonomous subjectivity, realism, humanism, are relics of a bourgeois past. I deny their major.

The essays herein embody in their own way the values deconstruction denounces, assuming the unity of the beleaguered subject, the personal depth of the writer and the corresponding acuity of the critic, who, in his better moments at least, reflects the "perception at the pitch of passion and expression as embracing as the air" that Henry James talks about. These essays assume, they tacitly posit, the reality of the individual writer's feeling *and* his thought, and, further, the fruitful integration of the two, even to the extent of the tandem essay (e.g., "Saul Bellow and the Example of Dostoevsky"), an essay comparing two focuses. Literature itself, then, becomes a way of asserting value judgments, of attempting to create a morally as well as an aesthetically coherent universe. The novel itself may become a form of criticism. "Novelists are often our best critics and nowhere more so than in the novel itself" begins my book on Bellow.[2]

What follows is a summary of the essays in this book, which sometimes uses direct quotation from them. Narcissus as Narcissus, perhaps. But the occasion demands. The first essay, "Ernest Hemingway, Literary Critic," points to a quality of mind of a writer ridiculed by Wyndham Lewis as "the dumb ox." The essay goes beyond thinking of "idea" as his typical confrontations, his dilemmas and resolutions, the topography of his fictional world—though, of course, it includes that—to a more nearly speculative function in which a particular prose or literary position or artist's reputation is under scrutiny, whether as direct comment or tangential remark. Hemingway can be seen as a literary compeer of Cervantes, Fielding, Mark Twain and others.

The essay on "Stevens and Santayana" speaks once again of the affinity between literature and ideas, in this case going the further step to philosophy itself. The exploration of thematic and imagistic influence is necessarily complex. Santayana's philosophy is poetic in itself, bringing with it a general imaginative coherence: philosophy as the art of thinking not the science of thought, vision more than argument. Santayana has said, "It is only when philosophy is good literature that it is good for anything."[3] It is no accident that Santayana is an excellent literary critic. This essay comes as an addition to my book, *The Comic Spirit of Wallace Stevens*,[4] which shows, as Leslie Fiedler remarked, that Stevens can be seen as a Nietzchean dandy. It is a young man's book, written mostly in my twenty-fourth year, and readers were more impressed with the first half of the book, the comic part, than the subsequent more philosophical half. So this essay tries to address that problem, to deal more justly with questions of idealization. [The Stevens book required the addition of a subtitle: *An Aspect of the Poet's Mind.* Similarly, Jonathan Wilson called the Bellow book, "By far the best account of Bellow as a mind," both descriptions suggesting as well that there were things the books did not do. *The Limits of Ferocity,* my third book, was literary and psychoanalytic about a postwar American mind shift. The deliberate ambiguity in the title of *Writers and Thinkers*—writers *and* thinkers, writers *as* thinkers—reflects this critical *gestalt.*]

Writers and Thinkers is broadly unified in this integration of literature and ideas but, historically speaking, the essays reflect a progression. The first two essays deal with high modernism; the essays that follow them deal essentially with the "contemporary." Hemingway and Stevens in different ways present a critique of tradition, a world of collapsing values and consequent means of expression. Hemingway's route is dark, drawn to nihilism (which it does not always resist), destructive of moral abstraction, drawn to a nocturnal anxiety. Stevens generally enters in broad daylight, defining change as either more in the nature of things or something that needs irreverent pressure to emerge as something better than what he calls "the rhetorical once." Stevens is pressured by boredom, not suicide. The contemporary essays deal with the redefinition of tradition, even the reconstitution of moral abstraction or at least the desire for its viability, certainly in Bellow and Malamud. Roth can be treated as a postmodernist in some of his work, but the power of his later fiction places Roth in a much more sympathetic relation to realistic tradition. The contemporary essays are mainly about American Jewish writers and their cultural impact after modernism.

The essay on "Bellow and Dostoevsky" shows how the contemporary can be influenced by the modern or, as Dostoevsky's work is sometimes called, premodern. Dostoevsky is a modern who clings firmly to aspects of tradition. In *Notes from Underground*, he establishes the genre of ideological comedy. For Bellow and Dostoevsky, the world that we know is in good measure a world of ideas, positions, solutions. Arnold Hauser rightly calls Dostoevsky "a romantic in the world of thought" in that in him the movement of thought has the same motive power and the same emotional, not to say pathological, impetus as "the flood and stress of feelings had in the romantics."[5] Bellow makes this lyricism of ideas his own. Underlying this way of dramatizing ideas in Dostoevsky's case is the strong affinity Bellow feels for the ideas themselves.

Not so with the essay on "Bellow and Freud." Here Bellow reacts to what he takes to be a modernistic determinism. At the same time, he is taken by Freud's imagination. Few thinkers have had more to do with "vision" than Freud, few novelists more to do with the meaning and emotional content of ideas than Bellow. Freud saw all systems of thought, including his own, as mythology. And the Bellow protagonist often breathes in what Bellow in his theatrical spoof of Freud calls "an environment of Ideas."[6] Ever the writer, Bellow sees the Freudian world in terms of "metaphors," as he sees all of philosophy from the point of view of imagination.

The Bellow/Grass essay is the only essay in the group that is journalistic—albeit journalism written by a cultural critic—an analysis of an event. It is concerned with the relationship between literature and politics, even actual politics, as the PEN Congress itself was, and points to the threats that politics may pose for literary creation.

The next two essays analyze single works. The essay on Malamud's *Dubin's Lives* sets the Jewish ethic up against the sexual one, a strategy to comment on the novel's very mixed results. Bellow's *More Die of Heartbreak* shows again that it may be hard to critique a Bellow work without writing cultural criticism. So many of his anxious protagonists are also thinkers. Once again Bellow depicts a world in which sex is more prominent than love, the detritus of a failed view. Once again this is presented with farcical overtones. Poe, Freud, Kojève, Blake—all vivify the frame of reference of our professor narrator. The process of cultural dehumanization given here makes him sound like one of the apocalyptic types Bellow used to ridicule.

"Identity and the Postwar Temper in American Jewish Fiction" is a brief literary history of the cultural significance of some distinguished writers. It shows the self becoming the soul in Bellow and Malamud, but with the reaching for individual awareness more than transcendent connection or belief. There is the dramatization of a plausible moral positivity, with due deference even to moral abstraction, a Jewish anti-Modernist trope. "The Holocaust and History in Bellow and Malamud" integrates the idea of narrative with the idea of history. This too is an adventure in cultural definition, which includes an attempt to define American Jewish sensibility and its role in postwar consciousness.

With the exception of the first essay in the collection, all of these essays were solicited either as lectures, as part of a special issue in a scholarly or literary quarterly or critical collection in a book, or both. In every case, the request elicited an essay that was in me, so to speak, that I really wanted to write.

The acknowledgements refer to the first presentation and/or publication of the essays as they appear in this book. I am grateful for permission to use them in this context. "Ernest Hemingway, Literary Critic," *American Literature* 36 (January 1965): 431–451; "Wallace Stevens and Santayana," *Patterns of Commitment in American Literature*. Ed. Marston

La France. University of Toronto Press, 1967: 135-164; "Saul Bellow and the Example of Dostoevsky," Principal lecture, Austrian American Studies Association, Schloss Leopoldskron, Salzburg, Austria, October 1975. *The Stoic Strain in American Literature*. Ed. Duane MacMillan. University of Toronto Press, 1979: 151-176. With minor changes in *Saul Bellow: Vision and Revision*, Duke University Press, 1984: 28-49, and "Bellow and Freud" (with minor revision), *Studies in the Literary Imagination* 17 (Fall 1984): 59-80; "Literature and Politics: The Bellow/Grass Confrontation," Lecture, Saul Bellow International Conference, University of Haifa, Israel, April 1987. *Saul Bellow: A Mosaic*. Ed. L.H. Goldman, Gloria Cronin, Ada Aharoni, Peter Lang, 1992: 49-57; Lecture, "More Die of Heartbreak: The Question of Later Bellow," International Symposium: Saul Bellow at 75. Deutsch-amerikanisches Institut (DAI), Heidelberg (and the Fritz Thyssen Stiftung of Cologne) July 1990. *Saul Bellow Journal* 11 Fall 1992: 21-34; "Identity and the Postwar Temper in American Jewish Fiction," *A Concise Companion to Postwar American Literature and Culture*. Ed. Josephine Hendin. Oxford: Blackwell Publishing, 2004: 238-262; "The Holocaust and History in Bellow and Malamud," *Critical Insights: Saul Bellow*. Ed. Allan Chavkin, Salem Press, 2012: 69-88. Used by permission of EBSCO Information Services, Ipswich, MA.

In writing, I have for some time used two major New York libraries. I wish to acknowledge the helpfulness of the reference librarians at Columbia University's Butler Library and the New York Public Library. I wish to acknowledge as well my local reference librarian *extraordinaire*, Agnes Kolben. They made work on this book (and the others) easier. Most helpful of all have been my wife Cara, who was there at every turn, and our daughters and colleagues Margot and Sabrina.

Notes

1. Daniel Fuchs, *The Limits of Ferocity: Sexual Aggression and Modern Literary Rebellion* (Durham: Duke University Press, 2011).

2. Daniel Fuchs, *Saul Bellow: Vision and Revision* (Durham: Duke University Press, 1984).

3. Daniel Fuchs, "Wallace Stevens and Santayana," *Patterns of Commitment in American Literature*, ed. Marston La France. (University of Toronto Press, 1967), 158.

4. Daniel Fuchs, *The Comic Spirit of Wallace Stevens* (Durham: Duke University Press, 1963).

5. Quoted in Daniel Fuchs, *Saul Bellow: Vision and Revision*, 38.

6. Saul Bellow, *The Last Analysis* (New York: Viking, 1965), vii.

1

Ernest Hemingway, Literary Critic

I

Though the critics have found many things to praise in Hemingway, his mind was seldom one of them. Dwight Macdonald, in a funny if unoriginal essay, seems to express the consensus in saying that there is little evidence of thought in his writing, that for all his sureness of "instinct" as a writer, he strikes one as not particularly intelligent.[1] And Leslie Fiedler points to a pervasive humorlessness, a shortcoming of mind, in him as a writer.[2] If the critics have been sharks to Hemingway's Santiago, it is also a case of man bites shark. Who more proudly flaunted his contempt of them? Who was the first to make megalomania part of the novelist's personal style—as if critical intelligence were exercised only by those who live life all the way from the neck up? Yet Hemingway was a writer whose diction, whose tone, whose very existence as an artist imply a relationship with literary culture no less certain than that of the mythical New York beasts he excoriates.[3] I am not speaking of his characteristic literary ideas, his typical confrontations, his dilemmas and resolutions, the topography of his fictional world, about which much has been said, but of a more purely speculative function in which a particular prose or literary position or artist's reputation is under scrutiny, whether in direct comment or tangential remark. Though this is an admittedly bookish approach to Hemingway, it is one he has still to gain by, and the very fact that it can be congenial indicates a kind of resilience to his intelligence that is not often associated with it. He was a critic in spite of himself. What is more, he had a more than tacit commitment to a particular cast of literary mind which in terms of his own preferences constitutes a tradition; this commitment makes clear the extent and quality of his humor.

For all his one-time modernity, for all his appropriation of a unique style, for all his Bohemianism, Hemingway is in a literary tradition as old as the novel itself. If we are looking for illustrious forefathers we may go as far back as *Don Quixote*. Leicester Hemingway, in his biographical reminiscence, recalls the following: "Ernest said there had been some wonderful men in the recent human past. These included Cervantes, Cellini and the Elizabethans."[4] And in *Death In the Afternoon* Hemingway tells us that he has "cared for" Cervantes, one of the very few writers who wrote before the nineteenth century whom he has made a point of complimenting.[5] Another is Fielding. He seems to have known Fielding well and felt the presence of a somehow kindred spirit to the extent that he quotes parts of the preface to *Joseph Andrews* as introductory squibs in his parody of Anderson, *The Torrents of Spring*. More than this, Fielding is the only author on Hemingway's fullest list of "musts" for young writers who wrote before the nineteenth century.[6] Along with the expected works of Stendhal, Flaubert, Tolstoy, we find him singling out *Joseph Andrews* and *Tom Jones* as part of the novel's most distinguished pedigree. His preference for Fielding should not surprise us, since he sees the unheroic hero in the world of his imagining and consistently mistrusts the elevated, the mystical, the glorious, the grand. In attacking Waldo Frank's *Virgin Spain* as "bedside mysticism"[7] he makes a remark which all innovators of realistic fiction would applaud: "All bad writers are in love with the epic."[8] (The comic epic in prose is another thing.) Parody, mistrust of the heroic, Cervantes, Fielding. The point I wish to make in this essay is that Hemingway is in what may be called the novel in burlesque tradition—burlesque conceived in its broadest range of sense, from explicit parody to implicit criticism. Hemingway is one of those writers who would not have written so well had others not written so poorly or, as the case may be, so differently, one of those novelists for whom the novel has been, among other things, literary criticism. Flaubert, Joyce, Mark Twain—all of whom he held in the highest regard—are others. All of these gave a new meaning to the word realism.

Ezra Pound once remarked that Hemingway is preeminently the wiseguy,[9] and though Delmore Schwartz dismisses this as an extravagance, Pound is here, as he often is, profoundly right about a literary peer. Hemingway's prose is indeed motivated by a comic contempt of standard English in its aspect of respectability, gentility, polite euphemism, though it never forgets it in its aspect of biblical plainness and repetition. Furthermore, as we shall have occasion to see, his wiseguy intransigence is manifest so often in the way he builds a scene, conceives a character, projects a vision, that it, as much as anything else, marks his characteristic style. This is at the heart of his critical sense. When this is understood, Macdonald's remarks, say, about Hemingway's affinity to his "opposites . . . Stendhal and Tolstoi—interesting that he should feel awed by them—who had no style at all, no effects"—will be easily countered. For example, what writer could we associate more with the battle initiations of Fabrice del Dongo and Nickolai Rostov than Hemingway? Hemingway's joke, his *Kunst*, lies in showing that things as they really are are different from what they are like in story books and political speeches, that the writer's duty is to cut away the imaginative dead wood, that realism is so often, in Tolstoy's phrase, "making things strange," that the wiseguy can be the source of an unexpected, bracing wisdom. Hemingway's distinction as a writer is that he considered this insight not only as matter but as manner. Macdonald speaks of him as if his writing were separable from his mind, which may be the reason he finds so little intelligence in him.

Hemingway, in short, like Cervantes, Fielding, Stendhal, Flaubert, Mark Twain, and Joyce, writes what is in this sense an anti-literary literature. Like that of many of the modernists of the twenties, Hemingway's work was at first hardly considered literature at all. Reminiscing about the early Paris days, he considers "all of the stories back in the mail that came in through a slit in the saw mill door, with notes of rejection that would never call them stories, but always anecdotes, sketches, contes, etc."[10] The genteel American response to his work was typified by his parents. His mother (a reader of Walter Scott who named her summer place "Windemere") and father returned In Our Time and were "bewildered and shocked" by The Sun Also Rises.[11] One need only teach In Our Time to observe even now the curious mixture of reverence and confusion in response to it.

Hemingway did not write better prose than that which appears in the In Our Time sequence (he has, of course, done worse), and it is this prose which registers as clearly as any his wiseguy stance. "On the Quai at Smyrna," which is an introductory sketch, exhibits a tension between the comfortable, genteel English of the English captain who is narrator and the war experience which it cannot seem to contain. Listening to the dispossessed women, he says, "The strange thing was . . . [how] they screamed at that time." They would be "quieted" by the searchlight: "That always did the trick." The dead ones had to be "cleared off" the pier. One was a "most extraordinary case"—the one whose legs drew stiff. Where English is capable of recording the shock of war it is in a Gulliver-like recording of detail. The euphemism, the detachment of the captain's manner is painfully modified by what he actually sees. But the captain seems to be aware of the inability of his language to express his feelings. Hence his irony in describing the harbor: "There were plenty of nice things floating around in it. That was the only time in my life I got so I dreamed about things." In his nervous matter-of-factness the Englishman sounds like a grown-up Huck Finn. "The Greeks were nice chaps too. When they evacuated they had all their baggage animals they couldn't take with them so they just broke their forelegs and dumped them into the shallow water. . . . It was all a pleasant business. My word yes a most pleasant business." The final turn of the screw is that his casual, genteel manner explodes in his face as his intended irony becomes indistinguishable from it.

This opening sketch about the Greco-Turkish war is connected to the final vignette in which Hemingway, or a surrogate, is interviewing the Greek king. A tension exists between the grim realities of revolutionary politics and the inanities of genteel conversation. Perhaps the best example of this deflationary technique is the Chapter IV vignette.[12]

It was a frightfully hot day. We'd jammed an absolutely perfect barricade across the bridge. It was simply priceless. A big old wrought iron grating from the front of a house. Too heavy to lift and you could shoot through it and they would have to climb over it. It was absolutely topping. They tried to get over it, and we potted them from forty yards. They rushed it, and officers came out alone and worked on it. It was an absolutely perfect obstacle. Their officers were very fine. We were frightfully put out when we heard the flank had gone, and we had to fall back.

Here again Hemingway observes the inadequacies of a language not equipped to deal with the destructive realities, an Englished language echoing from afar the terms of hunting and country festivities. Though the language is English, the way it is scrutinized is American. That the barricade is "perfect . . . simply priceless . . . absolutely topping" does not blend well with the murderous activity in which the English are both agents and victims. Then, too, being "frightfully put out" when the flank goes is something of a different order from a frightfully hot day. The docility of the language intensifies the panic, all of which is to the writer's credit. It may well be, as Carlos Baker informs us, that Hemingway is here imitating the speech of his friend Captain E. E. Dorman-Smith. But the use he is making of it has little relevance to friendship.

The most sustained piece Hemingway has done in this vein is the rarely noticed story, "A Natural History of the Dead." In conception a small *tour de force*, it is a montage of two violently dissonant prose styles: the first we are to take as standard English; the second as vintage Hemingway. The standard English style is not identifiable as the style of any of the four stooges named—W. H. Hudson, Gilbert White, Bishop Stanley, and Mungo Park: rather it is a mock-gentleman style which attempts to give us the essence of the English clubman's adventure story. The wiseguy irony implicit is that naturalistic adventure should be rendered so unadventurously, so prissily, as if Africa were an extension of the club. Mungo Park is quoted in pastiche; the stiff-upper-lip confidence of his prose is almost indistinguishable from Hemingway's parody.

When that persevering traveler, Mungo Park, was at one period of his course fainting in the vast wilderness of an African desert, naked and alone, considering his days as numbered and nothing appearing to remain for him to do but to lie down and die, a small moss-flower of extraordinary beauty caught his eye. "Though the whole plant," says he, "was no larger than one of my fingers, I could not contemplate the delicate confirmation [sic] of its roots, leaves and capsules without admiration. Can that Being who planted, watered and brought to perfection, in this obscure part of the world, a thing which appears of so small importance, look with unconcern upon the situation and suffering of creatures formed after his own image? Surely not. Reflections like these would not allow me to despair; I started up and, disregarding both hunger and fatigue, travelled forward, assured that relief was at hand; and I was not disappointed."[13]

In Hemingway's story Park is always "that persevering traveler" and he perseveres because, like Bishop Stanley, he knows that the study of Natural History is linked with an increase in faith, in "the protecting eye of that Providence." Park, who starts out (attempting to ascertain the course of the Niger) in a blue coat with yellow buttons and ends up two and a half years later naked, drinking at a trough between two cows, is more subject to despair than Hemingway will allow. Parody, however, is not known for its qualities of fairness. There is, in fact, a somewhat unwarranted calm about the Scot's prose and manner. It contrasts sharply with the hysteria, the *nada*, which Hemingway chillingly conveys in the second half of the story (after some funny transitions). Nor is Park's prose designed to record things memorably; an elephant is a "powerful and docile creature," a native a "poor untutored slave."

War is what Hemingway is talking about in the story. When he writes, "Let us therefore see what inspiration we may derive from the dead," he is attempting a *reductio* of the providential: "One wonders what that persevering traveler, Mungo Park, would have seen on a battlefield in hot weather to restore his confidence . . . and have any such thoughts as Mungo Park about those formed in His own image." Associating the providential and the idea of an ennobling death weighted with significance with the so-called Humanist literary movement, which in a mock-footnote he calls "an extinct phenomenon," Hemingway flaunts his first-hand experience of war like so many medals. If Hemingway's accusation that the Humanists were "dead in their youth of choice" is hysterical (it has its ironic point, e.g., Irving Babbitt arriving at his willed, fixed position in his twenties), few would dispute his feeling that the violence at the center of contemporary experience is one of the things that makes the Humanist categories seem inadequate. Moreover, the entire piece can be seen in terms of the old realistic priority placed on actuality.

The last section of the piece, all dialogue, emerges as the last refinement in actually being there. In this dialogue the writer records not only the disintegration of abstraction but of language as well. It need hardly be said that the negation expressed in the story does not leave the reader with a sense of all problems solved. What Hemingway succeeded in doing is making his reader more sharply aware of a dubious prose and the too comfortable assumptions supporting it. He has referred to this brutal story as being "written in popular style and . . . designed to be the Whittier's *Snow Bound* of our time." No "angels near at hand" in this frozen cave, no "harmless novel" this, but rather the mind of the writer engaged in the typical modernist stripping away of empty forms.

Probably the most famous passage in Hemingway does precisely this as it at the same time reminds us that this stripping down can be the underside of the coherence one may achieve in the face of its nihilistic potential. Frederick Henry tells us that abstract words like glory, honor, and courage seemed obscene beside the concrete names of villages. Hemingway's work can be seen as an attempt to redefine the actuality these abstractions might have. Pound could easily perceive the satiric thrust which this task inevitably entailed. He had written to Harriet Monroe that good writing needs ideas derived from seeing life in arrangement, the design in life as it exists, not the trying to see life according to an idea.[14] Pound taught his friends to go in fear of abstraction. Polite English became a victim. One of the characteristics of the twenties is that it gave rise to a number of highly stylized literary languages, testimony to the belief that the language, the civilization, needed reappraisal. The assumption that any writer uses English as if he were inventing it is much more relevant to the production of that era than it is to that of our own day. It is part of the orthodoxy of modernism.

II

Hemingway's disenchantment with polite English is generalized into a pervasive Anglophobia. Often this is fairly explicit, as in Frederick Henry's conversation with Count Greffi.

> "Oh, but when you are tired it will be easier for you to talk English."
> "American."
> "Yes. American. You will please talk American. It is a delightful language."[15]

This distinction between American and English is something which Hemingway felt deeply, if hyperbolically. It is, of course, more than a difference in diction and syntax. His very name—Hemingway—was to his wry sense of things too right-sounding, too English; he liked to be called Hemingstein and would sometimes sign his name in letters with even greater comic distortion. For Hemingway "English" often serves as a shorthand for the storybook ending, the providential, the public display, the political rhetoric, the disguise of privileged class, the pseudo-chivalric manner, the exacerbating euphemism of gentility. Occasionally the Hemingway hero will fall into it to his embarrassment as when Frederick Henry is told by Catherine that her fiancé was killed in the battle of the Somme. "It was a ghastly show," he says. "Were you there?" she asks. "No," he replies.[16] In *The Sun Also Rises* a Mrs. Braddocks introduces Robert Prentiss, a rising new novelist from New York by way of Chicago who had, Jake Barnes tells us, "some sort of an English accent." Jake's disgust is immediately evident. Prentiss asks Jake if he finds "Paris amusing?" and Jake is obviously angered. "Oh, how charmingly you get angry. I wish I had that faculty," says Prentiss, adding to Jake's animal repugnance of him. When Brett tries to brighten his mood he tells her that it has been a "priceless" evening. Brett herself is called Lady Brett when Jake holds her in contempt, when he considers her English-ness: "Brett had a title too. Lady Ashley. To Hell with Brett. To Hell with you, Lady Ashley."[17] And in *The Torrents of Spring*, we are given to believe that it is characteristically English to grace hastily the distinguished new Englishman, the dying Henry James, with the Order of Merit.[18] Similarly, the English tourist is the most removed for Hemingway, the most unreal. Arriving at the festival in Pamplona is a "sightseeing car . . . with twenty-five Englishwomen in it. They sat in the big, white car and looked through their glasses at the fiesta. . . . The fiesta absorbed even the Biarritz English so that you did not see them unless you passed close to a table." Of course, they are absurd at the bullfight: "The Biarritz crowd did not like it. They thought Romero was afraid."[19]

Some of Hemingway's best friends are English—or some of his most amiable characters: Harris in *The Sun Also Rises*, for one ("Take Harris. Still Harris was not of the upper classes," Jake notes). (Catherine Barkley is Scottish, not English. When asked by Rinaldi if she loved England, she replies: "Not too well.

I'm Scotch, you see.") It is the English in their aspect of decadent aristocracy that consistently elicit Hemingway's deflationary wit. "When you were with the English," Jake says, "you got into the habit of using English expression in your thinking. The English spoken language—the upper classes, anyway—must have fewer words than the Eskimo."[20] And the Hemingway hero must be some sort of expert on languages with few words. Nor is this aggression typical of only the younger Hemingway. No Hemingway hero is more contemptuous of the English than Colonel Cantwell of *Across the River and Into the Trees*: "'My lady has called twice,' the concierge said in English. Or whatever that language should be called we all speak, the Colonel thought. Leave it at English. That is about what they have left. They should be allowed to keep the name of the language." His young lady friend wants to learn "American." The Colonel's anti-English feelings are perhaps even more intense in his account of Montgomery: "I have seen him come into an hotel and change from his proper uniform into a crowd-catching kit to go out in the evening to animate the populace . . . he is a British General. Whatever that means." Cantwell adds to this description of "Field Marshal Bernard Law Montgomery" the information that he knew he was not great.[21]

It is as if the English were the source of most civilized evasions and distortions, a severe case, a monolithic instance of what Lawrence calls mental consciousness. Hemingway, too—in a parallel which does not imply an identity—encountered the dominant culture with disgust and aggression, countering respectability with an aesthetic primitivism, an intellectual Bohemianism. There is a balance in his work between primitivism and culture, between the physical ordeal, the victory of the code character and the brooding though anti-rational intelligence of the hero. He is, in Richard Chase's phrase, a highbrow-lowbrow;[22] or, to put it another way, he is a redskin half-paleface. He portrays defiance and grace in terms which are more than physical, making a raid upon a faltering cultural style. His Anglophobia is not to be strictly equated with a hatred of all things English so much as it is to be understood as a symbol of the failure of a gentility which results in a turning from life.

What is most inimical to Hemingway is the tradition of American literature he identifies as English. He maintains that "Emerson, Hawthorne, Whittier and Company wrote like exiled English colonials from an England of which they were never a part to a newer England that they were making. Very good men with small, dried and excellent wisdom of Unitarians; men of letters; Quakers with a sense of humor." What is perhaps most valuable in Hemingway's judgment is the clarity of his rejection in relation to his own writing. "All these men were gentlemen or wished to be. They were all very respectable. They did not use the words that people always have used in speech, the words that survive in language. Nor would you gather they had bodies. They had minds, yes. Nice, dry, clean minds."[23] If there is a broad truth in Hemingway's remarks it is of the kind that resides in John Jay Chapman's hyperbolic remark that the one thing a man in the future would not be able to know from our mid-nineteenth century writers (with Hawthorne an obvious exception here too) is that there were two sexes in America. But even the broad truth should not have completely blinded him to the fact that Emerson, albeit in a very different way, was very much engaged in the transformation of cultural values, in defining what was new world and how the new world was superior to the old. Extravagant as Hemingway's judgment may seem to be, it is more or less the going judgment of the polite, occasional, literary, picturesque, Europe-imitating schoolroom poets.

III

Hemingway's criticism comprehends, then, not only a renovation of language but in many cases an involvement with and judgment of other writers. *The Torrents of Spring*, the spirited but slight parody of Anderson in the role of victim of abstraction, almost succeeds in being as funny as *Dark Laughter* often is; it is a minor instance, more important as rehearsal than performance. Hemingway's confrontation of other writers was not merely in the vein of parody nor merely a presence in his minor work. The power of *A Farewell to Arms* is the power of negation, a negation which can be understood as his expression of ideas and evaluation of literary reputations that were very much in the air in the twenties. Carlos Baker mentions Hardy in connection with this novel; an explicit connection can be drawn. The sense of an indifferent cosmos, or even a cruel President of the Immortals underlies the work. The grim confusion of tragedy and farce is also Hardyesque. But Hemingway delineates this confusion in a burlesque dimension. He presents the brutal war as a series of jokes—it never happened this way in the books (except those of Stendhal, Tolstoy, Crane). Frederick Henry is no hero, not even a soldier, but an ambulance driver. And even in this capacity it does not matter whether he supervises the removal of the sick or not. The transference worked better when he was not there. Hurt in battle, he is "blown up while . . . eating cheese." Even if he had had notions of military glory he tells us that his gun jumped so sharply that there was no question of hitting anything. The Italian army itself is disorganized and disenchanted and appears like something out of a comic opera. The soldiers' helmets are not uniform; most of them are too big and come down almost over the ears of the men who wear them. The one "legitimate hero," Moretti, "bored everyone he met with his stories." The Italians fire on themselves. Frederick Henry is suspected of being a German in Italian uniform—the only alternative is the separate peace, the way of the anti-hero. And there is "Oh love, let us be true." But this is a Hardy-cum-Hemingway universe. The ill-omen rain, Catherine's fatalistic feeling about it, the sad, haunting folk refrain (O, western wind), the irrational fear justified by the indifference of the universe, the miscast woman made for a good providence—all these bring Henry to a Hardyesque explanation with a Hemingway twist: "If people bring so much courage to this world the world has to kill them to break them, so of course it kills them. The world breaks everyone and afterward many are strong at the broken places. But those that will not break it kills. It kills the very good and the very gentle and the very brave impartially." Or again, Henry on a modest version of the President of the Immortals: "They threw you in and told you the rules and the first time they caught you off base they killed you."[24]

If Hemingway's nihilism at this point seems lyrical at best or juvenile at worst, it gains in stature by comparison. Henry himself makes the judgments for us in his conversation with Count Greffi as the subject turns to war books. Greffi speaks first:

> "There is 'Le Feu' by a Frenchman, Barbusse. There is 'Mr. Britling Sees Through It [sic].'"
> "No, he doesn't."
> "What?"
> "He doesn't see through it. Those books were at the hospital." "Then you have been reading?"
> "Yes, but nothing any good."
> "I thought 'Mr. Britling' a very good study of the English middle-class soul."
> "I don't know about the soul."[25]

In the introduction to *Men at War* Hemingway adds to this: "The only good war book to come out during the last war was 'Under Fire' by Henri Barbusse. He was the first one to show us, the boys who went from school or college to the last war, that you could protest in anything besides poetry, the gigantic useless slaughter in generalship that characterized the Allied conduct of the war from 1915 to 1917. . . when you came to read it over to try to take something permanent and representative from it the book did not stand up. Its greatest quality was his courage in writing the book when he did. They had learned to tell the truth without screaming."[26]

Since both *Under Fire* and Mr. *Britling Sees It Through* ran through several printings in a short time in the United States, Frederick Henry was alluding to well-known books. Barbusse's sensational tone, his egalitarian grievances, his operatic manner, his pacifist editorializing—all give us something of the war that Hemingway does not. But in point of fable, answerable style, sustained psychological portraiture, and accuracy of observation, Hemingway has mastered a subject in part from noticing the shortcomings of Barbusse.

He thinks more kindly of him, however, than of H. G. Wells. Britling, an exemplary Britisher, a man of letters who inhabits the England of "Old John Bull," who considers the backstreets of London "an excrescence," and who believes that "one does not love women, one loves children," is of the genteel, complacent, mental sort that Hemingway likes to abuse. Britling, who despite ominous signs cannot imagine a world war, thinks of the Sarajevo murders as "something out of 'The Prisoner of Zenda.'" The war does break out, and Britling, responding to the narrator's call for a disciplined and clarified will, becomes a special constable. He rationalizes the war as the way the world reconstructs itself and the length of it by the notion that too brief a struggle might lead to a squabble for plunder. The protracted war brings nothing but the death of Mr. Britling's son, his subsequent breakdown, and, finally, his recovery with a wish for a world-federal-republic. If God means anything, thinks Britling, he means tenderness. Wells's novel suggests more than it dramatizes, and its appeal was largely a matter of timeliness. We are given a picture of complacency shattered. Some of the actuality of war is conveyed through the letters of Britling's son. Britling does, in Wells's view, see it through. Henry's point seems to be that he literally did not see much of it at all, or did only from the grandstands. And if Britling's hopeful internationalism and grasping at deity are illustrative of his middle-class soul, these are, for Henry, pale abstractions compared to the experience he has lived through. Henry's mistrust of abstraction, including the middle-class soul, obviously does not blind us to the fact that Britling's ideas are indeed alternatives. The literary point, however, is that in the novel they are almost offhand suggestions. Hemingway is typically associating writing well with telling the truth, the kind of truth *A Farewell to Arms* reveals.

Neither of these novels is important enough to focus Hemingway's main ideas very well. It would take his grappling with writers of greater moment to him than Barbusse and Wells for him to get at the center of his literary position. We have already encountered one of them.

IV

In 1925, Carl Van Doren, writing in the *Century Magazine*, spoke of "two men who have lately divided between them the honors of literary eminence" in England and France: Thomas Hardy and Anatole France.[27] How much of these then giant figures had Hemingway read? There is a juvenilia sketch done in the style of France called "A Divine Gesture,"[28] in which God, as much a tyrant as France's Ialdabaoth, convinces his wormlike followers that they must not squirm in dissent. The mingling of the mundane and the theological, the satire of religion with anti-Catholic emphasis, the non-representational quality of a whimsical idea-narrative indicate that Hemingway knew about *The Revolt of the Angels* even if he had not read it.

There is explicit mention of Anatole France and Hardy in *The Sun Also Rises*. Frances, Cohn's impatient mistress, is angry with him:

"You're thirty-four. Still, I suppose that is young for a great writer. Look at Hardy. Look at Anatole France. He died just a little while ago. Robert doesn't think he's any good though. Some of his French friends told him."[29]

Again the allusion to acknowledged greatness, this time with a difference. From the vantage point of the extreme right, the extreme left, and surrealism, new French writers pointed to Anatole France's vulnerability. For the Americans in Paris, the culture hero whose aesthetic would be the most serious indictment of France was Flaubert. Hemingway has said that he was "the one that we believed in, loved without criticism."[30] His control, his clarity, his rage, his irony—all of these were instructive to the advance-guard expatriates who were indifferent to the loosely strung idea-narratives, the insistent abstraction of the politically-minded later France.

There is a good deal of pastiche in *The Sun Also Rises*, with burlesque references to Mencken and Brooks among the most transparent.[31] There is, moreover, another allusion to Anatole France which is now somewhat obscure but particularly instructive. Bill Gorton tells Jake about "irony and pity"—"They're mad about it in New York"—words which were sacred to Anatole France. Bill and Jake are in Burguete for fishing and Jake is digging for the worms. Bill, thinking of Anatole France, fancies Jake a capitalist type:

"I saw you out of the window," he said. "Didn't want to interrupt you. What were you doing? Burying your money?"
"You lazy bum!"
"Been working for the common good? Splendid. I want you to do that every morning. . . ."

"Work for the good of all." Bill stepped into his under-
clothes. "Show irony and pity."
I started out of the room with the tackle bag, the nets,
and the rod case. . . .
"Aren't you going to show a little irony and pity?"
I thumbed my nose.
"That's not irony."
As I went downstairs I heard Bill singing, "Irony and
Pity. When you're feeling . . . Oh, Give them Irony and
Give them Pity. Oh, give them Irony. When they're feel-
ing . . . Just a little irony. Just a little pity . . ." He kept on
singing until he came downstairs. The tune was: "The Bells
are Ringing for Me and My Gal." I was reading a week-old
Spanish paper.
"What's all this irony and pity?"
"What? Don't you know about Irony and Pity?"
"No. Who got it up?"
"Everybody. They're mad about it in New York. It's just
like the Fratellinis used to be."[32]

The passage spoofs a well-known Anatolian phrase, the source
of which would have been much more familiar to literary men
of the twenties than it is to us today. It is from the important
prose ramble, *The Garden of Epicurus*.

The more I think over human life the more I am persuaded
we ought to choose Irony and Pity for its assessors and judges,
as the Egyptians called upon the goddess Isis and the goddess
Nephtys on behalf of their dead. Irony and Pity are both of
good counsel; the first with her smiles makes life agreeable;
the other sanctifies it with her tears. The Irony I invoke is
no cruel deity. She mocks neither love nor beauty. She is
gentle and kindly disposed. Her mirth disarms anger and
it is she who teaches us to laugh at rogues and fools, whom
but for her we might be so weak as to hate.[33]

Any discussion of France's irony is complicated by the fact that there are, generally speaking, three phases of it. The irony of *The Crime of Sylvester Bonnard*, an early work, is indeed indulgent and smiling. In *The Garden of Epicurus*, however, as in the contemporaneous *At the Sign of the Reine Pédauque*, the indulgence is more willed than felt. What is genuinely present is a disarmingly playful nihilism bordering on despair. Though there is still a verbal, or somewhat more than verbal, balancing of irony and pity in *The Garden of Epicurus*, by the time France writes the works which now seem his best or at least most popular, *Penguin Island* and *The Revolt of the Angels*, irony stands pretty much alone, stripped of indulgence. It is a bitter irony, the logical extension of the nihilism of *The Garden of Epicurus*. It is hardly likely, then, that "irony and pity" would be understood by literary men in the twenties in its earlier, gentle incarnation. *The Garden of Epicurus* must have been considered in the same context as the later works, a temptation to a despair it was only too easy to feel. Bill Gorton initiates the spoof and he is not only a good friend or even an alter ego, but a symbol of Jake's health.

If irony and pity were the rage in New York, or anything resembling it, Hardy, too, most explicitly in *The Dynasts*, would be a reason why. Though Hemingway would never dream of a spirit world, even as an artistic device, the Spirit of the Pities and the Spirits Ironic express a sense of life that paralleled and lent imaginative impetus to post-war themes. As we have seen, *A Farewell to Arms* is an expression of this world view. What does relate Hemingway to writers so very different from him as France and Hardy is the pose of the Ecclesiast. Solomon was an old man when he expressed the dim, retrospective view (France and Hardy were always old), but this did not inhibit the young American who, it is clear, had just cause for a pessimistic view. The discrepancy between venerable wisdom and eternal youth is one that would become telling when Hemingway would get only chronologically older.

Irony *is* an important element in Hemingway's fiction; and pity, too, is a subject for his defining. The irony may be the old irony of fate that we get in Catherine's death or Jake's wound or the sharks that plague Santiago. But more characteristic is irony as a matter of tone, as something controlled by Hemingway. That is, the spectatorial irony of France and Hardy, passive with some aggression on the one hand, cruel with some remission on the other, arises out of a sense of loss, a meaninglessness, which Hemingway and his surrogate heroes must do something about to survive. The older fatalism is replaced by stoicism; despite the threat of disintegration, the hero controls. To be sure, the hero is not a consummate expression of the mores and dominant conventions of his society; he finds his integrity in the face of them. But where the irony of Hardy and Anatole France issued into the absurd, the irony of Hemingway is, more characteristically, a sober naming of the ridiculous. The first implies loss, the second a minimal gain. The first is universal intendency, the second is more expressive of particular men at a particular historical moment. If Jake lacks much conviction, and the worst are full of passionate intensity, the difference between Jake and a character like Krebs, in "Soldiers Home," should be underscored. Jake's negation is selective (though sometimes provincial), a fact which itself implies a vantage point of stabilizing intelligence. Jake is, certainly, an observer; but he is also an actor in a novel whose lessons of morality and style are by now so clear that it emerges as Ernest Hemingway's Morality Play. As an observer, Jake is collaterally related to the straight-man voyagers of eighteenth-century fiction who indirectly expressed the irony of the author. The things they so factually observe! This, of course, is part of the central technical inspiration in *Huckleberry Finn*; as everyone knows, Hemingway owes much to Mark Twain's peculiarly American expression of it (the sensitive, responsible though apparently amoral initiate, the leaving of society, the violence giving over to bad dreams, the mistrust of abstraction, the deflation of the chivalric, the vernacular voice, the lonely equilibrium of self—though Jake is aware of any ironies and not mainly the agent for their indirect expression). It is also related to Flaubert's exemplary irony, which is at base nothing more than his being painfully, mockingly present in a world whose most common occurrences have their own kind of incredibility. The most common meaning the word now possesses in relation to literature is the one which originates in the venerable split between the writer and a society he knows only too well. The code characters notwithstanding, the real hero in Hemingway is his prose and those characters who are a surrogate for the disillusioned irony it expresses. His concept of the hero, accordingly, is one of his burlesque elements. Jake, for example, is not a great lover or a formidable fighter or a thinker who prospers in the rational order derived from a contemplation of disorder. His hero is the private, passive, ultimately modest man, a hero of abnegation, the very precariousness of whose selfhood qualifies him for minimal saintliness, for disinterested action. Yet, if the hero does not win, neither does he lose. If one may pursue the figure, he holds life to a draw, with, among others of a very different stamp, the almost feminine virtues of sensitivity, sympathy, intuition (he is sometimes afraid of the dark and even cries!). Hemingway's criticism of language, then, is also a criticism of personal style, just as it is a criticism of cultural assumptions. His characteristic irony, like that of the novelists in burlesque already named, involves a persistent attitude toward culture, toward books. This is nowhere more apparent then in *The Sun Also Rises.*

At Princeton Robert Cohn "read too much"; in Hemingway's world this is analogous to drinking too much. Cohn lives in a fantasy world.

He had been reading W. H. Hudson. That sounds like an innocent occupation, but Cohn had read and reread "The Purple Land." "The Purple Land" is a very sinister book if read too late in life. It recounts splendid imaginary amorous adventures of a perfect English gentleman in an intensely romantic land, the scenery of which is very well described. For a man to take it at thirty-four as a guide-book to what life holds is about as safe as it would be for a man of the same age to enter Wall Street direct from a French convent, equipped with a complete set of the more practical Alger books. Cohn, I believe, took "The Purple Land" as literally as though it had been an R. G. Dun report. You understand me, he made some reservations, but on the whole the book to him was sound.[34]

(Cohn's suggestion that he and Jake go off to South America together shows that he had not grasped Hudson's "loner" psychology very well.) If Hardy and Anatole France were a too apparent temptation to despair, W. H. Hudson represented a rainbow evasion of difficult considerations. Should it seem that Jake has too easy game in ridiculing *The Purple Land*, it is to be remembered that Hudson was considered one of the best writers of English prose by no less a judge than Ford Madox Ford.[35] First published in 1885, it was popular enough to be issued in The Modern Library in 1916. This does not prevent one from sharing Jake's opinion of the book. Richard Lamb's tendency to treat women as part of the local color, his wide-eyed primitivism, his political myopia, would support Jake's ironic view. And if Jake is not joking in saying that the scenery is very well described, perhaps he should be: "great plains smiling with everlasting spring; ancient woods; swift beautiful rivers; ranges of blue hills stretching away to the dim horizon. And beyond those fair slopes, how many leagues of pleasant wilderness are sleeping in the sunshine, where the wild flowers waste their sweetness and no plough turns the fruitful soil."[36]

Hudson's sentimentality, his too easy preference for the inanimate to the human, are symptomatic of the lack of personal responsibility that marks his narrator's debonair adventures. Cohn would be attracted. Jake, one of Hemingway's moral scorekeepers, would not be. Cohn is more of a throwback to the chivalric hero than is the flighty Richard Lamb. When we are almost ready to prefer Cohn's idealized preferences to the broken relationships of everyone else, we need only recall that Cohn is usually wrong in his judgments of others. "I don't believe she could marry anybody she didn't like," he says of Brett. "She's done it twice," Jake answers. Cohn is "ready to do battle for his lady love." Because "he was so sure that Brett loved him. He was going to stay, and true love would conquer all."[37] Part of Cohn's sentimentality is that he can love a woman only in an "affair." Brett is ultimately unattainable, hence desirable. In this sense she is a lost generation Dulcinea, nowhere nearly as perfect as Cohn imagines her to be. Cohn may be seen as a mean, distant relative of Don Quixote; his windmills are ladies, his giants the romanticizing of them. There must be a way other than schoolboy chivalry to dispel the cosmic ironies.

Though the ironies have excluded Jake from the final consummation, they cannot entirely reduce him. His decency remains intact. Though he has suffered a temporary collapse due to Brett's receptivity to all comers, the consequences of this receptivity are not something he could have entirely foreseen. He does what he can to keep Romero from her. The last fine of the book—"Isn't it pretty to think so?"—is a sign of Jake's sanity as well as his irony; it names Brett as another who, although she gave up Romero, lives essentially in fantasy. Despite the gloom of much of the book, a good part of it is pervaded by high spirits stemming from the peace of nature and the self-possession of those who have a clear object of ridicule. It should come as no great surprise that Hemingway regarded the book "as in part a humorous one";[38] or that he regarded the lost generation tag as splendid bombast.

Burlesque novelists in the past have often had more to sustain them—a return to happy normalcy, a love for the thing burlesqued. Hemingway has only an attenuated connection with this kind of affirmation; when it is made it is made most typically through the code characters who, in effect, ritualistically overcome a physical crisis analogous to the psychological one that confronts the hero. They overcome the ironies; they are not merely marionettes; their pain has meaning; they help to redefine glory, honor, courage. Hemingway's art is in this way confessional, yet the use of this adjective makes us hasten to add that he has less to say about the meaning of mental suffering. It is this, not the question of whether he had an intelligent encounter with culture, that renders him vulnerable. Hemingway *has* run Huck Finn through life, or part of life; he has stopped short of a maturity that would put him in the same ring with the greatest novelists—as he himself admits in his deferential remarks about Tolstoy. If Hemingway now reads, at times, too much like a classic writer of the twenties, if the artifice of understatement is once again giving over to a more open *cri de coeur*, if it is thought that the ironic brilliance of aesthetic realism fosters a paucity of human commitment, if it is felt that Hemingway sold the Romantic self short, if irony itself is viewed as the emblem of a Bohemian intransigence which the writer can no longer afford—whether he feels that there is no viable Bohemian community or he feels that identification with our most characteristic suffering is the way of transcending it—it is a tribute to him that a number of our recent novelists, Norman Mailer and Saul Bellow for example, still think of him as an angel to wrestle with, a father to kill. Considering the narrowness, even the exclusiveness, of his vision, it has had considerable endurance, attributable in good measure to the fact that he made his encounter with literature an inextricable part of it.

Notes

1. Dwight Macdonald, "Ernest Hemingway," *Encounter*, XVIII, 116–117 (Jan., 1962).
2. Leslie Fiedler, "Hemingway in Ketchum," *Partisan Review*, XXIX, 396, 398 (Summer, 1962).
3. For his most extreme statement on "New York literary reviews," sec Hemingway's Preface to Elio Vittorini's *In Sicily*. Nowhere in his work is there such a density of, shall we say, humanistic tropes.
4. Leicester Hemingway, *My Brother, Ernest Hemingway* (Cleveland, 1962), p. 171.
5. *Death in the Afternoon* (New York, 1932), p. 73.
6. *Esquire*, IV, 21, 174a, 174b (Oct., 1935).
7. *Death in the Afternoon*, p. 53.
8. *Ibid.*, pp. 35–36.
9. Quoted by Delmore Schwartz in *Ernest Hemingway: The Man and His Work*, ed. John K. M. McCaffery (Cleveland and New York, 1950), p. 114.
10. *Green Hills of Africa* (New York, 1935), p. 70.
11. *My Brother, Ernest Hemingway*, p. 100.
12. *The Short Stories of Ernest Hemingway* (New York, 1953), pp. 87–88, 113.
13. *Ibid.*, pp. 440–441.
14. From a letter of Ezra Pound to Harriet Monroe, in the Harriet Monroe collection in the University of Chicago Library, dated Dec. 15, 1915. Paraphrased with permission of the University of Chicago Library.
15. *A Farewell to Arms* (New York, 1929), p. 269.
16. *Ibid.*, pp. 18–19.
17. *The Sun Also Rises* (New York, 1926), pp. 21, 30.
18. *The Hemingway Reader* (New York, 1953), p. 51.
19. *Op. cit.*, pp. 205, 217.
20. *Ibid.*, p. 149.

21. *Across the River and Into the. Trees* (New York, 1951), pp. 195, 206, 134.

22. *The Democratic Vista* (New York, 1958), p. 52.

23. *Green Hills of Africa*, p. 21. Longfellow, too, is fair game: "Some-one with English blood has written, 'Life is real, life is earnest, and the grave is not its goal.' And where did they bury him? And what became of the reality of his earnestness?" The apparent objection is to Longfellow's abstract, moralizing quality. Yet the shrill, juvenile quality of the nihilism here expressed makes one think of Longfellow's virtues.

24. *A Farewell to Arms*, pp. 259, 338.

25. *Ibid.*, p. 270.

26. *Men at War*, ed. Ernest Hemingway (New York, 1942), p. 9.

27. *Century Magazine*, CX, 419 (Jan. 25, 1925).

28. *Double Dealer*, III, 267–268 (May, 1922).

29. *Op. cit.*, pp. 50–51.

30. *Green Hills of Africa*, p. 71.

31. See pp. 43, 115. Also worth noting is Jake's mention of A. E. W. Mason in that it expresses the old realistic ridicule of the marvelous: "I was reading a wonderful story about a man who had frozen in the Alps and then fallen into a glacier and disappeared, and his bride was going to wait twenty-five years exactly for his body to come out on the moraine, while her true love waited too" (p. 120). Jake also reads from Turgenieff's "A Sportsman's Sketches," which, in its unobtrusive crafts-manship, clarifies and makes sober; "I had read it before but it seemed quite new. The country became quite clear and the feeling of pressure in my head seemed to loosen" (p. 147).

32. *Ibid.*, pp. 113–114. The Fratellinis are the continental circus act. For Mencken and Brooks, see pp. 43, 115.

33. *The Garden of Epicurus*, trans. Alfred Allison (New York, 1923), p. 112.

34. *Op. cit.*, p. 9.

35. Hemingway includes *Far Away and Long Ago* in his list of exem-plary prose works in *Esquire* for October, 1935.

36. *The Purple Land* (New York, 1916), p. 12.

37. *Op. cit.*, pp. 178, 199.

38. Charles Fenton, *The Apprenticeship of Ernest Hemingway* (New York, 1954), p. 203.

2

Wallace Stevens and Santayana

I

That Stevens was influenced by Santayana has been often enough affirmed.[1] The pages which follow attempt to delineate the extent of this influence. There can be no doubt that Santayana was a benign presence in Stevens' literary career, from early to late. Yet Stevens was too autonomous a self to have been dependent on Santayana. Rather it is a question of cultural accord, the smile—not quite the shock—of recognition. Santayana is not Stevens' progenitor, but he is a memorable and fairly constant source. The connection between them was real enough for Stevens to have diverged from this source, and, of course, in the matter of poetry, to have transcended it.

Beginnings are at Harvard in the late 1890's where Stevens was a literary student and Santayana, a literary, somewhat avuncular, assistant professor of philosophy, had already written *The Sense of Beauty*. Many years later, on the occasion of Santayana's death, Stevens writes of this period to a friend:

I grieve to hear of the death of George Santayana in Rome. Fifty years ago, I knew him well, in Cambridge, where often he asked me to come to see him. This was just before he had definitely decided not to be a poet. He had probably written as much poetry as prose at that time.[2]

Stevens' letters confirm what he publicly stated: that Santayana's poems did mean a great deal to him. In a letter to Henry Church, to whom "Notes toward a Supreme Fiction" is dedicated, he gives a closer view of their Harvard connection: "I read several poems to him and he expressed his own view of the subject of them in a sonnet which he sent me, and which is in one of his books."[3] Holly Stevens possesses the handwritten copy of Santayana's sonnet as well as the handwritten copy of the Stevens sonnet to which it is a reply. The poems are Petrarchan sonnets which indicate that the movement and rhythm, the conventional touches of language, the *a capella* stance, would be characteristic of Santayana though not of the Stevens of *Collected Poems*. Yet a characteristic note emerges. Stevens' poem is about his preference of the rough, magnificent music of nature to the genteel, pleasing music heard in churches.

Cathedrals are not built along the sea;
The tender bells would jangle on the hoar
And iron winds; the graceful turrets roar
With bitter storms the long night angrily;
And through the precious organ pipes would be
A low and constant murmur of the shore
That down those golden shafts would rudely pour
A mighty and a lasting melody.
And those who knelt within the gilded stalls
Would have vast outlook for their weary eyes;
There they would see high shadows on the walls
From passing vessels in their fall and rise;
Through gaudy windows there would come too soon
The low and splendid rising of the moon.[4]

The first line is a witty conception. The supporting octave, focusing on sound, moves toward the "mighty and lasting melody" of the sea. The sestet, focusing on sight, concludes on "the splendid rising of the moon." Despite obvious difficulties, Stevens achieves the rise that the form calls for. Santayana's reply to this sonnet is instructive. It dramatizes the idea that religion, specifically Christianity, finds support in nature just as nature is conceived to be meaningful because of the mythological order religion imposes. For Santayana, all cathedrals are contiguous to the sea of experience.

CATHEDRALS BY THE SEA

Reply to a sonnet beginning "Cathedrals
are not built along the sea"

For aeons had the self-responsive tide
Risen to ebb, and tempests blown to clear,
And the belated moon refilled her sphere
To wane anew—for, aeons since, she died—
When to the deeps that called her earth replied
(Lest year should cancel unavailing year)
And took from her dead heart the stones to rear
A cross-shaped temple to the crucified.
Then the wild winds through organ-pipes descended
To utter what they meant eternally,
And not in vain the moon devoutly mended
Her wasted taper, lighting Calvary,
While with a psalmody of angels blended
The sullen diapason of the sea.[5]

The octave is hampered by the rather remote, melodramatic "she" and the crudeness of imagery in the last lines. But the sestet moves without a break rapidly through open vowels and liquid consonants to its fine concluding two lines. The thematic difference in these early poems reflects a difference in temperament which was to remain constant. Despite his naturalism, Santayana was not for long intoxicated with nature. For Stevens, the radiance of nature was often enough her own argument. In Santayana, nature is rather a more formidable mechanism when not made friendly by man's organized consciousness. Like some of his Harvard contemporaries, he expressed the *fin de siècle* "desperate naturalism"[6] which stemmed from the agonies of consciousness in a mechanistic universe, the sense that the natural world they wanted to believe in was a chaos which would paralyse this belief, rather than offering a harmonious, ordered world-view. But the tonal and thematic climate shared by these poems is more conspicuous than the differences they embody. Stevens, like Santayana, was concerned with the question of religion in a naturalistic world. This was the subject of Santayana's first sonnet sequence, as it appears in book form a makeshift narrative illuminating from different points of view Santayana's loss of faith in Roman Catholicism and consequent embracing of naturalism. In his Preface to his selected poems he affirms their autobiographical element. Making somewhat excessive apologies for the conventional, merely "literary," language, the lack of "fresh idiom," the "worn and traditional" prosody, the general "breathlessness and unction," he goes on to say that "their sincerity is absolute, not only in respect to the thought which might be abstracted from them and expressed in prose, but also in respect to the aura of literary and religious associations which envelops them." He admits to its being his "most authentic personal note," to its being the "confession of an actual spiritual experience."[7] The main segments of his selected poems are his two sonnet sequences. There is good reason to believe that most of this sincerity is attributed to the first sonnet sequence, not only because it contains the better poetry but because of Santayana's explicit remarks to his biographers Howgate and Cory about the second sequence, the "Platonizing sonnets" as he calls them. To Howgate he admits that the sequence is "somewhat of a literary exercise" in which "his mind if not his heart were touched";[8] to Cory he calls "the sublimated love sonnets . . . an evasion of experience."[9] It is the naturalistic sonnets which influenced Stevens.

It was not only the young Stevens who admired Santayana as a fellow poet, for in the late essay, "A Collect of Philosophy," Stevens recalls that Santayana "was an exquisite and memorable poet in the days when he was, also, a young philosopher."[10] Thematically the first sonnet sequence is close to Stevens' own concerns. The first, like the second and twentieth sonnets in the sequence, was written last—together they form an introduction and conclusion to the loose narrative pattern. The opening sonnet tells of Santayana's conversion from Roman Catholicism to nature.

> I sought on earth a garden of delight,
> Or island altar to the Sea and Air,
> Where gentle music were accounted prayer.
> And reason, veiled, performed the happy rite.
> My sad youth worshipped at the piteous height
> Where God vouchsafed the death of man to share;
> His love made mortal sorrow light to bear,
> But his deep wounds put joy to shamèd flight.
> And though his arms, outstretched upon the tree,
> Were beautiful, and pleaded my embrace,
> My sins were loth to look upon his face.
> So came I down from Golgotha to thee,
> Eternal Mother; let the sun and sea
> Heal me, and keep me in thy dwelling-place.

One may essentially agree with Santayana's devaluation of his poems and his later estimate: "Mine is not what English-speaking people now call poetry: it is not a dissolution and fresh concretion of language. . . . Where I break through convention . . . is in my themes or sentiments."[11] It is hard not to think that a good part of the hold these poems had on Stevens is attributable to the thematic content, for as Santayana himself acknowledged, the distinction of his poems is in their thought. An entry in Stevens' journal in 1906 bears out this speculation. He says that he has been reading poetry and is struck by "the marvelous poetic language" and "the absence of poetic thought. . . . We get plenty of moods . . . and so we get figures of speech, and impressions, and superb lines, and fantastic music." This is not enough: "But it's the mind we want to fill—with Life. We admit now that Truth is the warrior and Beauty only his tender hide." The poet who exemplifies this insight is Santayana. Stevens concludes that "Santayana's sonnets are far nobler and enduring in our eyes than [Stephen] Phillips' tragedies."[12] The first sonnet, serene, naturalistic, pious and irreligious gives over to a second which introduces a sharp note of vacillation:

> Slow and reluctant was the long descent,
> With many farewell pious looks behind,
> And dumb misgivings where the path might wind,
> And questionings of nature, as I went.
> The greener branches that above me bent,
> The broadening valleys, quieted my mind,
> To the fair reasons of the Spring inclined
> And to the Summer's tender argument.
> But sometimes, as revolving night descended,
> And in my childish heart the new song ended,
> I lay down, full of longing, on the steep;
> And, haunting still the lonely way I wended,
> Into my dreams the ancient sorrow blended,
> And with these holy echoes charmed my sleep.

The descent is from "Golgotha," the place of generic religious suffering, the mountain upon which Christ was crucified.

The misgivings, mollified by "Summer's tender argument," take over in the final two lines in the form of the "holy echoes" of the "ancient sorrow." One may readily think of the alternating moods of "Sunday Morning" when reading the first sonnet sequence: the poetry of argument, the serene naturalism, the doubts of secularism, the memories of Christianity there called in similar language "the holy hush of ancient sacrifice." The protagonist of Stevens' poem will "find . . . comforts of the sun" as the "I" of Santayana's says "let the sun and sea/Heal me"—though here too Santayana's grasp of nature is somewhat aesthetic and mental rather than direct and primitive. In the fourth sonnet, Santayana can only say, "I would I had been born in nature's day" and his feeling for the primitive is bookish, imitation Keats: "No unsung bacchanal can charm our ears/And lead our dances to the woodland fane." Compare this wistful thought with Stevens' "supple and turbulent . . . ring of men," The most joyful note in Santayana's sonnets is struck in celebration of nature but it is a subjective, psychological one. It is an assertion of imaginative independence, the primacy of secular selfhood in the same "unsponsored" world of "Sunday Morning," the same lovable, post-mythological "old chaos of the sun."

> There may be chaos still around the world,
> This little world that in my thinking lies;
> For mine own bosom is the paradise
> Where all my life's fair visions are unfurled.

This note is also struck in "Sunday Morning":

> Divinity must live within herself:
> Passions of rain, or moods in falling snow;
> Grievings in loneliness, or unsubdued
> Elations when the forest blooms.

The most desperate doubt of the naturalistic answers, a note more pervasive in Santayana than Stevens, comes, for example, in the often anthologized third sonnet, "O world, thou choosest not the better part," which shows Santayana's youthful disenchantment with the "uncritical common sense and science of the day." A few lines will suffice:

> Bid, then, the tender light of faith to shine
> By which alone the mortal heart is led
> Unto the thinking of the thought divine.

A like impulse of doubt is expressed in "Sunday Morning" when the protagonist muses, "But in contentment I still feel/The need of some imperishable bliss." Her doubts are ultimately dispelled, as are the doubts of Santayana's figure. Commenting on the movement of recovery in his sequence, Santayana sums up by saying that though the third sonnet is "solipsistic" and "immature" the poems move toward a "mature solution . . . in obedience to matter for the sake of freedom of mind."[13] The twentieth and final sonnet is unlike the first two sonnets in its direct didacticism. Where the first sonnet was a secular prayer and the second a kind of confession, the concluding sonnet draws the moral clearly. The poet asks the "great Mother" to open his eyes to her secrets, for

> The soul is not on earth an alien thing
> That hath her life's rich sources otherwhere;
> She is a parcel of the sacred air.[14]

Similarly a didactic, secular note is struck in the concluding stanza of "Sunday Morning":

> She hears, upon that water without sound,
> A voice that cries, "the tomb in Palestine
> Is not the porch of spirits lingering.
> It is the grave of Jesus, where he lay."

But if there are similarities in tone, world-view, rhythm and even snatches of diction in "Sunday Morning" and the first sonnet sequence, the differences between the two are equally important. We are, after all, comparing one of the masterpieces of twentieth-century poetry with a thematically original, distinguished but uneven and formally derivative sonnet sequence. It is on the count of "dissolution and fresh concretion of language" that Stevens' poem is of a higher order, for in his naturalistic, American appropriation of romantic blank verse he found the "fresh idiom" Santayana lacked. Stevens juxtaposes in "Sunday Morning" the conventional language he discards with the fresh concretion which is the dominant language in the poem.

> There is not any haunt of prophecy,
> Nor any old chimera of the grave,
> Neither the golden underground, nor isle Melodious,
>   where spirits gat them home,
> Nor visionary south, nor cloudy palm
> Remote on heaven's hill, that has endured
> As April's green endures

The dissolution takes place as the verbal equivalent of the logical content of the poem (chimera of the grave, etc., is an irreverent tag). What is wrong with Santayana's poetry, as he himself acknowledged, is that the language lags behind belief, the formal convention is not adequate to the theme.

Another illustration of how different levels of language function precisely in "Sunday Morning" is seen in the following:

> Death is the mother of beauty; hence from her,
> Alone, shall come fulfilment to our dreams
> And our desires. Although she strews the leaves
> Of sure obliteration on our paths,

The path sick sorrow took, the many paths
Where triumph rang its brassy phrase . . .
She makes the willow shiver in the sun
For maidens who were wont to sit and gaze
Upon the grass . . .

Once again a fresh version of romantic elevated diction (with its possible recollection of Keats's "Ode on Melancholy," though Stevens is serenely thinking of fulfilment where Keats, thinking of destruction, is left in anguish), is heightened by its juxtaposition with an archaic, here generically neo-classical diction. "Sick sorrow," and "triumph rang its brassy phrase" bring to mind other ways in which death is mythologized, confronted and made the subject of emotion. As the concessive "although" indicates, death was cause for despair in the older renditions of it, whereas his own naturalistic mythology accentuates its paradoxically benign effect on life. Here again, Stevens' characteristic use of language is made more poignant by the presence of a diction to be dissolved. Masterpieces like "Sunday Morning" and "Peter Quince at the Clavier" spring up almost out of nowhere. These are "early" poems, composed at about the same time he is doing poems which improve on Austin Dobson or poems which are precious versions of Imagism. He did well by these influences too. But it is not until Stevens makes use of some of the themes close to his Harvard friend that he breaks through to the major accent. Unlike Santayana, he finds a style wholly answerable to the moment of these themes.

If Santayana's poetry offers a thematic analogy to what Stevens was doing in some of his earlier work, so does his prose of that period add to the argument for influence. The prose works which Santayana wrote as a critic-philosopher at Harvard help to create the cultural ambience for Stevens' first breakthrough into major poetry. Santayana's moving essay on Lucretius, for example, delineates the naturalistic sense of nature as it appears not only in Lucretius and Santayana but, in essential respects, in Stevens as well:

> Nature remains always young and whole in spite of death at work everywhere; and what takes the place of what continually disappears is often remarkably like it in character. . . . To perceive universal mutation . . . is the condition for any beautiful, measured, or tender philosophy.

This is the sort of triumph over death, the sort of serious tenderness "Sunday Morning" gives us. The immediacy compounded with philosophical sweep of Stevens' poem is prefigured by such a sentiment as the following:

> We seem to be reading not the poetry of a poet about things, but the poetry of things themselves. That things have their poetry, not because of what we make them symbols of, but because of their own movement and life, is what Lucretius proves once for all to mankind.

In addition, the satiric dismissal of archaic concepts in "Sunday Morning" is anticipated: "Mythology, that to a childish mind is the only possible poetry, sounds like bad rhetoric in comparison. The naturalistic poet abandons fairy land because he has discovered nature, history, the actual passions of man." Naturalism is "the least poetical of philosophies."[15] Stevens liked to think of himself as being anti-mythological in this sense. I do not mean to suggest that Stevens is as Lucretian as Lucretius—his theme is not the vanity of life, and in his nature Venus usually has the last word—but that much of what Santayana says about nature in this essay must have struck a liberating note.

Santayana's preference of the naturalistic concept of nature to the romantic one is stated in these terms: "Nature has

depth as well as surface, force and necessity as well as sensuous variety. Before the sublimity of this insight all forms of
the pathetic fallacy seem cheap and artificial."[16] And he takes
no less a figure than Wordsworth to task on these grounds:

> When he talked of nature he was generally moralizing,
> and altogether subject to the pathetic fallacy; but when
> he talked of man, or of himself, he was unfolding a part
> of nature, the upright human heart, and studying it in
> its truth.[17]

Without going into the question of the accuracy of this
description, it is worth noting that when Stevens talks about
the "romantic" in its pejorative sense he is thinking of this
sentimental aspect. "The Snow Man," another poem, is
about the superiority of cold, naturalistic perception to the
false warmth generated by the pathetic fallacy. Here too,
Santayana, an exemplary mind of winter, taught him.

Reason in Religion is another of Santayana's early books
which bears directly on "Sunday Morning." Pointing to the
anthropological origin of magic, sacrifice and prayer, Santayana says that "if all went well and acceptably, we should
attribute divinity only to ourselves." The naturalistic narrator
of "Sunday Morning" insists that "Divinity must live within
herself" so that all may go well and acceptably. Santayana
adds to his proposition, however, that there are "ambiguous
regions of nature and consciousness which we know not how
to face."[18] These are the regions which account for magic,
sacrifice and prayer. "Sunday Morning" too accounts for
"ambiguous undulations," but is content to rest in the ambi-
guities. Stevens' rather ordinary "casual flocks of pigeons,"
like most Stevens birds in flight, sink "downward" towards
earth, a romantic naturalist counterpart of Shelley's skylark.
Although there is a chaste, Dionysian worship there is no

necessity for magic, sacrifice or prayer. If this worship is mythology, it is rather like the one Santayana describes the Vedic Indians as having: they "burst into song in the presence of the magnificent panorama . . . day-sky and night-sky, dawn and gloaming, clouds, thunder and rain."[19] "Sunday Morning" does allude retrospectively to a more conventional godhead, particularly in the somewhat puzzling passage which fuses classical and Christian mythology.

> Jove in the clouds had his inhuman birth.
> No mother suckled him, no sweet land gave
> Large-mannered motions to his mythy mind.
> He moved among us, as a muttering king,
> Magnificent, would move among his hinds,
> Until our blood, commingling, virginal,
> With heaven, brought such requital to desire
> The very hinds discerned it, in a star.

This passage finds its parallel and clarification in *Reason in Religion* (p. 64) where Santayana points out that "the incarnation of God in man, and the divinisation of man in God are pagan conceptions, expressions of pagan religious sentiment and philosophy." Jove and Christ in this sense come from a common source, the religious imagination. In both classical and Christian myth man is transformed, ennobled, by divine visitation. This is the way gods "move among us." Santayana writes (p. 30): "Men like to think that God has sat at their table and walked among them in disguise." But "Sunday Morning" leaves no doubt that incarnation is not the myth of the present.

Finally, "Sunday Morning" even subscribes to the prescriptive remarks Santayana makes about poetry in "The Elements and Function of Poetry," the important concluding essay of *Interpretations of Poetry and Religion*. In addition to the "visible landscape," which Santayana says "is not a proper object of poetry," it gives us what Santayana calls the "cosmic landscape." And it embodies what Santayana considered a necessity for relevant poetry—the element of prophecy. For Santayana, the poet must either express an existing religion or herald one which he believes possible. Despite the sense of exhaustion of conventional mythology, then, there is no despair. In a later work, Santayana puts it this way:

> The loss of faith, has no tendency to banish ideas . . . [it] lends to the whole spectacle of things a certain immediacy, suavity, and humour. All that is sordid or tragic falls away, and everything acquires a lyric purity, as if the die had not yet been cast and the ominous choice of creation had not been made.[20]

Another, perhaps *the* other, great "early" poem (1914) by Stevens, "Peter Quince at the Clavier," shares the Santayana air. Possibly the beginning—"Music is feeling, then, not sound"—recalls the typical sort of statement that Santayana makes in *The Sense of Beauty* to the effect that the aesthetic experience is dependent on emotional consciousness. But it is the meditation on Susanna's fate which clearly owes something to the chapter in *Reason in Religion* called "Ideal Immortality." Santayana has been discussing the two kinds of immortality. First, the belief in a future life, of which he says, "Such an immortality would follow on transmigration or resurrection, and would be assigned to a supernatural sphere." Second, ideal immortality, where he considers the way in which ideal compensations may console the self for its lost illusions. Santayana begins his discussion by saying that nature has not solved the problem of perpetual motion in the animal body, as nature has approximately solved it in the solar system. Nutrition should have continually repaired all waste, so that the cycle of youth and age might have repeated itself yearly in every individual, like summer and winter on earth. Nor are some hints of such an equilibrium altogether wanting.

For example, "a belated love" may bring about "a certain rejuvenescence in man prophetic of what is not ideally impossible—perpetuity and constant reinforcement of his vital powers" (p. 173). Immortality, the life cycle, permanence in flux, love out of season—we move towards the Susanna story, Stevens style. The elders of course are satirically given, yet their sense of "Susanna's music" is itself a poignant reminder of her beauty, the tone of the poem being relaxedly hedonistic rather than morally prescriptive. Susanna is immortal because she was beautiful in her day and lives in myth as a synonym of grace in the collective memory. For Santayana this is the meaning of immortality: "As it is memory that enables us to feel that we are dying and to know that everything actually is in flux, so it is memory that opens to us an ideal immortality. . . . It is an immortality in representation—a representation which envisages things in their truth as they have in their own day possessed themselves in reality." (p. 179) In both Stevens and Santayana, then, that which may take the place of future life or eternal beauty or spiritual immortality is the naturalistic sense of beauty—something existent, something remembered, something eternal in its perfection of a given moment. The representation of this beauty is the human equivalent of the eternal, the "perpetual motion in the animal body [which] nature has approximately solved" in the natural world:

Beauty is momentary in the mind—
The fitful tracing of a portal;
But in the flesh it is immortal.
The body dies; the body's beauty lives.
So evenings die, in their green going,
A wave, interminably flowing.

> So gardens die, their meek breath scenting
> The cowl of winter, done repenting.
> So maidens die, to the auroral
> Celebration of a maiden's choral.
> Susanna's music touched the bawdy strings
> Of those white elders; but, escaping.
> Left only Death's ironic scraping.
> Now, in its immortality, it plays
> On the clear viol of her memory,
> And makes a constant sacrament of praise.

Susanna's beauty is part of the poet's emotional consciousness, as she was that of the elders', and is in this sense
"music," which "is feeling, then, not sound." The praise of
such beauty, the perceived beauty of a young woman in the
flesh, has therefore a sacred character.

The thematic similarities between Stevens and Santayana
are easily translated into programmatic ones. There is a quality to some of Santayana's early utterances about the social
function of imagination which Stevens echoes early and
late in his prose and poetry. In *Reason in Art*, for example,
Santayana speaks, as Stevens would, of the revolutionary
quality of art:

> If what is hoped for is a genuine, native, inevitable art, a
> great revolution would first have to be worked in society. We
> should have to abandon our vested illusions, our irrational
> religions and patriotisms and schools of art, and to discover
> instead our genuine needs, the forms of our possible hap-
> piness. To call for such self-examination seems revolution-
> ary only because we start from a sophisticated system, a
> system resting on traditional fashions and superstitions,
> by which the will of the living generation is misinterpreted
> and betrayed. To shake off that system would not subvert

order but rather institute order for the first time, it would be . . . a setting things again on their feet.[21]

One could hardly find a better statement for Stevens' own imaginative imperialism. Stevens too, in "Imagination and Value"—in part, literally, a tribute to Santayana—alludes to "the imagination" as "the irrepressible revolutionist."[22] He too wishes to institute order; he too works for our only possible happiness to emerge from disillusion. Both see the imagination as "a principle *a priori*."[23] Santayana's sense of the imagination, however, is rather more exalted than Stevens', as when he says: it "must furnish to religion and to metaphysics those large ideas tinctured with passion, those supersensible forms shrouded in awe in which alone a mind of great sweep and vitality can find its congenial objects." Stevens' sense of the supersensible is more modest than Santayana's. "To the One of Fictive Music" offers his version of it. After describing how close the imagination is to the particulars of human life, the poet adds:

Yet not too like, yet not so like to be
Too near, too clear, saving a little to endow
Our feigning with the strange unlike . . .
Unreal, give back to us what once you gave:
The imagination that we spurned and crave.

The deliberately archaized language is consonant with Stevens' assumption of the priestly role, his indulgence in the supersensible. It is when he writes explicitly of the imagination that he comes closest to embracing the idealism he so clearly knows the limits of.

One of the advantages of studying Stevens and Santayana side by side is that Stevens' relation of idealization becomes clearly defined. How far does he go? Where does he approach

Platonism? Reject it? What sort of impact did Santayana's doctrine of essences have on him? What light does Santayana's development as a philosopher shed on Stevens' development as a poet? And, finally, what in Santayana was alien to Stevens? What did he modify or reject? To answer these questions we must delineate certain aspects of Santayana's philosophy more carefully.

II

There is a shift in Santayana from humanism to epistemological scepticism and systematic ontology, a shift from anthropological psychology to Being and the relation of essence to existence. There has been a tendency on the part of pragmatists to regard this shift as a weakening into Platonism, or even worse, mysticism, but Santayana's realm of essences is not Plato's. The distinction is nicely drawn by Irving Singer:

> In distinguishing essence from existence, Santayana aligns himself with the Platonic doctrine presented in the *Timaeus*. There the distinction is made between that which is self-identical, immutable, and definable and that which is in flux, unstable, and indefinable. But whereas Plato considered the Forms to be dynamic and causative, Santayana delegates all power and activity not to essence, but to the flux of existence. For him, essences are only "logical characters." As such, they constitute a different ontological realm from the underlying surd which they happen to characterize.[24]

For Santayana, "an essence is simply the recognizable character of any object or feeling, all of it that can actually be possessed in sensation or recovered in memory, or transcribed in art, or conveyed to another mind."[25] He states clearly that "what I call essence is not something alleged to exist in some higher sphere: it is the last residuum of scepticism and analysis."[26] If Santayana had the cursed Platonic strain in him, it was injected the wrong way. It seems that what gives the edge to Santayana's definition is its distinction from the Platonic doctrine to which it owes much. Indeed, it is probable that Stevens' sense of Plato—his version of I love Plato but I love truth more—is derived in good part from Santayana, who makes a materialistic critique of Plato. In accents very much like Stevens' he says that Plato "was preaching a crusade against the established church. For naturalistic deities he wishes to substitute moral symbols, for the joys of sense, austerity and abstraction."[27] The criticism moves from the anthropological to the ontological level in *The Realm of Essence*. Here Santayana says that geometrical figures, types of animal bodies or human institutions are indeed essences,

> but so also are all the qualities of sensation despised by Platonism and all the types of change or relation neglected by that philosophy. . . . To discern them only in natural or moral units, and to think of them as perfections towards which things aspire, is not merely to omit noticing them elsewhere but to regard them as natural magnets, as a background of metaphysical powers, more selective than nature itself, and constituting a world of substances behind the flux of appearance.[28]

It was in this sense that Santayana denied that he was a metaphysician. His sympathy is with the material flux. What motivated Platonism (and Santayana, like Stevens, does not say Plato was no Platonist) "was not love of nature at all but . . . a political, human good, and . . . so much in nature as might sanction it."[29] In short, Santayana laments the loss by the Platonic ideas of "the radiance and the music of Phoebus Apollo," concluding that the ideas "in establishing their absurd theocracy over nature, were compelled to bend their backs to that earth-labour, and become merely a celestial zoology, a celestial grammar, and a celestial ethics."[30] When we say that Stevens is antipathetic to a realm of essences or that he rejects ontological priority we mean essences and Being in the Platonic sense which Santayana has characterized. Santayana's realm of "materialistic" essences is a friendlier, more viable conception to Stevens, his ontology more close, more human. In his poem "To an Old Philosopher in Rome," Stevens characterizes this realm as "the celestial possible." The oxymoron here—the idea of heaven and the idea of what can actually exist—points to the difference in conception.

The closest Stevens comes to the Platonic road in Santayana's sense is a poem like "The Idea of Order at Key West." In this rhapsody on idealist impulse, to use Santayana's terms, essence is discriminated from sense data: "The water never formed to mind or voice,/Like a body wholly body" for "it was she and not the sea we heard . . ./And when she sang, the sea,/Whatever self it had, became the self/That was her song." The conclusion to this idealist epiphany is a sense of mysterious order. The essential song ends and the lights of Key West

> Mastered the night and portioned out the sea,
> Fixing emblazoned zones and fiery poles,
> Arranging, deepening, enchanting night.

The poem concludes with an apostrophe to the "Blessed rage for order," which will give our experience the heightening of "ghostlier demarcations, keener sounds." There is a passage in *The Realm of Essence* which is strikingly pertinent to this process:

> Sometimes sense itself, without any dialectical analysis, distinguishes essences from facts, and recognises them in

their ideal sphere . . . this labour of perception may be more or less welcome, pleasant, or life-enhancing, apart from its ulterior uses; and sometimes this incidental emotion is so strong that it overpowers the interest which I may have had originally in the external facts. . . . I am transported, in a certain measure, into a state of trance. I see with extraordinary clearness, yet what I see seems strange and wonderful, because I no longer look in order to understand, but only in order to see. I have lost my preoccupation with fact, and am contemplating an essence, [pp. 6–7]

The most characteristic, and one of the greatest, of his later poems, "Notes toward a Supreme Fiction," indicates more clearly the extent to which Stevens knew Santayana's later work. The shift in Santayana from the philosophy of history to systematic ontology is paralleled in Stevens by a shift from the sensuous world to a more mental conception of that world, from hedonist celebration to the mind corralling itself in never-ending meditation, from the tone of naturalistic elegy to ideas of order, from existence to its connection with essences, from primary colours to a general luminous quality, from comedy with a satiric edge to an elevated levity characterized by pathos and expansiveness. "Notes toward a Supreme Fiction" embodies most of these shifts.

At the same time it is related to Santayana in other ways. For example, it recalls Santayana's early programmatic statements about poetry. In *Interpretations of Poetry and Religion* (p. 290), after saying that poetry "must be" euphonious, euphuistic, sensuous and ideal, Santayana hopes for the fruition of "relevant fiction, of idealism become the interpretation of the reality it leaves behind. Poetry raised to its highest power is then identical with religion grasped in its inmost truth." This elevated sense of poetry is also Stevens'. The spiritedness with which *Three Philosophical Poets* concludes (pp. 189 f.) is also to the point: "Honor the most high poet, honor the highest possible poet. But this supreme poet is in limbo still," I do not mean to suggest that Stevens is the answer to Santayana's limbo, but that the impulse behind Santayana's rhetoric seems to have had a hold on Stevens. The two qualities that this rational art must possess Stevens understands. First, it should buttress—the way science, business, morality buttress our life—"it informs us about our conditions and adjusts us to them; it equips us for life; it lays out the ground for the game we are to play." Santayana adds that "the philosophical or comprehensive poet, like Homer, like Shakespeare, would be a poet of business. He would have a taste for the world in which he lived." Second, it should express "the ideal toward which we would move under improved conditions. . . . Who shall be the poet of this double insight? He has never existed, but he is needed nevertheless." The tentative, hopeful, not quite literal prophetic note recalls Stevens, as does Santayana's emphasis on the artist as a craftsman whose home should be in the midst of society, "not on its bohemian fringes, nor in some remote empyrean." "Notes toward a Supreme Fiction" as much as any of Stevens' poems and more than most is "philosophical" in the sense in which Santayana wanted poetry to be "philosophical." Santayana admires the poetry which contemplates the order of things or sees the anything in the light of the whole, pointing out that "poetry . . . is not poetical for being short-winded or incidental, but, on the contrary, for being comprehensive and having range" (p. 20).

In the interpretation of "Notes toward a Supreme Fiction" Santayana figures in various ways. Knowledge of his ontology is helpful in penetrating the difficult first cantos. "This invented world" implies the sort of historical relativism which both writers display in their sense of the progress of mythology, as when Santayana writes, in *Persons and Places* (p. 85), of his first awakening to this insight: "I was aware, at first instinctively and soon quite clearly on historical and psychological grounds, that religion and all philosophy of that kind was *invented*. It was all conceived and worked out inwardly, imaginatively, for moral reasons." The world in Stevens' poem must be invented since the idea of the sun, Being, is inconceivable; the realms of Being—matter, truth, essence—cannot be fully grasped by thought. The idea of the sun is inconceivable in the way Santayana says the realm of matter is: "the intrinsic essence of matter [is] unknown . . . all human notions of matter, even if not positively fabulous, must be wholly inadequate";[31] or in the way that the absolute truth is: "Possession of the absolute truth is not merely by accident beyond the range of particular minds; it is incompatible with being alive, because it excludes any particular station, organ, interest, or date of survey: the absolute truth is undiscoverable just because it is not a perspective";[32] or in the way the realm of essence is: it is not conceivable in that the realm of essence is all that Being could ever be or contain. To pursue Santayana's terminology, the spirit—an amalgam of feeling, thought, consciousness, imagination—may, through individual perception, make partial appropriation of essence, matter, and truth. This is what Stevens means when he says that the idea of the sun is inconceivable but that the idea of this invention may be perceived. For Stevens, as for Santayana, there is no first cause, no inventing mind as source of this idea; therefore, there is no necessity for sages of that concept. Though no mind can invent Being, man can "see" or intuit it in the serenity of privileged moments. Then, the comedy of mythological transience gives over to an apparently permanent intuition of Being.

> How clean the sun when seen in its idea,
> Washed in the remotest cleanliness of a heaven
> That has expelled us and our images . . .

The odd metaphor obscures the meaning but the same metaphor in Santayana, in a strikingly similar context, clarifies it:

> In order to reach the intuition of the pure Being, it is requisite to rise altogether above the sense of existence. . . . In other words, the proper nature of existence is distraction itself . . . so that it cannot be synthesised in intuition without being sublimated into a picture of itself, and washed clean of its contradiction and urgency.[33]

But in Stevens sympathy with this purity of intuition is short-lived. The stanza concludes with the denial of the permanence of such intuitions: "Phoebus was/A name for something that never could be named." The canto concludes with an existential dissonance:

> The sun
> Must bear no name, gold flourisher, but be
> In the difficulty of what it is to be.

The sun survives the myths. Being cannot be permanently dubbed this or that (though Stevens' sympathy with the attempt betrays itself in "gold flourisher"). Existence is in this sense difficult. Santayana has very much the same idea: "In so far as spirit takes the form of the love of truth . . . it must assume the presence of an alien Universe and must humbly explore its way, bowing to the strong wind of mutation, the better to endure and profit by that prevailing stress."[34]

The ephebe is the figure of youth as virile poet (and sometimes not so virile). This conception too might have had its origin in Santayana: "Throw open to the young poet the infinity of nature; let him feel the precariousness of life, the variety of purposes, civilizations, and religions even upon this little planet; let him trace the triumphs and follies of art and philosophy, and their perpetual resurrections."[35] This is clearly a figure of youth as virile poet, as a hero in the kaleidoscope of myth. The ephebe must become an "ignorant man" in that sense of second innocence that Stevens attributes to poets. Santayana too associates "the child of poetic genius" with "the ignorant heart."[36]

The second canto points to the inevitable "celestial ennui" which comes from the necessarily approximate rendering of the first idea. The great sun is reduced to an isolated fragment at times, a "hermit." The process, the sense of renewal, goes on. In canto III, the poem as fresh imaginative interpretation, as partial arresting of the first idea, has the sanction of primitive impulse. Santayana tells us that "Memorable nonsense, or sound with a certain hypnotic power, is the really primitive and radical form of poetry."[37] Stevens' stylized Arabian (and once-listened-to wood-dove) and nonsensical ocean embody this original and not yet extinct nexus of poetry. The "damned hoobla" and howling "hoo" will never cease; the integration of imagination and reality is a constant. Stevens is far from the hieratic tone of "The Idea of Order at Key West." It is characteristic of him to treat comically a theme he elsewhere treats in all seriousness.

The fourth canto alludes to Descartes, whose methodological doubt as a scaffolding to prove the existence of God is questioned. Stevens does not reach for a Platonic first cause but is content with a materialistic relativistic sense of "the" first idea.

There was a muddy centre before we breathed.
There was a myth before the myth began,
Venerable and articulate and complete.
From this the poem springs: that we live in a place
That is not our own and, much more, not ourselves
And hard it is in spite of blazoned days.

"Descartes," Stevens writes, "is used as a symbol of the reason. But we live in a place that is not our own; we do not live in a land of Descartes; we have imposed reason; Adam imposed it even in Eden."[38] Reason is used here in a special sense, as an equivalent to man's imaginative rendering of reality. The "not ourselves" is an allusion to what Stevens and Santayana conceive to be a romantic appropriation of nature, as in Stevens' "The Snow Man" or Santayana's essay on "The Genteel Tradition in American Philosophy," where he traces the evolution of Transcendentalism from "a conscientious critique of knowledge" to "a sham system of nature."[39] Eve and "her sons and . . . daughters"—an outgrowth of Adam— were the first to subvert reason emphatically by indulging in a sham system of nature. "The first idea was not to shape the clouds/In imitation. The clouds preceded us." For Stevens, as for Santayana, spirit is said to be transcendental but epiphenomenal—beyond the body, of the body, but not causally effective on matter. In Eve's view, nature is a reflection of human wishes: "They found themselves/In heaven as in a glass." How general does Stevens mean the indictment to be? He adds, in explication of this passage, "It is not the individual alone that indulges himself in the pathetic fallacy. It is the race. God is the centre of the pathetic fallacy."[40] The mirror is didactically replaced in Stevens by a hard, materialist perspective—"bare board." True consolation is the result of an only personal subjectivity, there being no celestial harmony: "Abysmal instruments make sounds like pips/Of the sweeping meanings that we add to them."

The fifth canto pursues this vein of self-irony, in the form of the ephebe as precarious, urban, introspective hero. Generally, the rest of "It Must Be Abstract" works towards the mythical possibility the ephebe has to work with. The supreme fiction and the ordinary man are reconciled in a triumph of abstraction.

The man
In that old coat, those sagging pantaloons,
It is of him, ephebe, to make, to confect
The final elegance, not to console
Nor sanctify, but plainly to propound.

The feeling here is comic, genuine, American and on first blush remote from the austere, patrician Santayana. Then one recalls his sympathetic essay on Dickens, or his essay, "Imagination," in which he thinks tenderly of a similar figure: "What dreams occupy that fat man in the street, toddling by under his shabby hat and bedraggled rain-coat?" Love? Religion? Politics? We are all "ruled by imagination."[41] Stevens' meditations on the first idea and mythology lead to an affirmation of ordinary life. His indulgence in abstraction only confirms his naturalism.

"It Must Change" works many of the familiar Stevens themes: the old seraph juxtaposed with the young girls with jonquils in their hair, the eternal generations of bees, the archaic statue, the harmony of natural opposites in a universe of change, the poignancy of the physical world. The sixth canto bears curiously on Stevens' relation with Santayana. It echoes—perhaps unconsciously—a line in Shelley's "Ode to the West Wind" which Santayana often quotes. "Be thou me, impetuous one," says the poet to the wind. Like Shelley, Stevens is concerned in this canto with the reaction of consciousness to change; but what is cosmic in Shelley is local in Stevens. Stevens' gloss on this passage, though, could almost literally be a gloss on Shelley's poem: "In the face of death life asserts itself. Perhaps it makes an image out of the force with which it struggles to survive. Bethou is intended to be heard; it and ké-ké, which is inimical, are opposing sounds. Bethou is the spirit's own seduction."[42] The last flourish takes us far from Shelley's idealistic appropriation of nature, though it has its own necessary, minimal idealism. The poem tells us that "bethou . . . is/A sound like any other. It will end." This seems to be an undercutting of Shelley. For Stevens, the flux clearly transcends any attempt by consciousness to penetrate it. With all his sympathy for the poet, Santayana, in his essay on Shelley, makes a similar point: "he will never be able to make nature the standard of naturalness."[43]

The final canto of "It Must Change" is a meditation in the manner of Santayana.

> A bench was his catalepsy, Theatre
> Of Trope. He sat in the park. The water of
> The lake was full of artificial things,
> Like a page of music, like an upper air.
> Like a momentary color, in which swans
> Were seraphs, were saints, were changing essences.

The mood is typical of Stevens though some of the language specifically recalls Santayana. The philosopher, who often uses the image of the theatre in his prose, defines trope as "the essence of any event, as distinguished from the event itself."[44] The psyche or soul itself is considered a trope in that it is potentiality rooted in a seed. The language of Santayana underscores the depth of the reflection. The poet is transfixed by meditation, marrying the world of sense to an accessible transcendence. The swans, the seraphs, the saints—none here has the ironic connotation that Stevens had earlier in his career given them. The west wind—Stevens' west wind—is not impetuous but animates the local bucolics and calls to mind the principle of constant change, "A will to make iris frettings on the blank." The "frettings," a late figure in Stevens, signify the internal intricacies of his later meditations. They are like the "damask" of "An Ordinary Evening in New Haven" (another poem with various flourishes out of Santayana); "the blank" is a version of the realm of essence, as is New Haven's "dominant blank, the unapproachable./This is the mirror of the high serious."[45] (A pun?) The element of change in nature is analogous to the transformations of the introspective self. Essences are revealed, Santayana tells us, only by the movement of matter.

"It Must Give Pleasure," after a series of familiar contrasts, leads to climactic utterance:

> To find the real,
> To be stripped of every fiction except one,
> The fiction of an absolute—Angel,
> Be silent in your luminous cloud and hear
> The luminous melody of proper sound.

Note, *an* absolute. Even what remains is recognized as fiction. The angel is imagination in its ideal aspect as a reflection of the realm of essence. Because of this it must listen to the actual melody of worldly sound to find expression. A Stevens angel, he "Leaps downward . . . Forgets the gold centre, the golden destiny," and thereby "grows warm." The luminous quality, the essential contingent on the existential, the sense of a multiplicity of possible fictions, the necessity to believe in imaginative transcendence and the necessity of imaginative transcendence to be derived from a mundane world—these are qualities central to Santayana as well, as when he writes of "innocent" essence:

> When actually given in intuition, every essence is *luminous* and not estranged . . . by any doubt or veil. Matter is neither luminous nor innocent; it is therefore no object of contemplation; but nevertheless there lie all his hopes [the hopes of essence]; hence he sprang, on that he feeds, and there he must leave his mark if he would render existence more friendly to the spirit. It is by shifts of matter, in the world or in the brain, that essences are revealed . . .

happy the man who, in bringing to light those which to him can be . . . congenial, leaves all the others to loom for ever in the distance, like ancient gods respected but not worshipped.[46]

Stevens' angel, not like all the others, is the necessary angel of earth; Stevens' poetry is compounded of the "luminous flittering" and "the concentration of a cloudy day," the "imagination's Latin" and the "lingua franca et jocundissima." As Santayana would have it, his poetry expresses the ideal towards which we would move as it informs us about our conditions and adjusts us to them.

"Notes toward a Supreme Fiction" moves towards conclusion as the whistling wren (no "be thous" here) offers natural counterpoint to the euphoristic poet who "can/Do all that angels can." The wren, cock and robin are bound by an only instinctive life to "mere repetitions." Yet the poet, with a comic bow to Coleridge, is left to muse whether the more elaborate activities of imaginative man are not themselves inevitably an analogous sort of repetitious activity, "One of the vast repetitions final in/Themselves and, therefore, good." Man's occupation is expansive rather than forced but he must repeat, must order the flux by naming it. The resultant clairvoyance of consciousness, the coalescence of essence and datum, is man's most characteristic pleasure. As Santayana puts it,

> Radical flux is indeed characteristic of existence . . . but the mind, even if describing only the series of its own illusions, attempts to describe it with truth: and it could not so much as fail in this attempt unless that series of illusions and each of its terms had a precise inexpungible character. . . . I may long ruminate upon it and impress it upon myself by repetitions, which to a lover never seem vain . . . the repetition serves to detach and to render indubitable the essence meant.[47]

"Notes toward a Supreme Fiction" concludes with the lover's essential consummation as he rests in an imaginative conception of his world: "flicked by feeling, in a gildered street,/I call you by name, my green, my fluent mundo." Stevens' flicks, glitters, flashes of gold, particles of nether-do are a figurative expression of Santayana's realm of essence. A knowledge of this concept dispels the fuzziness of numerous later poems. When, for example, in "A Primitive Like an Orb," Stevens alludes to "The essential poem at the centre of things," he is thinking of mythology as an essence, the sum of all poems. It stands in comic relation to the present artificers of the poem, "such slight genii in such pale air." This essential poem is not ontologically prior to poems; "it is not a light apart, up-hill." The giant in the poem is the collective poet, an inspiration to slight genii, "a large among the smalls/Of it, a close, parental magnitude."

Stevens makes a poet's appropriation of the realm of essence as a worthy mythology in itself. He is more concerned with imagination than cognition and essences are for him not so much a logical necessity as an aesthetic preference. Nor is animal faith a self-conscious doctrine in the poet. The strong tendency in Stevens to think of description as a product of imagination is consonant with Santayana's view, but the equally strong (until the last phase) and logically contradictory tendency (Stevens makes poetry out of this contradiction) to immerse himself with direct cognition, empirically, in the indubitable thingishness of things is not. Much of Stevens' poetry is an example of the "gay empiricism" which Randall Jarrell says is the characteristic quality of American poetry. The philosopher bridled at this confident American quality. Yet Santayana's sense of culture, his naturalism, his idealism, though not his epistemological scepticism nor his air of Olympian resignation, provide an analogy in reflection to Stevens' poetry. In addition, Santayana's philosophy is considered poetic in itself. His categories are valued for the satisfaction and general imaginative coherence they bring rather than for their factual accuracy. Santayana thinks of philosophy as the art of thinking rather than the science of thought, as vision rather than argument; he goes so far as to say that it is only when "philosophy is good literature that it is good for anything."[48] Such a philosophy served Stevens as a theoretical justification of the residual Plato in him.

III

Though Santayana has influenced Stevens' production in all these ways it is important to point to some essential difference. Stevens found an impetus to his later poetry in Santayana's ontology, but a major strain of his later poems is a clear departure from Santayana's aesthetics. *The Sense of Beauty* was written in 1896, yet when the subject of Stevens and Santayana is broached the impulse of critics is to show how Stevens—especially in his late masterpieces, "Notes toward a Supreme Fiction," "Esthétique du Mal"—is a poetic embodiment of that early book. Santayana's is a hedonistic aesthetics. And does not Stevens say of the supreme fiction that it must give pleasure? Not sybaritic, but tempered, mellow, naturalistic pleasure. Yet "Esthétique du Mal" seems to question even this accessible bliss. It is possible that Stevens thought of these two extraordinary works as contrapuntal, both dense meditations having the majesty of the *summa*, but "Notes" being to harmony and pleasure what "Esthétique" is to dissonance and pain.

What Santayana has to say about the aesthetic experience bears relation to the earlier Stevens and that considerable aspect of the later Stevens which relates to his viable hedonism. Santayana writes: "The appreciation of beauty and its embodiment in the arts are activities which belong to our holiday life, when we are redeemed for the moment from the shadow of evil and the slavery to fear, and are following the bent of our nature where it chooses to lead us."[49] For Santayana, pleasure is the essence of the aesthetic experience. Beauty is defined as "pleasure objectified" to distinguish it from pleasure derived from ordinary activity, pleasure in the adverbial sense. (In this sense hedonism is conspicuous in the philosophy of Aristotle himself.) In accents which may have made a permanent impression on Stevens, he speaks of the arena of pleasure. "To see it in the physical world, which must continually be about us, is a great progress toward that marriage of the imagination with the reality which is the goal of contemplation."[50] The sense of harmonious appropriation of the object by the subject, the gentlemanly tone, the aura of leisure, the refined hedonism—Santayana's aesthetics does take us directly into *Harmonium*, a good way into the gay melancholy of "Notes," and even into the last poems. But it does not take us very far into the dark italics of "Esthétique du Mal" and the many poems like it. For in these poems the idea that pleasure is not the essence of aesthetic experience is explored. Terror, dissonance, darkness, isolation—but not pleasure.[51] This represents a change in Stevens' thought and a break from Santayana's. In a late essay Stevens writes: "Men in general do not create in light and warmth alone. They create in darkness and coldness. They create when they are hopeless, in the midst of antagonisms, when they are wrong, when their powers are no longer subject to their control. They create as the ministers of evil."[52] This statement has none of Santayana's idealizing aesthetic impulse. It is quite the contrary of Santayana's saying that beauty "is never the perception of a positive evil, it is never a negative value,"[53] as is much modern literature contrary to his saying that "art does not seek out the pathetic, the tragic, and the absurd." Indeed, Stevens is not original in his meditations on beauty as a positive evil. Much of the serious literature of our time is immersed in the destructive element, just as much criticism has explored the relation between art and neurosis. It is not simply a question of the negative element being "imposed . . .

upon our attention." The crucial fallacious distinction here is the one Santayana makes in his discussion of expression, which is the quality acquired by objects through association (from judgment to revery). Expression consists of two terms, the manner (e.g., sound, rhythm, image) and the object itself; it is only by subordination of the second term to the first, Santayana tells us, that evil may be aesthetically represented, may be made "agreeable to contemplation." Santayana says that "we are not pleased by virtue of the suggested evils, but in spite of them."[54] While it is true that the gratuitous accumulation of painful stimuli renders a work of art horrible, the fact remains that a beauty whose essence is not pleasure is the inspiration of much modern art.

In "Esthetique du Mal" the sun is not majestic or clean, but faltering, imperfect, dressed "in clownish yellow, but not a clown." If it still represents the source of mythology, or the realm of essence, it is the apotheosis of *mal*. The "big bird [that] pecks at him," preferring spiritual to earthly food, essences to sensations, is Stevens' weirdest bird. He contents himself with the perfections of an imperfect paradise.[55] The moon in "Esthetique du Mal" is seen in its "comic ugliness," the landscape of the mind in its nightmare state,

> A man of bitter appetite despises
> A well-made scene in which paratroopers
> Select adieux; and he despises this:
> A ship that rolls on a confected ocean.
> The weather pink, the wind in motion; and this:
> A steeple that tip-tops the classic sun's
> Arrangements; and the violets' exhumo.

Whatever the protagonist of "Esthetique" experiences, it is not the normative, humanistic pleasure that Santayana writes about (except at the opening where he entertains more or less conventional ideas about tragedy and the sublime). If he is an epicure here, he is tasting "hunger that feeds on its own hungriness." Similarly, in "No Possum, No Sop, No Taters," Stevens exhibits his fascination with the negative second term: "The crow looks rusty as he rises up./Bright is the malice in his eye. . ." As the poet says, "Bad is final in this light." The first term, the manner in which this poem is expressed—with its monosyllables, short sentences, choppy tetrameters, abstract words, lack of colour, the very inversion of his standard *Harmonium* patterns—is remarkable. But the poem does not succeed despite its subject.

Though Santayana's aesthetics is rejected by the Stevens of the aesthetic of evil (Santayana himself seems to have set little store by *The Sense of Beauty* in his later years),[56] the tone and verbal ambience of his later writing is not. The very use of the word "comic" or "clownish" in Stevens' later poems to indicate the nothingness of disillusion, the precariousness of man, the confusions of history, the detritus of metaphysics and the relativity of the physical world is something he may well have picked up from Santayana, who frequently enough alludes to "the comedy of change," "the laughing firmament," "this motley world," this "endless comedy of experience."[57] Similarly, when, in canto xiii of "Esthetique," Stevens writes of "the unalterable necessity/Of being this unalterable animal," Santayana's materialist psyche comes to mind. When Stevens adds

> This force of nature in action is the major
> Tragedy. This is destiny unperplexed.
> The happiest enemy

we see that this happy tragedy is close to sad comedy and we may think of an analogous passage in Santayana:

> The tragic compulsion to honour the facts [determined or fixed natural conditions] is imposed on man by the destiny

of his body, to which that of his mind is attached. But his destiny is not the only theme possible to his thought, nor the most congenial. The best part of this destiny is that he may often forget it; and existence would not be worth preserving if it had to be spent exclusively in anxiety about existence.[58]

The perplexed calm of this insight is like the note on which canto xiii concludes, a note of difficult Mediterranean serenity which, as several critics have observed, brings Santayana to mind. The concluding lines of "Esthetique" issue into a whirling recessional, the ontological expression of which is the materialistic philosopher's realm of essence.

So many selves, so many sensuous worlds,
As if the air, the mid-day air, was swarming
With the metaphysical changes that occur,
Merely in living as and where we live.

A friend once asked Santayana why he no longer wrote poetry and he answered "that poetry was not congenial to the spirit of the age"[59] No doubt. But what Santayana did not adequately see was that poetry can be made of this very contradiction, poetry at least partially representative of the aggrandizing fiction he had speculated about as a critic. The result is a modernist experimentalism he generally could not or would not fathom, the ideational content of which was sometimes closer to his own interests then he knew. Though Santayana seems not to have remembered Stevens, Stevens seems never to have forgotten Santayana. Speaking of Santayana's "poetic way of writing," he says that "the exquisite and memorable way in which he has always said things has given so much delight that we accept what he says as we accept our own civilization. His pages are part of the *douceur de vivre*."[60] And Stevens does accept his civilization. The impressionism and piety of this remark are rendered more meaningful when we remember that Stevens has just been less complimentary in his estimate of Nietzsche's "poetry" and of Bergson's. It is Santayana whom he considers representative, inclusive, sweet. He pays similar tribute to Santayana in his essay, "Imagination as Value," both directly and indirectly. Indirectly, in that he shows distrust for the romantic conception of imagination as something having metaphysical value in the everperfecting poem of the universe, but trust in the imagination as metaphysics when considered "something vital" and "capable of abstraction"—or not metaphysical at all but simply a power of the mind over external objects, a force in arts and letters. Directly, when he says, in comparing the life which is thrust upon man to the life which exists by the deliberate choice of the man who lives it, "it may be assumed that the life of Professor Santayana" (he hadn't been a professor since 1912)

> is a life in which the function of the imagination has had a function similar to its function in any deliberate work of art or letters. We have only to think of this present phase of it, in which, in his old age, he dwells in the head of the world, in the company of devoted women, in their convent, and in the company of familiar saints, whose presence does so much to make any convent an appropriate refuge for a generous and humane philosopher.[61]

Stevens remembered the man and had read the first two volumes of the autobiography. Taken together this is the life to which he refers, a life self-conscious, austere, detached, harmonious with itself. It seems an instance of normality in an abnormal time and is in this sense analogous to the problem which any recent imaginative effort is likely to encounter. "To an Old Philosopher in Rome" is a tribute to that life. Written before the publication of the third volume of Santayana's autobiography and just before his death, the poem depicts the later "spiritual" Santayana, the spectator of time and eternity. Of course, this had since his youth been a congenial stance for Santayana. But his definitive utterances about the life of the spirit occur in his later work. There he says, with residual Christian emphasis, that the "kingdom [of the spirit] is not of this world" and he eulogizes its power of renunciation in portentous prose rhythms: "understanding too much to be ever imprisoned, loving too much to be in love." He hastens to add, however, that "its distinctive object is not pure Being in its infinity, but finite being in its purity."[62] Yet the emotional meanings which attach to spirit are an index of the temperamental difference between Stevens and Santayana. It is the difference between Connecticut and Rome. Though both are hermitic, Apollonian, spectatorial, elegant, and wise, though both came to prefer places to persons,[63] the element of renunciation, of superiority to merely worldly triumph and sensuous indulgence is what typically distinguishes the exile from the American. But Stevens' later theme of *mal* bridges this gap considerably. The old Santayana seems often as close to the old Stevens as the young Santayana was to the young Stevens. Both remained to the last "impenitent" as to the eternal and were, in the end, "most penitent" about life itself.

"To an Old Philosopher in Rome" reflects Santayana's dualism, his distinction between essence and existence, in a series of threshold parallels: the figures of the street, the figures of heaven; Rome, the more merciful Rome beyond; the inch and the mile; the banners and the wings; the human end and the spirit's greatest reach; the known and the unknown; the newsboy's muttering and another murmuring; the smell of the medicine and a "fragrantness" not to be spoiled; the light on the candle tearing against the wick and a hovering excellence. (Even the "bird-nest arches" and "rain-stained vaults" extend the threshold imagery, both being intermediary, in nature and church, between earth and heaven.) The realm of essence, "your particles of nether-do," arrests the flux. As Being comes near, the senses cling to "men growing small in the distances of space," the "smaller and still smaller sound" of their singing, the candle which evades sight. It is a remarkable rendering, its relentless abstraction a testimony to the interior distance Stevens has covered in his lifetime meditation as a poet. Here is delineated a human apprehension of the "celestial possible," the transcendence which is the qualitative dimension of existence itself. Santayana, in his heroic, philosophical absorption in the tragi-comedy of existence is Stevens' "master and commiserable man." The author of *Realms of Being*, this "inquisitor of structures," is a capable representative of the existential "poverty," the naturalistic disillusion, Stevens came to write much about. Santayana knows too, "It is poverty's speech that seeks us out the most./It is older than the oldest speech of Rome." The consolation of Rome is a fictive one; "mercy" is not "a mystery/Of silence" but the reverberations of the bells. That this "total grandeur at the end," this "total edifice," this scene so adequate to the meaning of life, was chosen by the philosopher "For himself" is characteristic of the way in which Santayana's life was a work of the imagination.

The interior landscape is exquisite but it is not quite Stevens'. Rather it is an expression of empathy for a kindred spirit. The very titles of Stevens' stunning last poems show a deliberate diminution of grandeur: "On the Way to the Bus," "As You Leave the Room," "Farewell without a Guitar." The embodiment of Stevens' desire and apperception in the mystical realm of essence takes typically a less churchly, a more spiritually subdued, more ordinary, more spontaneous, more exclusively naturalistic form. This distinction in heart's desire is rather like the one figured in their early

sonnet dialogue. Now, in its essential gold and fire, we envis-
age Stevens' final bird.

> The palm at the end of the mind,
> Beyond the last thought, rises
> In the bronze distance,
> A gold-feathered bird
> Sings in the palm, without human meaning,
> Without human feeling, a foreign song.
> You know then that it is not the reason
> That makes us happy or unhappy.
> The bird sings. Its feathers shine.
> The palm stands on the edge of space.
> The wind moves slowly in the branches.
> The bird's fire-fangled feathers dangle down.

The exquisiteness of the representation, here and in other last
poems, indicates a sense of tempered recovery, the grasp of
naturalistic sanity, the possibility that pleasure may really be
the last word, the final tribute to the intuitions of aesthetic
normality. The poem is called "Of Mere Being," (OP) the
irony intending to show that Being is contingent upon existence. For Stevens, even more that Santayana, knows that
eternity is in love with the productions of time.

Notes

1.   See Joseph N. Riddel, "The Contours of Stevens Criticism," *Eng-
      lish Literary History*, XXXI (March, 1964), 131 n. Samuel French
      Morse, in a letter to me, Nov. 12, 1965, confirms that Stevens
      was familiar with Santayana's poetry and prose, and "owned a
      good many of Santayana's books." What remains of his library
      includes Santayana's *Sonnets* (1896), *The Hermit of Carmel and
      Other Poems* (1901), and the three volumes of the autobiography.
2.   In a letter to Barbara Church, Sept. 29, 1952, no. 842 in MS
      of *The Letters of Wallace Stevens*. Since this essay was written *The
      Letters of Wallace Stevens* has been published (1966) in the United

States by Alfred A. Knopf, Inc., and in England by Faber and Faber. All quotations from the *Letters* by permission of Holly Stevens, Alfred A. Knopf, Inc., and Faber and Faber.

3.   Dated Oct. 15, 1940, no. 413. In this letter Stevens also writes: "I did not take any of his courses and never heard him lecture." Stevens' transcript shows that he took no philosophy courses at all, but did take seven English and comparative literature courses and a few composition courses, in addition to history and government.

4.   "Cathedrals are not built along the sea," *Harvard Monthly*, XXVIII (May, 1899), 95.

5.   In *The Hermit of Carmel and Other Poems* (New York, 1901), p. 122. The sonnet was not included in subsequent collections of Santayana's poems.

6.   Herbert W. Schneider, *A History of American Philosophy* (2nd. ed., New York and London, 1963), pp. 352–71. Cf. William Vaughn Moody's "Gloucester Moors."

7.   George Santayana, *Poems* (London, 1922), pp. vii-xiv *passim*.

8.   George W. Howgate, *George Santayana* (Philadelphia, 1938), p. 57.

9.   Daniel Cory, *Santayana: The Later* Years '(New York, 1963), p. 208.

10.   Wallace Stevens, *Opus Posthumous* (New York, 1957), p. 187. Hereafter cited as OP. All quotations from Opus *Posthumous*, copyright © 1957 by Alfred A. Knopf, Inc., and from *The Collected Poems of Wallace Stevens*, copyright © 1955 by Alfred A. Knopf, Inc., by permission of Alfred A. Knopf, Inc. and Faber and Faber.

11.   "The Middle Span" (originally published 1945) in *Persons and Places* (New York, 1963), II, 164.

12.   Letter no. 117: a Journal entry dated May 29, 1906.

13.   "The Background of My Life" (originally published 1944) in *Persons and Places*, I, 241.

14.   The following numbered sonnets of Santayana have been quoted in this order from his *Poems*: sonnet II, p. 4; IV, p. 6; XIV, p. 16; III, p. 5; XX, p. 22.

15.   *Three Philosophical Poets* (New York, 1953), pp. 28 f., 39 ff., 60. Copyright © 1910 by Harvard University Press. All quotations by permission of Harvard University Press.

16.   *Ibid.*, p. 39. Santayana writes elsewhere (Daniel Cory, ed., *The Letters of George Santayana* [New York, 1955], p. 408):

"Naturalism . . . is something to which I am so thoroughly wedded that I like to call it materialism, so as to prevent all confusion with *romantic* naturalism like Goethe's, for instance, or that of Bergson. Mine is the hard, non-humanistic naturalism of the Ionian philosophers, of Democritus, Lucretius, and Spinoza."

17.   Three Philosophical Poets, p. 59. Cf.: M. H. Abrams, *The Mirror and the Lamp* (New York, 1958), pp 291 f.; Geoffrey H. Hartman, *Wordsworth's Poetry, 1787–1814* (New Haven, 1965). Cf. also an anonymous review of Santayana's Interpretations of Poetry and Religion (New York, 1957) in *Harvard Advocate*, LXIX, no. 2, 31 f.: to one "drowsy with the warm scent of mystic Ones and transcendent Experiences in which all differences are merged, the eminently sane and rational view of life and its meaning which Mr. Santayana sets forth will come as a breath of clear cold air." Stevens was president of the *Harvard Advocate* at this time.

18.   *Reason in Religion* (New York, 1962), p. 25.

19.   *Ibid.*, p. 47.

20.   *Scepticism and Animal Faith* (New York, 1955), p. 67. Naturalism does not preclude for Santayana, as it does not for Stevens, the private enactment of religious rituals. Indeed, both men feel the poignancy a naturalist may feel for them.

21.   *Reason in Art* (New York, 1962), p, 152.

22.   In *The Necessary Angel* (New York, 1951), 152. Hereafter cited as NA. Copyright © 1951 by Alfred A. Knopf, Inc. All quotations by permission of Alfred A. Knopf, Inc.

23.   Santayana, *Interpretations of Poetry and Religion*, p. 10.

24.   *Santayana's Aesthetics* (Cambridge, 1957), p. 3. Copyright © 1957 by Harvard University Press. Quoted by permission of Harvard University Press.

25.   "Proust on Essences" in Irving Singer, ed., *Essays in Literary Criticism* (New York, 1956), p. 241.

26.   "On the Unity of My Earlier and Later Philosophy" in *Works of Santayana*, Triton Edition (New York, 1937), p. xiii.

27.   *Reason in Art*, p. 68.

28.   New York, *1927*, pp. *30–31*.

29.   *Platonism and the Spiritual Life* (New York, 1987), p. 310.

30.   "Ideas" in Soliloquies in England and Later Soliloquies (New York, 1923), p. 232.

31. *The Realm of Matter* (New York, 1930), pp. vii f.
32. *The Realm of Essence*, p. xiii. *The Realm of Truth* was published in 1938, "copyright 1937, 1938." The central idea is that truth is the sum "of all true propositions, what omniscience would assert, the whole system of qualities and relations which the world has exemplified or will exemplify. . . . If views can be more or less correct, and perhaps complementary to one another, it is because they refer to the same system of nature, the complete description of which, covering the whole past and the whole future, would be absolute truth." This living truth is no living view, no actual judgment, "but merely that segment of the realm of essence which happens to be illustrated in existence" (*The Realm of Truth*, pp. vii, viii). It is perhaps interesting to speculate whether Stevens' poems about "The truth," published in the autumn of 1938 and embodying different aspects of this insight, came on the fresh reading of Santayana. See "The Man on the Dump," "On the Road Home," "The Latest Freed Man," "Connoisseur of Chaos."
33. *The Realm of Essence*, p. 47 f.
34. *The Realm of Matter*, p. 206.
35. *Three Philosophical Poets*, p. 186.
36. *Interpretations of Poetry and Religion*, pp. 259 f.
37. *Reason in Art*, p. 67.
38. In a letter to Hi Simons, tan. 12, 1943, no. 469. The allusion to Descartes may be an acknowledgment as well, for Stevens knew Descartes and his *Meditations* supply us with a possible source of imagery in these cantos, e.g., "we must finally reach a first idea, the cause of which is an archetype (or source):" See *Meditations* (Indianapolis, 1960), pp. 38–40.
39. *Winds of Doctrine* (New York, 1957), p. 195.
40. In a letter to Hi Simons, March 29, 1943, no. 479.
41. *Soliloquies in England*, p. 122.
42. *In a letter to Hi Simons, Jan. 28, 1943, no. 472.*
43. *Winds of Doctrine*, p. 166. See also: Interpretations *of Poetry and* Religion, p. 145; Paul Arthur Schilpp, ed., *The Philosophy of George Santayana* (New York, 1951), p. 282; *The Sense of Beauty* (New York, 1896), p. 244 f.; "My Host the World" in *Persons and Places*, II, 1 f., originally published posthumously (1953) ten years after "Notes toward a Supreme Fiction." In this last,

Santayana contrasts unrepentant "transcendental spirit" with his own limited penitent psyche.

44. *The Realm of Matter*, pp. 101 f. Whitehead's *Science and the Modern World* is close in idea to *The Realm of Essence* and *The Realm of Matter*. In the postscript to *The Realm of Essence*, Santayana points to the similarity of their respective concepts of essence. Whitehead's concept of "event" is equally close to *The Realm of Matter*.

45. An Ordinary Evening in New Haven," which is about the integration of mundane fact and essences, shows various intimations of Santayana: "The metaphysical streets of. the physical town," "The difficulty of the visible/To the nations of the clear invisible . . . gets at an essential integrity"—even the unpromising "tink-tonk/Of the rain in the spout . . . is of the essence not yet well perceived." Moreover, the theoretical remarks about the function of poetry recall the Santayana of *Interpretations of Poetry and Religion, Reason in Religion, Three Philosophical Poets*: "The poem is the cry of its occasion,/Part of the res Itself and not about it." Or, even more emphatically:

> This endlessly elaborating poem
> Displays the theory of poetry,
> As the life of poetry. A more severe,
> More harassing master would extemporize
> Subtler more urgent proof that the theory
> Of poetry is the theory of life,
> As it is, in the intricate evasions of as,
> In things seen and unseen, created from nothingness,
> The heavens, the hells, the worlds, the longed-for lands.

46. *The Realm of Essence*, p. 72.
47. *Ibid.*, pp. 5 f.
48. *Scepticism and Animal Faith*, p. 254.
49. *The Sense of Beauty*, p. 25.
50. *Ibid.*, p. 136. For Santayana's critique of his early, empirical "definition" of beauty (from "pleasure objectified" to "a vital harmony felt and fused into an image under the aspect of eternity") see Singer, *Santayana's Aesthetics*, pp. 42 ff. Pleasure is still the essence of the aesthetic experience.

51. Cf. Marshall Cohen, "Aesthetic Essence" in Max Black, ed., *Philosophy in America* (Ithaca, 1965), pp. 115-33, for a challenging analysis of different views on aesthetic essence and the difficulty in establishing such a category.

52. "Two or Three Ideas" in *OP*, p. 210.

53. The *Sense of Beauty*, p. 49. In an engaging essay, "The Fate of Pleasure: Wordsworth to Dostoevsky," Lionel Trilling assesses the moral consequences of the "negative transcendence" of modern literature, of its attraction to "unpleasure," with late romantic nostalgia for the career of pleasure in literature. In Carroll Camden, ed., *Literary Views* (Chicago, 1964), pp. 93-114.

54. The *Sense of Beauty*, pp. 222 f.

55. Cf. William Burney, "Wallace Stevens and George Santayana," unpublished Ph.D. dissertation (State University of Iowa, 1962), ch. 4. Burney points to a connection between this canto and *Scepticism and Animal Faith*, p. 85.

56. Cory, *Santayana*, p. 17.

57. *The Realm of Essence*, pp. 109, 92; *Scepticism and Animal Faith, pp.* 3, 53. There are some recurrent images in Santayana which Stevens may have found there—the candle, the book, the small bird, nature as mother who has a philosopher as child.

58. The *Realm of Essence*, p. xii. Burney suggests that the protagonist of "Esthetique du Mal" is probably Santayana. In "My Host the World," Santayana does visit Naples (Vesuvius is on the bay), does think about sublimity in Sicily and elsewhere, does write a letter home (from the Holy Land). However, this final volume of *Persons and Places* was originally published in 1953, ten years after the poem.

59. John Herman Randall in Corliss Lamont, ed., *A Dialogue on George Santayana* (New York, 1959), p. 29.

60. "A Collect of Philosophy" in *OP*, p. 187.

61. NA, pp. 136 ff., 147 f. When Stevens adds that the imagination is "a miracle of logic and that its exquisite divinations are calculations beyond analysis" and then, quoting anonymously, says, "If so, one understands perfectly the remark that 'in the service of love and imagination nothing can be too lavish, too sublime or too festive'" he is quoting from the second volume of the autobiography ("The Middle Span," pp. 2 f.). Santayana's

statement is actually more complex and typical of his later tone: "Baroque and rococo cannot be foreign to a Spaniard. They are profoundly congenial and Quixotic, suspended as it were between two contrary insights: that in the service of love and imagination nothing can be too lavish, too sublime, or too festive; yet that all this passion is a caprice, a farce, a contortion, a comedy of illusions." Santayana spent his last years at the Blue Sisters' Nursing Home in Rome.

62.   *Platonism and the Spiritual Life*, pp. 257, 304, 293.

63.   cf. "Persons yielded in interest to places" says Santayana of the years 1897–1913 ("The Middle Span," p. 111). In *Adagia* (*OP*, p. 158) Stevens writes, "Life is an affair of people not of places. But for me life is an affair of places and that is the trouble."

3

Saul Bellow and the
Example of Dostoevsky

I

It is no longer possible to say that all modern American literature comes from *Huckleberry Finn*. In a literal sense it was never possible, whatever *éclat* Hemingway's famous hyperbole has had. In view of recent developments in the novel, it sounds with the resonance of another era. True, Salinger is oblique witness to the life of a tradition that includes Anderson, Hemingway, Lardner, and Faulkner, but the figure of the innocent initiate cannot be the only iconographic center of a literature which is focused on the adult genital ego in culture, and on its corresponding mental sweat. It was once possible to think of a pure adolescent heart as symbolic of hidden virtue still resident in the young country, a natural, redeeming reality deeper than all worldly appearances. But the difference between Huck and Holden Caulfield is instructive: solitude has become isolation, traumatic experience fullblown neuroticism, lighting out for the territory retiring to the mental institution. Adolescence is no longer an example but a case. Salinger is on Mark Twain's side, on his far side—civilized life is scarcely worth living—but we no longer have the freedom of the asexual idyll; we have urban, claustral impotence. Holden's grey hair symbolizes the end of an American myth, a time when America comes of middle age.

There are, however, advantages to growing all the way up, fallen though that state may be; what is lost in innocence is gained in knowledge. Though this moral has often been full of possibility in American literature, the force of it is no longer widely considered to be dramatic in itself. America has moved closer to Europe, and much, not "all," contemporary American literature comes from Flaubert or the Russians if it "comes from" anywhere. We have seen what the Flaubert tradition affords.

Bellow, on the other hand, seems to be the leading contemporary exponent of the "Russian" way. The idea of a writer as teacher rather than martyr, citizen rather than artist, journalist rather than aesthetician; the idea of literature that is flexible enough to be tendentious and broad enough to be inspiring; a literature that refuses to adopt the pose of objectivity, detachment, and disenchantment with life in quest of the compensatory salvation of form and avoids comparing the artist with God—all this bears witness to the Russian influence. The Russians would never think of art as religion, yet moral feeling in their work is charged with an energy, a yearning, a hope, that may finally be described as religious. Their art respects, indeed thrives, on mental effort and expresses, as Irving Howe has remarked, "that 'mania for totality' which is to become characteristic of our time."[1]

The postmodern Jewish writers have brought to American literature a dramatics of the mind which, generally speaking, recalls the Russians. V. S. Pritchett has suggested that there is an affinity between the American writers of Yiddish background and the Slavs. They know what the western writers have long ago forgotten, says Pritchett, "the sense of looseness, timelessness and space."[2] Pritchett's impressionistic remark acknowledges the essentialist affirmation, desperate though it may be, of irreducible moral truths that define a sort of rhythm of the ethical sphere. The artist-god comparison implies the need for a total subjective originality that denies the reality of this timelessness. These generalizations may be illustrated by a comparison between Bellow and the Russian master whose example is most instructive to him, Dostoevsky.

The central impetus in both writers, in periods marked by ideological confusion and in novels full of explainers, is the quest for what is morally real. Ivan Karamazov's "if there is no God everything is permitted" is the sort of immoralist proposition that they must refute. When Dostoevsky says of the "enthusiast," Belinsky, "He knew that the moral principle is at the root of everything,"[3] we have a statement in tune with Bellow's idea of "axial lines." To begin with a conventional illustration, both writers use the image of the child as the embodiment of innocence—sometimes offering it with an unabashed naiveté. We recall, for example, Augie's *après vu* of his fatherhood, or Myshkin's story of the peasant woman with a baby who says, "God has just such gladness every time he sees from heaven that a sinner is praying to Him with all his heart, as a mother has when she sees the first smile on her baby's face."[4] While such an image may embarrass the properly jaded reader, we know that a character like Myshkin could not exist without such sentiment. The contemporary reader has, perhaps, less difficulty with Ivan's conception of the child as victim, as symbol of unspeakable injustice, as is seen in incidents of child beating so vividly represented that even Alyosha agrees that the sadistic perpetrator should be shot. Similarly, a courtroom re-enactment of child beating is a blow sufficient to turn the civilized Herzog to murderous thoughts. Of course, child abuse has a seductive force in Dostoevsky, who is sometimes called the Russian Sade; but its thematic effect inverts Sade in order to expose nihilism, not to promote it. The poetry of crime—fully orchestrated and directly dramatized in Dostoevsky, muted and usually the subject of a lyric polemic in Bellow—comes to serve as a last-ditch proof of the existence of God or, at least, of the existence of moral imperatives since, in modern literature, God typically enters through the back door. The creator of Raskolnikov might almost have written (though it was actually Bellow) that "there are friendships, affinities, natural feelings, rooted norms. People do on the whole agree, for instance, that it is wrong to murder. And even if they are unable to offer rational arguments for this, they are not necessarily driven to commit gratuitous acts of violence."[5]

To be sure, the words of the Grand Inquisitor to Christ—"Dost Thou know that the ages will pass, and humanity will proclaim by the lips of their sages that there is no crime, and therefore no sin; there is only hunger?"[6]—carry great force in an age of behavioral environmentalism. We are familiar with Brecht's paraphrase of "Feed men, and then ask of them virtue." And it develops into the argument of Mailer's "The White Negro" where he excuses the murder of a storekeeper by young killers. *Anomie* issuing in desperate boredom does link characters like Stavrogin and Mailer's Marion Faye. Stavrogin wishes to "put powder under the four corners of the earth and blow it all up"[7]—as does Marion in similar words. The difference is that Dostoevsky, like Bellow, ultimately has a contempt for the immoralist Stavrogin, whereas Mailer's essential sympathy lies with the immoralist (now hipster) Faye.

Even greater is Dostoevsky's contempt for the radical Pytor Verkovensky, whose vision of the revolution come to pass is one of crime as the norm. Speaking to Stavrogin, he counts his troops: "The lawyer who defends an educated murderer because he is more cultured than his victims and could not help murdering them to get money is one of us. The schoolboys who murder a peasant for the sake of sensation are ours. The juries who acquit every criminal are ours. The prosecutor who trembles at a trial for fear he should seem advanced enough is ours, ours." Pytor concludes that "crime is no longer insanity, but simply common sense, almost a duty; a gallant protest."[8] True, in Czarist Russia any protest was credible, but what we get in Pytor is a prefiguring of Stalinist manipulators. On his part, Bellow has always been mistrustful of the clairvoyance of radical solutions, but it is not until Mr. *Sammler's Planet* that he dramatizes a comparable political hysteria.

Dostoevsky's attack on nihilism, then, is political as well as ethical. Not confined to hysteria, the assault often expresses itself as comedy at the expense of ideology, which is seen to be utilitarian, socialist, individualist, western. The underground man is, perhaps, the most conspicuous illustration of the assault on the radicalism of the 1860s (as opposed to the more humanitarian radicalism of the 1840s with which he has some ambivalent sympathy, as did Dostoevsky himself), which is imaged as the wall, the piano key (determinism), the ant hill, the chicken coop (the urban mass and that utilitarian haven, the apartment house), and the Crystal Palace (the new cathedral of utilitarian perfection). As Ralph Matlaw says, Dostoevsky is attacking the utopia of Chernyshevsky, Fourier, and Saint-Simon, which tried to reconcile Hegel and Rousseau, the world historic process and the man of feeling, historical determinism and individual will.[9]

In *Notes from Underground* and elsewhere Dostoevsky makes no distinction between ideology and utopia, which he uses in its pejorative sense. The uncensored version had intimations of Christian belief; however, the censor seems to have done well in deleting them if his aim was the dramatic coherence of the work. Despite the underground man's brilliance and authenticity, he is trapped in the atom of his ego, unable to love, unable to be more than a caricature of the "freedom" he claims to represent. But with *Notes from Underground* the genre of ideological comedy is established. The ruthless, loud honesty, the intellectual acuity, the comic dramatization of mental suffering—all these appear earlier in Diderot's *Rameau's Nephew*, but the full head of self-consciousness, historical awareness, and philosophical depth is Dostoevsky's addition. The underground man knows more than the nephew and enjoys less; he is isolated and, generally, impotent.

Ideological comedy—which is to have an impact on Bellow—is not confined to *Notes from Underground*. In *Crime and Punishment*, for example, there is the marvellous Lebeziatnikov, a rarely noticed character. After describing the "anaemic, scrofulous little man," the usually neutral narrator tells us that he was "really rather stupid; he attached himself to the cause of progress and 'our younger generation' from enthusiasm. He was one of the numerous and varied legion of dullards, of half-animate abortions, conceited half-educated coxcombs, who attach themselves to the idea most in fashion only to vulgarize it and who caricature every cause they serve, however sincerely." Lebeziatnikov is a theoretician and, in a wildly comic scene, expounds Fourier and Darwin to the smug bourgeois Luzhin who despises him as a man of no connections. Luzhin, ready for any praise, accepts Lebeziatnikov's commendations for being ready to contribute to the establishment of a new "commune," for abstaining from christening future children, for acquiescing "if Dounia were to take a lover a month after marriage, and so on." Luzhin, who is the most tyrannical, self-absorbed, money-mad character in the book!

When Luzhin asks to make certain that Sonia is a prostitute (later the sinister depth of this request is revealed), Lebeziatnikov says, in the tone of airy emancipation that Dostoevsky scorns, "What of it? I think, that is, it is my own personal conviction that this is the normal condition of women. Why not? I mean, *distinguons.* In our present society, it is not altogether normal, because it is compulsory, but in the future society it will be perfectly normal, because it will be voluntary. . . . I regard her actions as a vigorous protest against the organization of society." From Dostoevsky's point of view—and from her own—Sonia's life of prostitution is a martyrdom. This point of view is conservative, sympathetic to monogamy, privacy, Christianity, chastity. It is characteristic of Dostoevsky to scorn "advanced" ideas, to characterize them as utopian schemes masking the self-interest of the idea-monger. (Lebeziatnikov does "wait in hopes" of Sonia.) Dostoevsky, profoundly mistrusting meliorist realism, often sees the cause itself as the caricature. Lebeziatnikov says, "I should be the first to be ready to clean out any cesspool you like . . . it's simply work . . . much better than the work of a Raphael and a Pushkin, because it is more useful,"[10] and thus gives us the first statement of a theme which becomes major in *The Possessed.* Here, as elsewhere, Dostoevsky treats the ideologue as the buffoon. When, in his concern about the distraught Katerina, Lebeziatnikov tells Raskolnikov that "in Paris they have been conducting serious experiments as to the possibility of curing the insane, simply by logical argument,"[11] we have a delicious reduction of the excessive faith in rationalism which Dostoevsky condemns as western.

Dostoevsky's rare allusions to America suggest that he believes that the new land is about as western as you can get. In *The Possessed* it is for the fop Lebyadkin to sing its praises. He speaks glowingly of an American millionaire who "left all his vast fortune to factories and to the exact sciences, and his skeleton to the students of the academy there, and his skin to be made into a drum, so that the American national hymn might be beaten upon it day and night."[12] The experience of Shatov and Kirillov in America gives this rationalist optimism the lie. America, with its capitalism, its science, its utilitarianism, is, in Dostoevsky's mind, a desperate place. He must sometimes have thought that Russian culture by comparison was concerned with the smiling aspects of life.

In Bellow and Dostoevsky the world that we know is in good measure a world of ideas, positions, solutions. The letters of Herzog are only the most celebrated instance of the endless interplay of explanation which strikes Bellow as the most salient characteristic of an anxious age. Some of the ideas are worthy of Lebeziatnikov—like the theory of the Bulgarian aesthetician Banowich, who believes that telling someone a joke means that you want to eat him, or, more seriously, the various Sadean theories of negative transcendence which espouse creative criminality. Basteshaw, Dahfu, Bummidge, Lal are among those heavy theoreticians in Bellow in whom ideology is open to the charge of utopianism. Dostoevsky's attack is centered on the utilitarian and the revolutionary; while not excluding these, Bellow's is directed at more recent utopian attitudinizing, including the psychoanalytic, the technocratic, the modernist visionary. The mold is the same but the material has changed somewhat, partly because Bellow has a common-sense sympathy for a number of the liberal utilitarian propositions which Dostoevsky burlesques. For Dostoevsky suffering is the mother of human consciousness; Bellow is willing to grant this, provided one holds, as he does, that pleasure is its father. Still, both writers reduce the Babel to a comic dimension from the point of view of a more traditional truth to be told. Both take confidence from older, "obsolete" truths, residues of a religious tradition.

II

Bellow's outlook is analogous to that of social theorists such as Raymond Aron and Edward Shils. A *précis* of their key arguments sheds a clearer light on his aims, and on those of writers like him.

Raymond Aron's *The Opium of the Intellectuals* implies in its title the reduced attraction of the Marxist ideology and revolutionism that had once greatly appealed to a number of the post-war liberal revisionist writers in America. Aron maintains that revolutionism had benefited from the prestige of aesthetic modernism, that the artist who denounced the philistines and the Marxist who denounced the bourgeoisie could consider themselves united in a battle against a single enemy. Aron notes, however, that none of the big literary movements was allied with the political left. Exceptions seem tangential and only prove the rule: "Sartre's itinerary toward quasi-Communism appears to be dialectical. Man being a 'vain passion,' one is inclined in the last analysis to judge the various 'projects' as all equally sterile. The radiant vision of the classless society follows on the description of the squalid society of today."[13]

Bellow shares his view not only of high culture, but also of the mythicized proletariat, of whom Aron writes: "Servant of the machine, soldier of the Revolution, the proletariat as such is never either the symbol or the beneficiary or the leader of any regime whatsoever. . . . The common source of these errors is a kind of visionary optimism combined with a pessimistic view of reality."[14] As for the justification of such pessimism, Aron points out that by comparing the division of wealth and the standards of government of a century ago with those of today, we can see that "the growth of collective resources makes societies more egalitarian and less tyrannical. They remain, nonetheless, subject to the old, blind necessities of work and of power and, *ipso facto*, in the eyes of the optimists, unacceptable."[15]

This "doctrine of sustained tensions" with its emphasis on "the courage . . . to endure," as R. W. B. Lewis describes it, in a review of Lionel Trilling's *The Liberal Imagination*,[16] gives us what Lewis calls "the new stoicism," which is analogous to the Burkean view of history. Though the word has little of its original meaning, there is a similarity between the "old" Stoic rejection of Platonism in favor of sense perception and the late forties' stoic rejection of Marxism in favor of a pragmatic sense of possibility. Both posit a dignified self-sufficiency in a world of failed illusion. In Aron's dichotomy the essentialists and the utopians are at odds. We have seen Professor Herzog lecturing in a similar vein on the modernist *"new utopian history, an idyll, comparing the present to an imaginary past, because we hate the world as it is."*[17]

Along with Aron, perhaps the clearest exponent of the stoical view is Edward Shils, a student of Karl Mannheim, sociologist and Bellow's colleague at the University of Chicago. Bellow would seem to admire the tone that these men assume—totally unapologetic—in their critique of modernist utopianism. Like Aron, Shils must place the Marxist view in what he feels is its proper perspective. He points out that Trotsky thought "the average human type will rise to the heights of an Aristotle, a Goethe or a Marx. And above this ridge, new peaks will rise." But Shils feels that the working class, even where it is Communist, is uninterested in revolution, in the moral transformation of itself and the rest of the human race. Shils believes that all ideologues (e.g., Marxists, French monarchists, Southern agrarians) are hostile to human beings as they are. A revulsion against their own age makes intellectuals think of the elevated cultural life and dignified peasantry of a non-existent past (e.g., Tönnies, Simmel, Sombart, Marcuse). He denies the validity of the *Gemeinschaft/Gesellschaft* distinction, since it assumes a small-scale, perfectly consensual, theological society that never existed.

Shils does not believe that bourgeois individualism, urban society, and industrialism are an impoverishment of life. For him, as for Bellow since *Dangling Man*, the "fundamental problems of humanity are the same as in antiquity." He wants a pluralistic society rather than a completely integrated one, with a bow to British utilitarianism and Burke's critique of ideological politics, and with another to the British liberals, like Milton and Locke, who saw that society could be effective even if it had no uniformity of belief, no unifying ideology, and to Mill who, taking the next step, held that diversity of viewpoint was a necessity for a healthy society. Moreover, Shils believes that in mass society there is actually "more of a sense of attachment to the society as a whole, more sense of affinity with one's own fellows, more openness to understanding, and more reaching out of understanding among men than in any earlier society of our western history or in any of the great oriental societies of the past"; that is, "it is the most consensual." Indeed, the "uniqueness" of mass society is its "incorporation of the mass into the moral order of its society." Since the mass means more to the elite than in other societies, we see an enhancement of the dignity of ordinary life. Again, with a bow to Weber, "the unique feature of the mass society is . . . the dispersion of charismatic quality more widely throughout the society" (e.g., working class, women, youth, ethnic groups previously disadvantaged). Shils does attribute some truth to the view which he is compelled to deny, saying that while there is alienation, there is another side to the conventional Marxist critique of mass society. The other side of alienation is disenchantment with authority; of egotism and hedonism, the growth of sensibility; of the decline of local autonomy, a more integrated society. Beyond all this dynamism the primordial attachments—kinship, locality, sexuality—will change but persist.[18]

Shils attacks "ideology," a term that he defines with strict constructionist precision. Ideology is a highly systematized pattern of belief integrated around a few pre-eminent values—salvation, equality, ethnic purity. Political coherence overrides every other consideration, with supreme significance going to one group or class—the nation, the ethnic folk, the proletariat, the party leaders. It has a Manichean cast, positing uncompromisable distinctions between good and evil, sacred and profane, left and right, we and they; the source of evil is a foreign power, an ethnic group, or a class (e.g., bourgeois). There is a distrust of traditional institutions—family, church, economic organizations, schools, conventional political alignments. Shils distinguishes ideology from outlooks (e.g., Protestantism), which are pluralistic, containing creeds which shade off into ideology but do not take a sharply bounded and corporate form, and have much less orthodoxy. He also contrasts ideology with systems and movements of thought, which, like ideologies and unlike outlooks, are elaborate and internally integrated, but do not insist on total observance in behaviour, complete consensus among its adherents, or on closure vis-à-vis other intellectual constructions. Ideology, too, is distinct from programs, which involve specification of a particular limited objective, often in the form of a passionate rejection of one aspect of society.

Opposed to ideology is civility or civil politics; civility is the virtue of the citizen who shares responsibility in his own self-government. It is compatible with other attachments to class, to religion, to profession, but it regulates them out of a respect for tradition and out of an awareness of the complexity of virtue, an awareness that every virtue costs, that virtue is intertwined with vice. With characteristic benignity Shils, writing in 1958, says that "There is now in all strata, on the average, a higher civil sense than earlier phases of Western society have ever manifested." In the manner of civility Shils does not believe that ideology should be "completely dismissed"—the desire for greater equality, the distrust of authority, the need for heroism, all have "some validity." It is not the substance but the rigidity of ideological politics that does damage. Ideologies fail in their notions of global conquest because "normal" values assert themselves, compromises are made, and the world changes. As for the phrase "end of ideology," it applied only to a very specific time and in a very specific way; it did not mean that ideology could never exist. It was wrongly taken to mean that ideals, ethical standards, and general or comprehensive social views and policies were no longer either relevant or possible. Both sides failed, at times, to distinguish between ideology and outlook and between ideology and program. No society can exist without a cognitive, moral, and expressive culture; there can never be an end to outlooks and creeds, movements of thought and programs.[19]

It is worth briefly noting objections to these views which, like the views themselves, bear on a comprehension of Bellow and Dostoevsky. Needless to say, historical events of the late sixties represented an anger, a sense of injustice, that does violence to the tonality of these remarks and to a number of the propositions themselves. This is not the place for a weighing of arguments. To an amateur observer, however, it appears that Americans now and in the past have often been passionate about what Shils defines as programs, and that ideology is a concept resonant with the struggles of *Mitteleuropa* from which a number of liberal and radical intellectuals derive perhaps too much of their vocabulary. Ideology, as Shils defines it, is as bad as he says it is. But it is difficult to gainsay Dennis Wrong's questioning of the total view: "If 'ideology' is by now, and perhaps with good reason, an irretrievably fallen word, is it necessary that 'utopia' suffer the same fate? . . . [Utopia] is the vision of a *possible* society, a vision that must deeply penetrate human consciousness before the question of how it might be fulfilled is seriously considered—and by that time we will already have advanced a long way towards its fulfillment."[20]

The impatience or dislike shown by radical readers (adherents, say, of C. Wright Mills) for a book like Mr. *Sammler's Planet*, in which "ideology" is presented as brutality, or a book like *Herzog*, whose hero feels that the "occupation of a man is in duty, in use, in civility, in politics in the Aristotelian sense," not in ideology or politics in the Marxist sense, is another way of drawing the lines. One recalls Lenin's view of *The Possessed*: "great but repulsive." Bellow has his own personalist, novelist's point of view, but his explicit utterances about ideology, by which he means what Shils means, are in the manner of Aron and Shils: "Ideology is crippling to attention. It has no finite interests but makes a wholesale distribution of innumerable human facts. Its historical or biological schemes dispose of human beings by classification." In support of a deeper, contrary wisdom, he then quotes Dostoevsky, who writes in an accent Bellow comes to adopt: "We cannot exhaust a phenomenon, never can we trace its end or its beginning. We are familiar merely with the everyday, aparent and current, and this only insofar as it appears to us, whereas the ends and the beginnings still constitute to man a realm of the fantastic." The moral is then drawn by Bellow: "Ideology commands an end, imposes a law, speaks the first and last words and abolishes confusion. But it has no interest in the miracle of being which artists endlessly contemplate."[21] This "mystery of mankind," as Bellow is later to call it, this inexhaustibility, is indicative of the personalist, anti-ideological view.

Even more so are Dostoevsky's critical remarks on *Anna Karenina*. Addressing himself to the question of Anna's guilt, Dostoevsky repudiates the "physician-socialists," saying that, for the Russian author, "no ant-hill, no triumph of the 'fourth estate,' no elimination of poverty, no organization of labour will save mankind from abnormality, and therefore—from guilt and criminality . . . that in no organization of society can evil be eliminated, that the human soul will remain identical; that abnormality and sin emanate from the soul itself, and finally, that the laws of the human spirit are so unknown to science, so obscure, so indeterminate and mysterious, that, as yet, there can neither be physicians nor *final* judges, but there is only He who saith: 'Vengeance belongeth unto me; I will recompense'" (the epigraph to the novel). This is deeper than environmentalism, which says, "inasmuch as society is abnormally organized, it is impossible to make the human entity responsible for its consequences. Therefore, the criminal is irresponsible and at present crime does not exist." But, Dostoevsky continues, Tolstoy knowing in this case the consequences of adultery and equal "crimes," expresses his older wisdom in an "analysis of the human soul."[22] Though Bellow is far more sympathetic than Dostoevsky to the environmentalists, he gives us in Alexander Corde of *The Dean's December* a man who does not want to see crime go unpunished. And Corde is sorry that in the murder of a white woman by a black psychopath, "Nobody actually said, 'An evil has been done'" (*DD*, p. 202).

One of the truisms of Dostoevsky criticism is that the writer who excoriated the ideology of political radicalism himself embraced the ideology of pan-Slavism with its belief in the messianic mission of the God-bearing Russian people, the truth of Russian orthodoxy and the falsehood of western Roman Catholicism, the sanctity of the Russian soil, and the even more sacred quality of the Russian peasant; here we have the we—they, sacred—profane dichotomy, which Shils says characterized the ideologist. But Dostoevsky scarcely knew the peasants he idealized. And, as Philip Rahv has said, the manner in which he embraced orthodoxy was so apocalyptic as to undermine orthodoxy, subvert dogma, shatter the notion of institutionalized religion itself.[23] If, in *The Possessed*, he saw the failure of revolutionary ideology, he was too honest not to portray the nihilistic vacuum which revolution must fill. Perhaps anyone viewing political reality in Czarist Russia with a clear eye would see a chaos beyond the politics of civility to set right. Dostoevsky dreaded the Antichrist whose arrival he intuited, which accounts for the gloom behind the comic balance of the book. As for his belief, does he ever really convince us of anything more than Shatov's "I—I will believe in God"? And for all his sweet clairvoyance, the final point about Myshkin is that he fails.

III

Above all, the dramatic force of Dostoevsky's art often works against his didactic intention with a brilliance that illustrates the subtle uniqueness of literature—the exposition, in action, of ambivalence, the complex of feelings in the face of which any idea must be a simplification. The underground man, Raskolnikov, Ivan—all characters whom Dostoevsky fundamentally rejects—are creations of a child of light who saw best in darkness. But the metaphor should not confuse. Dostoevsky was nothing if not a personalist. In saying of him that "nobody was less preoccupied with the empirical world. . . . His art is completely immersed in the profound realities of the spiritual universe,"[24] Nicholas Berdyaev gives us what is, at best, a half-truth. How can one be a non-empirical psychological genius? More to the point is the description by Strakhov, who knew Dostoevsky intimately: "All his attention was upon people, and all his efforts were directed towards understanding their nature and character. People, their temperament, way of living, feelings, thoughts, these were his sole preoccupation."[25]

This personalism is consonant with the intellectual depth of his work; for he is, as Arnold Hauser puts it, "a romantic in the world of thought" in that "the movement of thought has the same motive power and the same emotional, not to say pathological, impetus in him as the flood and stress of the feelings had in the romantics."[26] In this lyricism of ideas combined with a centrist conception of character Bellow finds Dostoevsky the acknowledged master. Typically, in a Bellow novel, an essentially urban man—usually "cracked," often intellectual, portrayed in his solitude or isolation, usually unemployed in one way or another, whose business turns out to be personal relationships—is thrust forward at the moment of intense subjective crisis. Everyday apprehension is shattered by a welling up of the demonic. What George Steiner says of Dostoevsky also applies to Bellow: his "characters—even the neediest among them—always have leisure for chaos or an unpremeditated total involvement."[27] Virtuosi in mental suffering, these characters embody the heady balance of disequilibruim. When Dostoevsky, in his famous letter to Strakhov, wrote, "I have my own view of art, and that which the majority call fantastic and exceptional is for me the very essence of reality," he was a pioneer, not aware that he was writing a motto for much of the literature of the future. It is this merging of realism and fantasy in a context of pained, obsessive, often funny subjectivity—this art, as Philip Rahv has it, of psychic distortion, moral agitation, and resentment,[28] the way of Gogol rather than the "objective" way of Pushkin—that Dostoevsky and Bellow take as their aesthetic norm. Herbert Gold called the author of *Henderson the Rain King* the "funniest sufferer since Gogol,"[29] to which one can only add, with the possible exception of the creator of *The Double, Notes from Underground,* and *The Eternal Husband.*

"All Dostoevsky's heroes are really himself,"[30] says Berdyaev, offering a version of the distinction between Dostoevsky, a writer of subjectivity and obsession, and Tolstoy, one of objectivity and proportion. This is a distinction of convenience, but it is a contrast that can tell us something about Bellow as well. Both present a theater of self-realization where the heart is laid bare in the act of defining what is real. In this personal quest sociological categories are secondary to the spiritual. If this implies a distance between object and subject, society and self, action and temperament, it is a distance which both writers feel must be bridged. In both, brotherhood is a refrain whose melody they are trying—and often failing—to recapture. Both attempt to break out of what Edward Wasiolek has called *"the circle of hurt-and-be-hurt,"*[31] the network of sado-masochism, which appears to be a governing principle in Sammler's era. *But, in both, meekness or mildness is largely its own reward. Caritas* is typically confounded by Eros in a scenario where man-woman relationships testify to the potency of moral tenuousness or disintegration. In Dostoevsky, as Berdyaev says, "The mystery of marriage is not consummated," and in Bellow the marriage is consummated, but the mystery is not dispelled. For both, in Berdyaev's phrase, "love serves only as an index of . . . inner division."[32]

Yet the delineation of similarities points significantly to differences, for Dostoevsky presents us with a drama of extremes, a moral *chiaroscuro,* an acting out in fact of what in Bellow often remains fantasy or suggestion. Raskolnikov commits the murder; Herzog does not. Herzog thinks of and, in some ways, embodies the strength of mildness; Myshkin is its apotheosis; hit by a block of wood and his senses clarified, Henderson says that truth comes in blows, but when Dmitri Karamazov says, "I understand now that such men as I need a blow," he has been condemned for a parricide he wished for. The self-willed in Dostoevsky are pathological, the meek incredibly self-effacing. And sometimes both extremes inhabit the same soul. Corde skeptically, reluctantly admits that he cannot accept such paradoxes: "It was foreign, bookish—it was Dostoevsky stuff that the vices of Sodom coexisted with the adoration of Holy Sophia" (*DD*, p. 130). When a "murderer-saviour" type appears in *The Dean's December* in the person of Toby Winthrop, Bellow does not do much more than include him as part of the grim local color. Respecting his male-nurse qualities, he nonetheless considers him a "case," part of abstract modern consciousness rather than Christian miracle. Still, in his articles, Corde finds it necessary to mention the Antichrist.

Czarist Russia had a way of rendering fantasy literal, making for a dramatic, even operatic, quality which in a kindred comtemporary spirit more usually comes out as *opéra bouffe*. Dostoevsky's ideological preferences lent substance to an often Manichean opposition of forces. The outcome in Dostoevsky is typically tragic in overtone, a Dionysian coming to grips with the demonic, leaving one with a sense of waste nobler than the hidden cause. In Bellow even the Dionysian inspiration—e.g., Henderson, Herzog—is ultimately comic in that the painful, headlong quest is inseparable from knowledge that constitutes the self—the western, Dostoevsky-doubted ego, the last court of appeals; the self that, in its constant exposure, cannot be taken as seriously as it once was, yet is most of what we have to take seriously. Where Dostoevsky dramatically records the disintegration of the self, Bellow tentatively assumes it, and the tragic is converted into the comic. In Bellow, accordingly, more often than in Dostoevsky, the soul is finally restored to a firm outline.

The one point at which the two winters would seem to differ most is the apprehension of the self in its full sensual regalia. Here Bellow appears to be positively Tolstoyan. A character like Stiva Oblonsky, in *Anna Karenina*, lives in the literary love of an author whose judgment is otherwise morally proscriptive of him. Many of Bellow's characters exist in this way. Ramona, for example, illustrates the delights of inner division. The observation of sensuousness implies the "normal" world, but the dramatic situation implies the Dostoevskian "extreme." It is precisely this integration of opposites which describes a good part of the course of the current literary *Zeitgeist*, for what we see in Bellow, and in other recent writers, is the normalization of the extreme—making it comfortable, cozy, charming. "If I'm out of my mind, it's all right with me," says Herzog and any reader of the book would understand him.

IV

Bellow's work offers some extended illustrations of the Dostoevskian influence—unconscious or otherwise. It has not been noticed, for example, that the dialogue between Joseph and the Spirit of Alternatives in *Dangling Man* is a low-keyed recasting of the apparition of the devil to the hallucinated consciousness of Ivan Karamazov. Ivan recognizes that the devil is his double: "You are the incarnation of myself, but only one side of me . . . of my thoughts and feelings, but only the nastiest and stupidest of them" (*BK*, P. 775). The devil appears as a shabby genteel Russian, whom Dostoevsky sees as a type. They "have a distinct aversion for any duties that may be forced upon them, are usually solitary creatures, either bachelors or widowers. Sometimes they have children . . . brought up at a distance, at some aunt's. . . . They gradually lose sight of their children altogether" (*BK*, p. 773). That is, the devil is worldly self-absorption divorced from the essential ties. Child abandonment, while not quite the equivalent of child abuse, is closely related.[33] Yet this prince of darkness is a gentleman, "accommodating, and ready to assume any amiable expression," possessing, in Dostoevsky's view, the complete western veneer and the basic western wisdom. He does not know if there is a god; he knows only *je pense, donc je suis* and, Descartes's "proof" of the existence of God to the contrary notwithstanding, its attendant solipsism (a sort of fantasy extension, in

Dostoevsky's view, of the rationalistic, ego-oriented west): "Does all that exist of itself, or is it only an emanation of myself, a logical development of my ego which alone has existed for ever" (*BK*, p. 781).

Goethe was enough of a traditional humanist to create a Mephistopheles who desired evil but did only good; Dostoevsky's Mephistopheles, however, operating in a universe much more attuned to the modern saturation of alienated consciousness, sees that he desires good but does only evil— which perfectly describes Ivan's predicament (culminating in his harrowing scenes with Smerdyakov, whose suicide he hears of immediately after the apparition vanishes). Ivan realizes at the outset that the devil embodies his "stupidest" thoughts, yet so attractive are they that they threaten to destroy his "intelligent" ones. "God is dead," "the man-god," "will," "science," "all things are lawful," "the old slave man," parade so tantalizingly before his hallucinated view that Ivan can dispel them only in the way Luther with his inkstand set the devil to rout—he throws his glass at him. If this is a breakthrough for Ivan, the devil himself remains *déclassé*. Konstantin Mochulsky notes that "in his *Legend* Ivan represented the devil in the majestic image of the terrible and wise spirit, and here he has proved to be a vulgar hanger-on. . . . The spirit of non-being is an imposter: this is not Lucifer with singed wings, but . . . the incarnation of world boredom and world vulgarity."[34] Precisely. And it is this note of boredom and vulgarity that Bellow strikes in his ostensibly reasonable, genteel representative of non-being, the Spirit of Alternatives. There is no nightmare, no sickness here—at least in the first meeting. Consistent with the meandering movement of the work itself, the encounter is "relaxed." So reasonable is the Spirit, so plausible to the dangling man are his alternatives, that he is also called "On the Other Hand" and *"Tu As Raison Aussi."* Yet it is clear that in his equivocal manner, his indeterminacy, his inevitable drift to the negative, the alienative, his flirtation with ideology, his attitudinizing in a vacuum of conviction, and above all, in his compulsion to the center of indifference, to death, he is the dangling man's devil-double in the same sense that the apparition is Ivan's—a representation of his own worst, his own "stupidest" ideas and tendencies. (Joseph, we recall, is already separated from the older, benevolent, rational, Enlightenment Joseph.) This apparition is even quieter than Joseph; his point must be elicited, but when it is seen to be "alienation," Joseph retorts that "it's a fool's plea." Not that there is no alienation, but "that we should not make a doctrine" of it.

Trying another route, the Spirit suggests "changing exis-tence" through politics, but Joseph rejects the revolutionary and even politics per se. He does, however, admit the value of "a plan, a program, perhaps an obsession." When the Spirit converts this typically American ad hoc impulse into "an ideal construction," Joseph notes the "German phrase," and wonders about the ideological exemplar or type. He concedes that an "obsessive device" may be "the only possible way to meet chaos" and sees the apparent "need to give ourselves some exclusive focus, passionate and engulfing," but the essentialist in him asserts itself: "what of the gap between the ideal construction and the real world, the truth? . . . Then, there's this: the obsession exhausts the man. It can become his enemy. If often does." When the Spirit has no answer to this, apparently having no real convictions to defend, Joseph drives him out, flinging "a handful of orange peel" at him (*DM*, pp. 137f.).

Like Ivan, Joseph seeks that which "unlocks the imprison-ing self," and in order to escape being "self-fastened" he him-self is willing to entertain the "highest 'ideal construction,'" though, more or less, as a passing fancy. Still, he feels that *Tu As Raison Aussi* stands refuted; Joseph has confidence that the "final end" of everyone is "the desire for pure freedom," which he defines in Dostoevskian fashion, not simply as free will but as will defining itself as spirit, "to know what we are and what we are for, to know our purpose, to seek grace" (*DM*, p. 154). This is as far as Joseph will go towards religion. But the resolution is offhand and represents only a moment of equilibrium.

Joseph's depression worsens, and in the next encounter the Spirit appears as an almost old-style Mephistopheles, the Spirit that Denies, tempting Joseph to "give up," to succumb to indifference, to die, to "worship the anti-life." Joseph recognizes his "inability to be free," and this is the cause of his "weariness of life." Unmistakably, and despite his noble wish to share the pain of his generation, Joseph joins the army in the same way one joins the Grand Inquisitor's church: "We soon want to give up our freedom . . . we choose a master, roll over on our backs and ask for the leash" (*DM* pp. 167f.). When Joseph utters the hollow cry, "Long live regimentation!" he is aware that he is "relieved of self-determination, freedom cancelled" (*DM*, p. 191). This conclusion has little of the ambiguity sometimes attributed to it. In the end Bellow's devil-double emerges as one who ascertains one's doubt of selfhood, uniqueness, "separate destiny." Joseph is rendered almost as pale, sickly, chilled, and enervated at the end of his encounter with the double as Ivan is with his.

The dramatization of guilt leading to confrontation with the double becomes conspicuous in comparing Bellow's *The Victim* with Dostoevsky's *The Eternal Husband*. This comparison has not gone unnoticed, but the context of extended comparison here affords us a wider view of its meaning. Actually, Dostoevsky's *The Double* is the precursor of both. A solitary spirit in a dreary urban landscape is the necessary beginning to each crisis of subjectivity. In *The Double* "the damp autumn day, muggy and dirty, peeped into the room through the dingy window pane with such a hostile, sour grimace that Mr. Golyadkin could not possibly doubt that he was not in the land of Nod, but in the city of Petersburg, in his own flat on the fourth story of a huge block of buildings in Shestilavotchny Street" (*D*, p. 477). If his living is compartmentalized, so is his job, for Golyadkin is a result of the dehumanizing Russian bureaucracy. The crisis in his life breaks out when the moral qualities that the system exacts of its lesser lights—bootlicking, toadying, a fidgety, manipulative quality, a nastiness masking as playfulness, a choreographed self-interest—appears in the shape of Golyadkin Junior who, like Ivan's devil-double, is the embodiment of Senior's worst self.

As the story begins, we see Golyadkin "satisfied" with the "insignificant" face and bald head he views in the morning mirror. He feels so good that he counts his money. Beware!—a sure sign of anal-retentive meanness in Dostoevsky is viewed here as a sign of life in the bureaucracy. A volatile mixture of self-esteem and self-abasement (before his superiors, or any other male authority figure), this isolated, hostile, sado-masochistic urban bachelor is Dostoevsky's first underground man. "Sick," he goes to see a physician, palpitating before the meeting but greeting him with a schizoid "figuratively crush-ing" glare. He is suffering from "the perfumed compliment," the "masquerade" (*D*. p. 485), and a sense of his own unim-portance; this feeling of insignificance is intensified when a rival in love, with better bureaucratic connections, wins out. In one of those scenes of comic humiliation of which Dostoevsky is in a class by himself, Golyadkin is rebuffed at the entrance to an important party only to stand in an obscure corner near the garbage—for three hours! Attempt-ing to crash the party and dance with his beloved Klara, he is thrown out. Shaken, even his "secure" office life seems to be disintegrating. At this point the doppelgänger appears, full of Schilleresque sentiment. Raggedly clothed, he tells a three-hour story which makes Golyadkin sob, "even though his visitor's story was the paltriest story" (*D*, p. 530). Senior, on his part, confesses his personal torment, saying, "It's from love for you that I speak, from brotherly love" (*D*, p. 532). But the very next day Junior is formal, official, self-important, a hypocritical mask-wearer who usurps Senior's place and wipes his hand from Senior's handshake; later he condescendingly pinches Senior's cheek and finally has him committed. His attempt at *Bruderschaft* and all the worthy emotions a failure, it is no wonder that Senior goes crazy.

The Eternal Husband presents us with another comedy of self-exposure, another crisis in the life of an ostensibly well-ordered existence, another confrontation with the double. Where Golyadkin represented the harassed little bureaucrat out of Gogol, Velchaninov is the smug bourgeois; in Wasiolek's terms, where Golyadkin was the "mouse," the underground man, the sexual loser, Velchaninov is the "bull," the sort who abuses him, the sexual winner. He is confident, muscle- and ego-bound, apparently immune to suffering or guilt. Mysteriously, he is smitten by an attack of "higher ideas." For a long time he had felt a vague malaise, a nervousness, a hypochondria; for an equal time solitude has replaced his social life. The "higher ideas" are the kind "he could not laugh at in his heart," but are forgotten the next day.

Aware that his night thoughts are radically different from his day thoughts, Velchaninov consults a doctor friend about his sleeplessness and is informed that being "too conscious of the double nature of [his] feelings" is a symptom of approaching illness. Why is it that he forgets the recent past but remembers things that happened fifteen years ago? "Why did some things he remembered strike him now as positive crimes?" (*EH*, p. 348). His vulnerability to conscience, among other things, distinguishes him from unfeeling characters like Luzhin or Totsky. Like Ivan, like Golyadkin, he is pursued by the embodiment of his worst thoughts. This embodiment takes the elusive form of Pavel Pavlovitch Trusotsky, whom Velchaninov finally confronts, recognizing in this changed man the cuckold of nine years ago. Attempting to redeem his idle life, Velchaninov is genuinely moved to do what he can for his natural daughter.

Pavel is the buffoon, the mouse, the sado-masochist, who had been cruel to the child—though his cruelty once took the oddly reflexive form of hanging himself before her—out of resentment. *Ressentiment* is the key to his character, explaining his alternate wallowing in bland *Bruderschaft* and intimations of revenge. As with Golyadkin and the underground man, he is seized by a compulsion to humiliate the humiliator. But between the guilty and the shamed there is some question about who the real predator is. Pavel tells the story of Livtsov, the best man at Golubenko's wedding, who was insulted by Golubenko and who lost out in love to him; he stabs Golubenko (but does not kill him) at the wedding, saying, "Ach! What have I done!" When Pavel says, "he got his own back," Velchaninov roars "Go to Hell!" (*EH*, pp. 405–6), and their understanding is clear.

Pavel invites Velchaninov to meet what he hopes will be his fifteen-year-old bride-to-be, and the situation threatens to be a repeat of their original one. Velchaninov pulls back: "We are both vicious, underground loathesome people" (*EH*, p. 443), he tells Pavel, recognizing a grim mutual dependency. Pavel later appreciates Velchaninov's not telling him about the girl's true feelings for him and nurses him with tea and compresses when he, exhausted and suffering from chest pains, seem to have a constitutional breakdown. "You are better than I am! I understand it all, all" (*EH*, p. 455), says Velchaninov shortly before embarking on a sleep from which he nearly never awakens. Pavel attempts to murder Velchaninov with a razor in a not precisely premeditated act: he "wanted to kill him, but didn't know he wanted to kill him." Velchaninov sees that "it was from hatred that he loved me; that's the strongest of all loves" (*EH*, pp. 460–1).

Though Bellow's *The Victim* is strikingly similar in certain respects, the emphasis is almost as much metaphysical as it is psychological. Whereas, for example, the child-victim of *The Eternal Husband* dies as a result of humiliation derived from the guilt of both men, the child-victim in *The Victim* dies from a fated physical disease. Accordingly, the double here is not so much a projection of a particular guilt as it is a conception of suffering. In *The Eternal Husband* Velchaninov is clearly at fault; his subconscious wells up for release. With Bellow's Leventhal it is much more a question of obligation or responsibility, in that disillusioned, late-forties sense. An illustration of the end-of-innocence stoicism of liberal ex-radicals—like Trilling's *The Middle of the Journey* and Mary McCarthy's *The Groves of Academe*—*The Victim* gives us a picture of the victim as victimizer, the tyranny of the disadvantaged and outcast. To complicate the tough-mindedness, *The Victim* also subverts the image of the benevolent Jew of popular fiction dealing with anti-Semitism.

The general scene of *The Victim* can fairly be called Dostoevskian: the hallucinatory, nocturnal, numinous quality; the unpromising urban backdrop; the steps, the room, the heat; the hide-and-seek beginning; the protagonist wishing to be decent but caught up in a petty bureaucracy which is a temptation to the contrary; the urban "bachelor" (Leventhal is married, but his good wife is necessarily out of town). But there are differences: where Velchaninov was directly guilty, Leventhal's real guilt is in unfeeling. His eyes are indifferent, not "sullen but rather unaccommodating, impassive" (V. p. 20). Physically large, he has none of the *amour-propre* of the Dostoevskian bull for, unlike him, he has not had a privileged life. On the contrary, it is not the softness but the "harshness of his life [which] had disfigured him" (V, p. 22). Meeting with the modest success of a respectable job and marriage, he tells his wife, "I was lucky. I got away with it," having avoided "the part that did not get away with it—the lost, the outcast, the overcome, the effaced, the ruined" (V, p. 26).

Allbee represents precisely this reality, as Leventhal comes to realize, but in a way that makes it very difficult for one to accept responsibility, even if direct in an attenuated way. Allbee is a victim of his own inadequacies and circumstances rather than any malicious action on Leventhal's part. Since Allbee is a determinist, his claim on Leventhal is more a gesture of revenge on conditions than it is an argument for individual agency: "The day of succeeding by your own efforts is past. Now it's all blind movement, vast movement, and the individual is shuttled back and forth. . . . Groups, organizations succeed or fail, but not individuals any longer . . . people have a destiny forced upon them" (V, pp. 68–9). Determinism is the cuckoldry of thought, but we are far from the direct guilt of *The Eternal Husband.* (And even there one can argue that Pavel needs Velehaninov and feels a sexual attraction to the man who brings him such masochistic undoing.) For his part, Leventhal will accept responsibility. (Allbee was fired as an indirect result of a scene between Leventhal and his boss.) But Allbee plays so heavily on the sentiment of guilt that it comes out as self-righteousness, despite the fact that he is not so much Leventhal's psychological double as he is, so the speak, a metaphysical one; for, as the story develops, he comes to represent, in Leventhal's mind, a necessary allegiance to those who are not lucky, the ruined. This is the meaning of the two epigraphs to the novel. Responsible or not, we are responsible. There are, after all, these faces in a sea of suffering.

Allbee claims an ideal relationship with his ex-wife, but the more we know about it, the more sentimental it seems to be. He cries when he sees the picture of Leventhal's wife because she reminds him of his own. It seems that their relationship was so good that she left him, because, he claims, he could not get a job. True love? Did Leventhal then break up his marriage as well? It turns out that Allbee had been fired at a number of places before and that his drinking really is something like the problem that the excessively restrained Leventhal thinks it is. His alleged depth of feeling for his wife is refuted by his not attending her funeral. (Pavel did not attend the funeral of his "daughter.") They were separated; it was hot; he would have had to see her family. Surely this is one of those instances, common in Bellow and Dostoevsky, where fine sentiment is travestied by contrary action. For both writers it is a *spécialité de la maison*. In *The Eternal Husband* Pavel attempts to kill Velchaninov after effusiveness, tea, and hot compresses: "it's just with a Schiller like that, in the outer form of a Quasimodo, that such a thing could happen," says Velchaninov. "The most monstrous monster is the monster with noble feelings" (*EH*, pp. 46–7). Velchaninov might just as well be speaking of Allbee.

Part of Allbee's "nobility" is hereditary. The depth of his *ressentiment* stems from his being the dispossessed Wasp, a *ressentiment* from above, deeper socially than Pavel's is from below. It explains his gloomy determinism, his excessive drinking, his difficulty in performing well at a job. When Allbee accuses Leventhal of ruining him "out of pure hate" (V, p. 74), we see an instance of pathology. Even more pathological is Allbee's virulent anti-Semitism; in New York "the children of Caliban" run everything, whereas "one of my ancestors was Governor Winthrop" (V, p. 131). He asserts that his "honor" tells him not to ask Leventhal for damages—though this is what he is doing, and then some—because he does not want to act like a "New York type." If things were not bad enough, books on Emerson and Thoreau are written by people with names like Lipschitz (V, p. 131). Later Leventhal finds Allbee in his own bed with another woman, and the degradation of the sentimental widower proceeds apace. Ousted, the resentful Allbee sets the gas jet in Leventhal's apartment. He "tried a kind of suicide pact without getting my permission first," thinks Leventhal; and in a rare judgmental remark, never quoted by those critics making a case for Allbee, the narrator says, "He might have added, fairly, 'without intending to die himself'" (V, p. 249).

Leventhal does err on the side of suspicion—though Allbee shows that this is sometimes impossible to do. Leventhal has none of the charm and little of the energetic temperament of later Bellow central characters. *The Victim* is the only longer work of Bellow with no comic element to speak of. There is a scrupulous meanness in the description of the milieu— between father and son, brother and brother—which goes with the Flaubertian-Joycean texture of the whole. Leventhal notices that the lights over the Manhattan building are "akin to the yellow revealed in the slit of the eye of a wild animal, say a lion, something inhuman that didn't care about anything human and yet was implanted in every human being too, one speck of it" (V, pp. 52–3). If this is the aura of sinister New York, it is also an intimation that the sympathetic heart is in danger of being lost.

Allbee is the double of Leventhal's impassivity—both are finally overcome, exorcised by Leventhal. When Leventhal finds out that—because of the office dispute (his boss "made [him] out to be a nothing," something he could ill afford to hear)—he was indirectly responsible for Allbee's losing his job, he wonders if he unconsciously wanted to get back at Allbee for some of his anti-Semitic jibes. Leventhal dreams of missing a train and of trying to catch the second section of it, from which men divert his path. His face is covered with tears. On awakening, "he experienced a rare, pure feeling of happiness. He was convinced that he knew the truth . . . [that] everything without exception took place as if within a single soul or person." Yet "he knew that tomorrow this would be untenable." Still, he recalls the recognition in Allbee's eyes, which "he could not doubt was the double of something in his own" (V, p. 151), a natural sympathy. Bellow, like Dostoevsky, does not end with a tearful wallowing in *Bruderschaft*. Despite the occasional closeness, even physical intimacy of a sort, the gain for Leventhal is in consciousness, not in a new relationship.

Like *The Eternal Husband, The Victim* ends with a coda which affirms the dubious character of the double. In a scene which takes place a few years after the main action Allbee, like M. Trusotsky, seems to be reincarnated—fancy clothes, wealthy woman, and all. Cantankerous, accusing, Jew-baiting by habit, pushing his lady around but speaking of her in ideal terms, denying any guilt in the murder attempt—he is changed only in circumstance, and Leventhal notices an underlying decay. Unlike Leventhal, Velchaninov does not seem to have changed: money, good food, and other creature comforts once again define his life. Pavel remains the eternal husband, subservient, harassed by infidelity, resentful of Velchaninov.

In a well-known speech in *The Victim*, which has no counterpart in *The Eternal Husband* but does in Dostoevsky's general outlook, wise old Schlossberg say, "It's bad to be less than human and it's bad to be more than human. . . . I say choose dignity. Nobody knows enough to turn it down" (V, pp. 127f.). These are sentiments to which the creator of Raskolnikov, the underground man, and Dmitri Karamazov would say "Amen." "More than human" is like that "sense of Personal Destiny" leading to "ideal constructions" for wisdom, bravery, cruelty, and art, which the dangling man thinks about. The man Leventhal meets in the men's room during a Karloff movie comprehends the type: "He really understands what a mastermind is, a law unto himself" (V, p. 96). Similarly, Caesar is Schlossberg's illustration of "more than human" in his idealized bravery (self-overcoming, casting out any human weakness) and his aspiration "to be like a god" (V, p. 121).

There is an attraction-repulsion in both writers to the "ideal construction," the "obsession [which] exhausts the man," superman transcendence, as there is to underground-man envy, self-laceration, and unfeeling (e.g., Golyadkin and Pavel, Joseph and Allbee). Leventhal, Bellow writes, "disagreed about 'less than human.' Since it was done by so many, what was it but human?" He adds: "he liked to think 'human' meant accountable in spite of many weaknesses—at the last moment, tough enough to hold" (V, p. 139). A nice touch this, recognizing as it does the common denominator of secular selfhood and its attendant anxiety, it establishes more-than-human/less-than-human as a continuum of gain and loss, up and down, in the struggle for subjective freedom. This is something of what Nietzsche meant when, in a remark attributed to him, he claimed that Dostoevsky's underman and his overman were the same. But this famous admirer of Dostoevsky's psychology misconstrued the Russian's relation to his character, for his transvaluation of morals, unlike that of Dostoevsky or of Bellow, was not related to Judeo-Christian roots. Did Nietzsche understand the anguished cry of the underground man—"They won't let me—I can't be good"?

Notes

1.   Irving Howe, "Dostoevsky: *The Politics of Salvation*," in *Politics and the Novel* (New York: Meridian, 1957), p. 51.
2.   V. S. Pritchett, review of Alfred Kazin's *Bright Book of Life*, in *New York Times Book Review*, 20 May 1973, p. 3.
3.   Philip Rahv, "The Legend of the Grand Inquisitor," in *The Myth and the Powerhouse* (New York: Farrar, Straus and Giroux, 1965), p. 159.

4. Fyodor Dostoevsky, *The Idiot*, trans. Constance Garnett (New York: Modern Library, 1935), p. 208. Quotations from Dostoevsky's novels are from the Garnett translations (Modern Library editions, though the Garnett translations of Dostoevsky's *The Double* [hereafter cited as *D*] and *The Eternal Husband* [hereafter cited as *EH*] are in *The Short Novels of Dostoevsky* [New York: Dial Press, 1951]). For *Notes from Underground*, I have used the Matlaw translation (New York: Dutton, 1960). The Bellow editions from which I have quoted are as follows: *Dangling Man* (New York: Meridian, 1960); *The Victim* (New York: Signet NAL, 1965), hereafter cited as *V*; *The Dean's December* (New York: Harper & Row, 1982), hereafter cited as *DD*; all other quotations from Bellow are from the Viking editions of his works.

5. Saul Bellow, "Cloister Culture," *New York Times Book Review*, 10 July 1966, p. 45.

6. Dostoevsky, *The Brothers Karamazov* (1960), p. 300; hereafter cited as *BK*.

7. Dostoevsky, *The Possessed* (1959), p. 705.

8. *The Possessed*, p. 247.

9. *Notes from Underground*, p. xiii.

10. *Crime and Punishment* (1956), pp. 354f.

11. *Crime and Punishment*, p. 411.

12. *The Possessed*, p. 268.

13. Raymond Aron, *The Opium of the Intellectuals* (New York: Norton, 1962), p. 80.

14. *Aron*, p. 96.

15. *Aron*, p. 100.

16. R. W. B. Lewis, "Lionel Trilling and the New Stoicism," review of Lionel Trilling's *The Liberal Imagination*, in *Hudson Review* 3 (1950): 317.

17. *Herzog* (New York: Viking, 1964), p. 163.

18. Edward Shils, "Daydreams and Nightmares: Reflections on the Criticism of Mass Culture," *Sewanee Review* 65 (1957): 587–608 passim; "The Theory of Mass Society," in *America as a Mass Society*, ed. Philip Olson (Glencoe: Free Press, 1963), pp. 30–47 passim; "Social Sciences and Law," in *Great Ideas Today* (Chicago: Encyclopedia Britannica, 1961), pp. 245–89 passim.

19. Shils, "The Concept and Function of Ideology," *International Encyclopedia of Social Science*, VII (New York: MacMillan and Free Press, 1968), 66–76 passim; "Ideology and Civility: On the Politics of the Intellectual," *Sewanee Review* 66 (1958): 450–80 passim.

20. Dennis Wrong, "Reflections on the End of Ideology," in *The End of Ideology Debate*, ed. Chaim L. Waxman (New York: Funk & Wagnalls, 1968), p. 123.

21. Bellow, unpublished Notebooks, C.2.7., p. 6, untitled draft for a lecture on the novel.

22. Dostoevsky, *The Diary of a Writer*, trans. Boris Brasol (New York: Scribner's, 1949). P. 787.

23. Philip Rahv, "Dostoevsky in *The Possessed*," in *Image and Idea* (Norfolk: New Directions, 1949), p. 90.

24. Nicholas Berdyaev, *Dostoevsky* (Cleveland/New York: .Meridian, 1964), p. 25.

25. Berdyaev, p. 40.

26. Arnold Hauser, *The Social History of Art* (New York: Vintage, 1958), 4: 152.

27. George Steiner, *Tolstoy or Dostoevsky* (New York: Vintage, 1961), p. 154.

28. Rahv, "Dostoevsky in *The Possessed*," p. 101.

29. Herbert Gold, review of *Henderson the Rain King*, in *The Nation* 188 (21 February 1959): 172.

30. Berdyaev, p. 21.

31. Edward Wasiolek, *Dostoevsky: The Major Fiction* (Cambridge, Mass.: MIT Press, 1964), p. 54.

32. Berdyaev, p. 113.

33. The one mitigating factor in Pytor Verkovensky's dossier is his father's relationship to him as a child. Stepan Verkovensky, a caricature of the airy, literary, liberal, may think fondly of Pytor, "the fruit of our first still unclouded happiness," but on the death of his wife, as the MacAndrew translation has it, "the fruit of their happiness was immediately packed off to Russia and his education entrusted to some distant relative residing in a remote backwater" (*The Possessed* [New York: Signet NAL, 1962], p. 13). Similarly Fydor Karamazov disposes of his own, with results even more patricidal in intention. Though there

seems to be no evidence of it, Dostoevsky may have wryly contemplated, in a book he knew well, the spectacle of western egotism in Rousseau's *Confessions*, a book whose self-analytical hero abandons his five children and goes on to write a book, a great book, about child rearing.

34.   Konstantin Mochulsky, *Dostoevsky: His Life and Work*, trans. Michael A. Minihan (Princeton: Princeton University Press, 1973), pp. 623–4.

4

Bellow and Freud

I

Like many writers and intellectuals of his generation, Bellow was genuinely involved with psychoanalysis. "Off the couch by Christmas" was a common hope or familiar joke in literary circles. Bellow himself tried a variety of approaches stemming from Freud and Reich. "I've had all the psychiatry I can use," Moses Herzog tells Dr. Emmerich.[1] Though much as been made of his switch from Freud to Reich, Bellow's connection with the utopian Reich was short-lived. Freud was the more enduring presence, the genius of psychoanalysis, the therapeutic and ideational father for whom Bellow expressed the inevitable love-hate. He has learned from Freud but essentially opposes him. To say that Bellow knows Freud very well is no exaggeration. There was a period when Freud was his nightly bed-time reading, and Bellow's frequent references to Freud in his fictive works, his notebooks, and his essays reveal an easy intimacy not only with major works but also with minor ones. As for the legitimacy of comparing an artist with a thinker, few thinkers have had more to do with "vision" than Freud, few novelists more to do with the meaning and emotional content of ideas than Bellow. Freud saw all systems of thought, including his own, as mythology. And the Bellow protagonist often breathes in what Bellow, in his spoof of Freud, has called "an environment of Ideas" (*LA*, viii).

Moreover, Bellow does not encounter in Freud an arcane scientist or offbeat mind. Freudian perceptions are at the heart of twentieth-century life. Freud gives us a view of man which is new, denuding, disillusioned, which is radically subjective and iconoclastic, which is, in short, modern. Bellow's resistance to Freud begins in opposition to the terms with which these views are given. Freud is a prime instance of modernism, against which Bellow has mounted a sustained critique.

"I didn't want to be what he called determined," says Augie March (*AM*, 117). He is thinking here of the environmental determinism warned against by Einhorn and extending it to a defense of personal autonomy, a goal that he or anyone else can only partially achieve. Though fully aware of the forces that oppose it, he insists on the reality of autonomy. There is always a margin of self-definition. Rather than determinism there are the irrepressible Bellovian asserters (Augie, Henderson, Herzog, Bummidge). But Freud introduces a determinism deeper than any Augie could imagine, the determinism of the unconscious mind. "What a man thinks he is doing counts for nothing," writes Bellow in a draft of Herzog. "All his work in the world is done by impulses he will never understand—sinful to the priest, sexual to the psychiatrist."[2] Freud said that character was essentially fixed by the age of six, that everything in character was essentially determined by that time. "In most cases," as Philip Rieff says, "Freud insists that character does not change deliberately, through taking thought or through decision; our character is, so to speak, changed for us, by returns from oblivion."[3] This applies to genius as well. So when a Leonardo abandons art for science, it is because his infantile past has gained control over him. The biblical Moses may be considered an heroic exception of conscious self-determination in Freud, and this is a reason

why *Moses and Monotheism* has not been influential with
the orthodox Freudians. Needless to say, the discovery that
childhood experiences are of the greatest importance and
that their effects are unconscious is momentous. Yet Freud's
emphasis on these truths almost precludes autonomy. Thus
the Freudian revisionists withdraw from his determinism.
"Freud did not envision people in terms of developing powers and as total personalities," says Clara Thompson. "He
thought of them much more mechanistically—as victims of
the search for the release of tension."[4] In their critique of
determinism and victimization, the revisionists are expressing a humanist concern, one similar to Bellow's, and they do
so with an ambivalence not unlike his. For the revisionists,
Freud often mistakes cultural phenomena for instinctual
ones. Bellow, as we shall see, does not regard the matter
with such anthropological detachment, which substitutes
a cultural for a biological determinism. But for him, as for
the revisionists, the root of the problem is the nature of the
Freudian unconscious.

By *unconscious* Bellow means the place first indicated by
Freud in the final chapter of *The Interpretation of Dreams* and
made more emphatic in *The Ego and the Id* and *New Introductory Lectures*; in other words, the dynamic unconscious which
implies a function, not merely the descriptive which implies
a quality. If it is a place, it is not an especially pleasant one.
"The desire to murder is actually present in the unconscious,"
says Freud.[5] The Bellow protagonist is not unfamiliar with
that desire. A central theme in Bellow is the overcoming
of that impulse, an impulse which is for him indicative of
nihilism. In *Totem and Taboo*, murder (the Oedipal killing
of the father, the primal crime) does take place, followed
by a complex reaction expressing the primal ambivalence
and thereby the beginnings of civilization. Professor Herzog
addresses himself to just this issue as he waits in his dreary

cell after his traffic accident: *"If a primal crime is the origin of social order, as Freud, Roheim et cetera believe, the bond of brothers attacking and murdering the primal father, eating his body, gaining their freedom by a murder and united by a blood wrong, then there is some reason why jail should have these dark tones."* But the perception is fleeting: *"All that is nothing but metaphor. I can't truly feel I can attribute my blundering to this thick unconscious cloud. This primitive blood-daze."* Indeed, his actions, superior to violence and murder, suggest that he should not. This is why he writes in "cheerful eagerness." Herzog sees something other than murderous egotism in the deepest recesses of the unconscious, something which refuses to disappear. *"The dream of man's heart, however much we may distrust and resent it, is that life may complete itself in significant pattern."* Freud may agree with this in the last analysis, but not in the first, and therein lies a great difference. The congenital optimist, Herzog knows that *"you got one last chance to know justice. Truth* (H, 303). Characteristically, he puts things in traditional, moralistic terms. He does not deny the existence of an unconscious, only its Freudian character.

Bellow has said, "the unconscious is anything that human beings don't know. Is there any reason why we have to accept Freud's account of what it is that we don't know?. . . . Is it possible that what we don't know has a metaphysical character and not a Freudian, naturalistic character? I think that the unconscious is a concept that begs the question and simply returns us to our ignorance with an arrogant attitude of confidence, and that is why I am against it."[6] Bellow is not giving us a positivist unconscious. In this view the unconscious is that of which we are *ex hypothesi* unaware; therefore nothing can be said about it; it is, then, effectively non-existent. Bellow's metaphysical unconscious is taken on what Santayana calls animal faith. This faith assumes a First Cause which may be called God. Rieff rightly call Freud's unconscious a "god-term" (Kenneth Burke's words) or "Freud's conceptual ultimate, a First Cause, to be believed in precisely because it is both fundamental to and inaccessible to experience."[7] In effect, Freud attempts "to eliminate religious experience by paralleling it."[8]

Bellow reverses the primary burden of the unknown, choosing to make upward rather than downward comparisons, outward, not just inward comparisons. He wants feeling without symbols, where Freud could not do without symbols. Dreams are, for Freud, the language of determinism, the truth of a totally symbolic, amoral chaos of an unconscious. Freud saw the drama of sleep but not so clearly the drama of being awake. If, as Rieff suggests, free association proves that we are never free, the primacy of dream symbolism implies a stereotyped psychological incarceration, a permanent state of house arrest. Kafka is the great novelist of this mood. Bellow suspects that symbolic interpretation may be an abrogation of free will, a way the unconscious can tyrannize over consciousness, the obscure motive over spontaneity. The result can be a scholasticism which infects not only the Freudian world but the literary world as well. "Deep readers of the world beware," Bellow once warned. "You may never again see common daylight."[9] Freud tells us that though the ego appears autonomous and unitary, marked off distinctly from anything else, it really is "continued inward, without any sharp delimitation into an unconscious mental entity which we designate as the id and for which it serves as a facade."[10] The downward and the inward movement is honorific in Freud, the true source, but the upward and outward is on a tight leash of sublimation. The metaphysical, the religious— these are, for Freud, ways of wrapping the self in a batting of excelsior.

Herzog's resistance to the Freudian unconscious issues into an engaging insight. In a letter to Spinoza, he agrees with the philosopher that thoughts not causally connected may cause pain. *"It may interest you to know,"* he writes, *"that in the twentieth century random association is believed to yield up the deepest secrets of the psyche"* (H, 181). While free association may be the ultimate insult to rational purposiveness, the process itself can yield some of the mysteries of the deep. One can argue that Spinoza overvalued reason; in any case, Freud surely knew something that Spinoza did not. Whether, or to what extent, the unconscious is Freudian, it is certainly there. Free association, like the psychopathology of everyday life, is, much more than chaos, a triumph over it. Herzog knows the rules but does not want to play the game, *"believing that reason can make steady progress from disorder to harmony and that the conquest of chaos need not be begun anew every day"* (H, 181f.). But isn't there such "progress" in psychoanalysis? Herzog is saved from smugness here by the precariousness of his claim: "How I wish it! How I wish it were so! How Moses prayed for this" (H, 182). The yearning for moral clarity even more than the clarity itself is the characteristic Herzog note. His prayer for reason is humanism in the defensive position.

A draft of Herzog's letter to Spinoza undermines the foundation of Freud's unconscious by dismissing its current post-Freudian expression. Freud holds that "what decides the purpose of life is simply the programme of the pleasure principle. This principle dominates the operation of the mental apparatus from the start." Rather than happiness, however, this brings unhappiness through an elaborate sequence of repression and renunciation. "One feels inclined to say that the intention that men should be 'happy' is not included in the plan of 'Creation'," says Freud.[11] Adhering to a different view of the pleasure principle, the post-Freudians have given us Freud without pain. Bellow rejects the biological determinism of both by denying the cardinality of pleasure. That he has to complain to Spinoza may be ominous. But is there anyone better around to talk to? Herzog writes, *"I subscribed at one time to the theory that it was pleasure and pleasure only that gave one the strength to be moral, that pleasure was fundamentally a question of health, and that the only possible source of goodness and happiness was instinctual gratification. I no longer believe this to be true."* He communicates with Spinoza as he and Ramona embrace. She bites his lip in ecstasy. *"This theory did me a lot of harm,"* he continues. The comedy of contemporary life does not keep his moralism down: "I think that John Stuart Mill was absolutely right: happiness cannot be a direct object. Must be a by-product" (B. 20.40, 180). Marriage to Ramona would be an ideological misalliance. Not the pleasure principle but self-directed purpose ought to determine. Something close to this opposition was made some time ago by Aristotle, who distinguished between pleasure as sensation and pleasure as activity. The latter in Bellow's humanistic view has more to do with happiness.

Freud's conception of the eternal recurrence of the Oedipal drama reduces religion to psychology and history to nature. History becomes a sort of secular predestination, with the unconscious as a weedy Garden of Eden, the primal crime as Original Sin. For Bellow, Freud minimizes and perhaps destroys pure motive[12] in a way that victimizes the Christian as well as the natural man. *"Charity,"* Herzog write to Edvig, *"as if it didn't have enough trouble in this day and age, will always be suspected of morbidity—sadomasochism, peversity of some sort. All higher or moral tendencies lie under suspicion of being rackets"* (H, 56). Herzog is angry at Edvig's indifference to his attempted *agape* in dealing with Mady, an indifference which destroys an aspect of the Judeo-Christian tradition he believes is real. *"If my soul, out of Season, out of place, experienced these higher emotions, I could get no credit for them anyway. Not from you with your attitude toward good intentions. I've read your stuff about the psychological realism of Calvin. I hope you don't mind my saying that it reveals a lousy, cringing, grudging conception of human nature. This is how I see your Protestant Freudianism"* (H, 57f.).

The friction between humanism and the Freudian unconscious surfaces again in Freud's view of history. Since history is nature and the unconscious determines, pre-history is more important than history in the conventional sense. Though psychoanalysis is an historical process for the individual patient, it also aims to uncover the individual equivalent of pre-history. Accordingly, Freud's writings on culture are more concerned with myth than history. "For the very reason that Hegel thought Africa no proper subject for the historian, Freud thought it most proper," Rieff says.[13] Bellow's Africa, on the other hand, is really an affirmation of traditional morality. And in much of his work Bellow is involved with historical reality as such. His time is chronological, not mythological. The momentous event has not occurred in an archetypal past but is unfolding before our contemporaneous eyes. We know what the momentous event is for Freud.

Anyone reading Freud with a clear eye will see that the Oedipus complex cannot be explained away in mollifying cultural terms. Freud really means it. However tentative and delicate his rhetorical poses, he never comes up with anything more suited to his purpose, and suggestion soon becomes fact. He sees nothing in history to cause him to change his mind. "*Homo homini lupus*," says Freud in *Civilization and Its Discontents* (a sentiment uttered in manuscript by Bellow's Winkelman of *The Last Analysis* as he thinks about contemporary reality in Balzacian terms). "Who in the face of all his experience of life and of history, will have the courage to dispute this assertion."[14] Bellow longs to accord to human nature the value that Freud grants to civilization. Renunciation is Freud's heroism. Bellow sees its importance, but he resents the parsimony implied by its prevalence in the Freudian system.

II

Comparing Bellow and Freud as thinkers points up perhaps more clearly than anything else can the religious tendency of Bellow's humanism. Bellow's hostility to Freud may be seen as the obverse of Freud's hostility to the religious tempera-ment. He explicitly attacks Freud's "A Religious Experience" for displaying systematic rigidity comparable to that of Marx: "Once you've given yourself over to one of these systems, you've lost your freedom in a very significant degree." Here then is Freudianism-as-ideology criticized from the point of view of humanist independence. Bellow recognizes that Freud was "a great genius" and recalls what "my feelings were quite early in life when I began to read Freud. It was hard not to see the world in terms of instinct and repression, not to see it in terms of concavity and convexity, not to see it in terms of the struggle of the child with his parents, and so on." Ever the writer, he sees these as "metaphors," as he sees all philosophy from the point of view of imagination. The individual must be moved, and Freud has moved him. "A Religious Experi-ence" has crystallized his contempt. An American doctor had read *The Future of an Illusion* and writes to Freud saying, "I too at one time lost my faith" when as a medical student the body of a "very beautiful old woman" was brought into the dissecting room. He "could no longer believe in a god" who would do such a thing. But the doctor thinks about it and recovers his faith, recommending that Freud too "postpone a final decision on the existence of God for a time." Bellow is outraged by Freud's response, which equates the cadaver with the doctor's mother. "At this moment," he says, "I expe-rienced a violent reaction against Freud. Was it not possible to experience beauty or pity without thinking of your mother, or without the Oedipus complex? The rigidity of this repels me. I felt that it was coarse and cruel. It's this sort of thing that I think of when I think of Freud."[15]

There is more to Freud's piece than Bellow's recollection of it, and what is left out, to be analytic about it, may be as much the reason for Bellow's having selected this minor essay from among many more obvious illustrations. The piece is more explicitly Oedipal than Bellow seems to remember. "Why was it," Freud asks, "that his indignation against God broke out precisely when he received this particular impression in the dissecting room?" Freud equates "his desire to destroy his father" with "doubt in the existence of God." Bellow speaks of the purity of human motive, but, given his own preferences, he might almost as well have spoken of the purity of belief. Freud concludes with just the sort of certitude that repels him: "The new impulse, which was displaced into the sphere of religion, was only a repetition of the Oedipal situation and consequently soon met with a similar fate. It succumbed to a powerful opposing current. . . . The conflict seems to have been unfolded in the form of hallucinatory psychosis: inner voices were heard which uttered warnings against resistance to God. . . . The outcome . . . was a kind predetermined by the fate of the Oedipus complex: complete submission to the will of God the Father."[16] Lying supine is a posture which invites the devil, warns the beleaguered Monsignor Sheen in his book on psychoanalysis. Freud's explanation rivals that of his sometime explanation of love, remembered by Herzog as a "a psychosis, usually brief" (B. 16.1). Is belief psychosis? Bellow thinks not. Yet it is significant that the humanistic rather than the religious content of the piece most sharply elicits Bellow's ire.

"Is it not true," asks Freud in *The Future of an Illusion*, "that the two main points in the modern educational programme are the retardation of sexual development and the early application of religious influence?" Freud laments this Victorian asymmetry and wonders how people "dominated by thought prohibitions" will "attain the psychological ideal, the primacy of the intelligence."[17] But what if the situation is reversed? What if the spiritual is more repressed than the sexual? The id triumphant and the superego underground? Body open and soul furtive? This may be said to have been the situation in America at least from the mid-sixties through the seventies. The consequences for psychoanalysis were great. A Freudian analyst speaks of this topsy-turvy swing of history. Virginity was once a value, notes Henry Lowenfeld; now perhaps it is a taboo.[18] He cites the case of a patient who broke her hymen with a shampoo bottle. As for the psychoanalytic ethic of honesty, there is the young woman who invites her four-year-old son to watch her sexual performance with different lovers. Lowenfeld believes that children do not introject parents anymore but parents introject children. The decline of the superego is the root of the problem, signifying the weakened role of the father and the eclipse of religion. The Oedipus complex is not resolved. Rather than hysteria or obsessional neurosis, the neurotic constellations of sexual liberation are depression, emptiness, inability to love. There is a problem for libido theory. You can cure frigidity but what can you do for promiscuity? Much of Bellow's writing since *Herzog*—the sexual grotesquerie might almost have come out of *Mr. Sammler's Planet*—responds to this second reversed reality. To speak of religion in Bellow, then, is to speak of it in a cultural predicament quite different from Freud's. Freud was slaying a dragon; Bellow is preserving a dinosaur. Though he has little sympathy for ritual orthodoxy, he has far less for Freud's description of religion as universal obsessional neurosis. Herzog rejects just this term. For Bellow, as for the religious man, superego is not primarily equated with a usually repressive society, not part of the Oedipal drama writ large. Aware of "the harm done by people of high principles," Herzog nonetheless records his dissent from the psychoanalytic view: "Instead of laying the blame as Freud does on the excess of superego, I would say that the doing of good relieves the poor burdened human soul" (B 20.40,195). For Bellow, conscience remains intact as a means of individual assertion, in an age where many have confused it with pleasure. Like the believer, Bellow thinks that psychoanalysis undermines morality. Freud advocates nothing. D. H. Lawrence was right in saying that this is why he can never "get down to the rock on which he must build his church."[19] Rieff puts it precisely in saying that Lawrence charges Freud with having "forgotten the prayerful attitude that man ought to have toward himself."[20] Bellow's Gonzaga puts the contemporary lack of moral intensity more dramatically: "*Go away. You have no holy ones*" (*SD*, 175). Though certainly not in Lawrentian terms, it is fair to say that Bellow desires to express the prayerful attitude. Augie March's sense of the *amor fati* as blessedness rather than indifference, Tommy Wilhelm's funeral parlor transfiguration, Henderson's self-proclaimed "mediumistic and attuned" soul, Herzog's addressing God as "Thou," Sammler's knowledge of the contract, Citrine's musing on Humboldt's transcendence—all of these attest to the prayerful attitude.

What, then, is the quality of Bellow's belief? Erich Fromm's distinction between authoritarian and humanistic religion takes us close to the answer. The first involves self-abasement, subjection of the individual to a higher end, the "fear and trembling" of contrition. The powers of the self are projected onto God. The soul or self is slight compared to life after death or the Fatherland. Humanistic religion, on the other hand, is "centered around man and his strength." It does, of course, imply a oneness with the "All," and it is "theistic"; however, it insists that "God is a symbol of *man's powers.*"[21] Spinoza is an example. He affirmed God's immanence but denied his transcendence (for which, we may note, he was excommunicated). In the humanist perspective, as Fromm sees it, the teachings of Buddha, Isaiah, Christ, Socrates and Spinoza are the same. In humanistic religion, "conscience is not the internalized voice of authority but man's own voice, the guardian of our integrity. . . . Sin is not primarily sin against God but sin against ourselves."[22] Obedience is not the issue.

As a Jew out of the synagogue, a man who defines religious feeling largely in reaction to a profound lack in the secular life in which he is saturated, Bellow is certainly distant from authoritarian religion. Some may think that he is distant from religion altogether, lacking in the commitment (which may necessarily include institutional involvement) that makes it a way of life. Be that as it may, Bellow is more attuned to tradition than Fromm's distinctions will allow. For Bellow, God is not merely a symbol of man's powers or a symbol of anything. God is not simply immanent but transcendent and, usually, the Jewish God. He is "Thou" but he is not, as Herzog puts it in manuscript, "God the Father, above the clouds. I don't believe in that" (B.18.12, 131). Conscience is man's own voice but a voice with a transcendental yearning.

The ending of *Herzog* is perhaps the clearest case in point. Herzog is not without some self-abasement ("*My face too blind, my mind too limited, my instincts too narrow*"), but God, somehow personal, is defined in terms of Herzog's emotional response to Him ("*Thou movest me*"). There is always the humanistic questioning ("*But this intensity, doesn't it mean anything? Is it an idiot joy that makes this animal, the most peculiar animal of all, exclaim something?*"). Yet reason will take him only so far ("*But I have no arguments to make about it*"). Just as his faith receives support from Nature ("*Something produces intensity, a holy feeling, as oranges produce orange, as grass green, as birds heat.*"), his God concludes in man ("*I am pretty well satisfied to be, to be just as it is willed, and for as long as I may remain in occupancy*") (H, 340).

If Fromm's sense of the unity of spiritual worthies is rather indiscriminate, we may recall that Sammler's fascination with Eckhart and Citrine's with Rudolf Steiner is no less universalizing. Bellow's is not the belief of perfect faith. Faith may even surprise the Bellow protagonist, issuing usually from an unshakable sense of the ethical. "I wilfully misread my contract," thinks Herzog in a characteristic metaphor of obligation. "I never was the principal, but only on loan to myself," he continues, using a metaphor that Hattie Waggoner of "Leaving the Yellow House" also uses. She is on loan from her real, that is, unconscious self, the reservoir of her spirit. Herzog, however, is on loan from above rather than below: "Evidently I continue to believe in God. Though never admitting it. But what else explains my conduct and my life?" (*H*, 231). His subsequent recoil from murder is to make that explanation even more clear. Having reached a plateau of moral clarity, Herzog earns the right to correspond with God—a humanist assumption! The man of letters in the religious world. His words to God are very much those of humanist religion. "*How my mind has struggled to make coherent sense,*" says our seeker of the morally real. Contemporaneous as his words are, they have a trace of humility: "*I have not been too good at it. But have desired to do your unknowable will, taking it, and you, without symbols. Everything of intensest significance*" (*H*, 325f.). God is emotionally charged meaning, value, an immediate experience, an authentic illumination not to be diluted by constructs standing for something else (e.g., Freudian symbolism). This is not authoritarian religion but the humanist religion that equates God with the highest, purest feeling. He adds, with the post-Romantic, postmodern psychological fatigue not to be confused with religious self-abasement: "*Especially if divested of me*" (*H*, 326). Herzog's salvation is freedom from the cult of sensibility. In a draft of a letter to Monsignor Hilton, Herzog writes: "*If I had to *put it in my own* way," and he always does, *"I would say that to be inescapably closed up in a world of one's own making is hell"* (B.18.10). Herzog knows the condition first-hand, and he calls the transcendence of it God.

"Love thy neighbor as thyself"—Fromm says that this is the essence of religion. But he didn't count on an era of self-hatred. There seems to be nothing in the humorless analyst that would put him in touch with our wrenching comedy on this subject. Herzog does pay more than lip-service to "our employment by other human beings and their employment by us" as the "real and essential question" (*H*, 272), but he does not have the answer. Nor do any of the later Bellow protagonists, much as they may want it. Cain and Abel, rather than Oedipus, are central to the Judeo-Christian tradition. The issue of responsibility for the other person has always been a difficult one. "Am I my brother's keeper?" is, in its original context, a rhetorical question raised by a maniac. All the more reason that the answer must be yes. If the mutual love of brothers is difficult, how much more difficult is that of neighbors. In *Civilization and Its Discontents*, Freud says the Golden Rule is "impossible to fulfill." Bellow would have to agree that "such an enormous inflation of love can only lower its value,"[23] but he would reject Freud's contention that it is "a commandment which is really justified by the fact that nothing else runs so strongly counter to the original nature of man."[24] While not so optimistic as Fromm, he is not so pessimistic as Freud.

Freud has contempt for what Fromm defines as humanist religion, the poetized religion of 'as if,' God as symbol in a universe of tolerant cultural relativism. The pious neurotics at least had belief, not just spiritual need. On this point it is important to emphasize that Fromm's humanism excludes actual belief but Bellow's does not. Bellow easily meets Fromm's criteria for the religious mentality: (1) wonder

(2) "ultimate concern" (Tillich) (3) oneness of separate self with All. The first two the Bellow protagonist typically exhibits, the last less fully, though Bellow dramatizes it shamelessly, if wryly, in *Humboldt's Gift*. Freud would have said that Citrine can't let go of poppa and thus exhibits the infantilism of the oceanic feeling. As for "ultimate concern," Freud writes to Marie Bonaparte that, "The moment a man questions the meaning and value of life he is sick, since objectively neither has any existence."[25] Man may seek the light but it will only give him another insight into darkness. On this assumption, wonder cannot be pristine but only an experience of darkness overcome. Bellow would counter that these are prime illustrations of the usual psychoanalytic reductiveness. "You're a hard-nosed man," shouts Bummidge to his "analyst." "Why do you prefer the ugliest interpretations? Why do you pollute all my good impulses?" (LA, 27).

Freud does acknowledge the civilizing tendencies of religion, even in its most primitive form. In *Totem and Taboo* he writes, "It is difficult to resist the notion that, long before a table of laws was handed down by any god, these savages were in possession of a living commandment: 'Thou shalt not kill,' a violation of which would not go unpunished."[26] Freud sees religion as the origin of ethics. Curiously, Freud comes back every now and then to the one religious (cultural) commandment that most fascinates Bellow, one that provides a stay against nihilistic chaos. Even a tyrant or a dictator, says Freud in *The Future of An Illusion*, "has every reason to want others to keep at least one cultural commandment: thou shalt not kill." The alternative for Freud is intolerable. "How short-sighted," he says, "to strive for the abolition of culture! What would then remain would be the state of nature, and that is far harder to endure."[27] The state of nature for Bellow is not so nearly Hobbesian, though in *Mr. Sammler's Planet* and, particularly, in *The Dean's December*, it almost is. In any case, the prohibition against murder does not amount to religion.

There is an important distinction to be drawn in the ways Bellow and Freud view the act of murder. Freud sees all murder as part of the Oedipal drama, thereby shedding a brilliant light on, say, the Oedipal Dostoevsky. In his essay "Dostoevsky and Parricide," Freud considers *The Brothers Karamazov, Oedipus Rex* and *Hamlet* as Oedipal dramas which, being three of the greatest works of literature, lend indirect support to his interpretation of psychological experience. Of the murder in Dostoevsky's novel Freud writes, "It is a matter of indifference who committed the crime; psychology is interested only in discovering who desired it, and who welcomed it when it was done, and for that reason, all the brothers are equally guilty." Because of the Oedipal reality, in Dostoevsky, "the criminal is to him almost a Redeemer, who has taken on himself the guilt which others would otherwise have had to bear. One need not now commit murder, after he has committed murder, but one must be grateful to him, because without him, one would oneself have to have been a murderer."[28] This interpretation can be documented in *The Brothers Karamazov*, which gives us a father well worth killing. But Freud makes virtually the same point in his discussion of tragedy in *Totem and Taboo*, where he speaks of the tragic hero in general. The primal crime underlies all: "In the remote reality it had actually been the members of the Chorus who caused the Hero's suffering; now, however, they exhausted themselves with sympathy and regret, and it was the Hero himself who was responsible for his own sufferings. The crime which was thrown on to his shoulders, presumptuousness and rebelliousness against a great authority, was precisely the crime for which the members of the Chorus, the company of brothers, was responsible. Thus the tragic Hero becomes, though it might be against his will, the redeemer of the Chorus."[29] Here as elsewhere, the brilliance of Freud's perceptions makes one feel that, anthropological evidence to the contrary notwithstanding, there must be a rightness to what he says.

Yet a crucial moral distinction remains. For Bellow, and for humanism generally, there is all the difference in the world between committing a murder and wishing to do so, between impulse and deed. Bellow has said that this is a distinction between the Jewish and Christian points of view: "The Jewish outlook is that unless you have actually committed the crime you are not guilty of it, no matter what you have thought or dreamed."[30] This is also the humanist and liberal view. Man may be vulnerable, the capacity for evil (yetzer ha-ra in the old Hebrew expression) may be always present, but so is the capacity for good (yetzer ha-tov), and in the struggle between them lies the reality of moral life. For Freud and for a certain kind of Christianity, determinism or predestination essentially obliterated the distinction between wish and act. Nowhere are Bellow's humanist sympathies vis-à-vis Freudianism more clearly drawn in terms of moral emphasis. The assertions of free will in Bellow may be small but there is, for example, a crucial difference between Herzog's desire to murder and his decision not to. It is the criminal who is guilty, but we are not "equally guilty" (as Freud puts it). The problem is complex, for as Freud says in "Dostoevsky and Parricide:" "A moral man is one who reacts to the temptation he feels in his heart without yielding to it."[31] In other words, Freud does make a distinction between what psychology is "interested in" and what morality is "interested in." Psychology is not ethics; health values are not moral values. Granted. But any system has moral implications and there is a key difference here: in Bellow there is the attraction of the good, in Freud the renunciation of the bad. As Rieff puts it: "Freud could not speak of the desire to be good in the same sense that he could speak of desiring what we have to renounce for the good. Surely this is one-sided. Aspiration may be as genuine as desire, and as original."[32] With his emphasis on the sway of the unconscious, Freud is nothing if not profound. But there can be the greatest depth in the obvious. Freud sees this when he considers biological desire (e. g., the babe at its mother's breast) but does not when he weighs moral desire. His dark view of human nature misses the profundity of simplicity. If the good can ever be considered simple.

Yet Bellow and Freud share a skepticism about the extremity of Dostoevskian goodness, that "rage for goodness so near to vileness and murderousness," as Albert Corde puts it (DD, 161). Neither is satisfied with the "murder-saviour" type, which Corde sees in the relatively moderate Toby Winthrop, and both see in Raskolnikov and Stavrogin. "It was foreign, bookish—it was Dostoevsky stuff that the vices of Sodom coexisted with the adoration of Holy Sophia," says Corde (DD, 130). Bellow characterizes this as abstract modern consciousness, but Freud has a clearer explanation of the phenomenon in its acute Dostoevskian manifestation. He is skeptical of penitence which "becomes a technique to enable murder to be done."[33] In The Future of an Illusion he states the social raison d'être for "the sublime conclusion" of Russian mysticism "that sin is indispensable for the full enjoyment of the blessing of divine grace, and therefore fundamentally. . . pleasing to God." Freud says, "It is well known that the priests could only keep the masses submissive to religion by making these great concessions to human instincts."[34] Freud attacks the holy sinner as part of his argument to undermine religion, which he sees as authoritarian. Bellow, in his humanist stance, never without some skepticism about religion even in Sammler and Citrine, has Corde say, "So what was this pure-in-spirit bit? For an American who had been around, a man in his mid-fifties, this beatitude language was unreal" (*DD*, 130). Religion must meet the humanist requirement of reason.[35]

III

Despite this point of similarity, Freud's essay on "Dostoevsky and Parricide" illustrates still another sharp difference between Bellow and Freud, their relationship to art, literature in particular. Brilliant as it is, Freud's piece treats Dostoevsky more as a case than a writer. Freud finds Dostoevsky fascinating for the clarity with which he confirms the Oedipal drama. Freud's interest in content, then, is of a special kind. He has no interest in formal or stylistic matters and not even much interest in thematic ones. *The Brothers Karamazov* is mainly an instance of Dostoevsky's personality, particularly his neurotic configurations and how they damaged his artistic mission. The illumination of a psychoanalytically relevant pattern takes the place of moral and aesthetic evaluation of a work, which is why Freud may make much of a work that has little literary significance (e. g., Jensen's *Gradiva*). Freud gives us dazzling insights into Dostoevsky the neurotic, but he cannot really tell us why his work is good or bad, great or mediocre. In these ways, Freud's treatment of Dostoevsky is similar to his treatment of Leonardo.

Freud is, in fact, uneasy with art. Otto Rank maintained that Freudian theory could not cope with the creative artist. And Freud seems to agree with him. It is in the essay on "Dostoevsky and Parricide" that Freud issued this famous disclaimer: "Unfortunately, before the problem of the creative artist, analysis must lay down its arms."[36] Why is this so? Because there is something about art that eludes the theory of unconscious determinism, there is something that is larger than Freud's system. This has for a long time been Bellow's opinion. And art is not, in his view, the only thing that is larger than Freud's system. As Herzog puts it (in manuscript), referring to just this remark, "Freud confessed he laid down his arms before the problem of art. He should have surrendered to all the mysteries of high inspiration, including the work of moral genius" (B.17.8). Again Bellow insists that there is an area of freedom that Freudian rationalism does not comprehend.

Lionel Trilling has written of the similarities between literature and psychoanalysis, which is "a science of tropes, of metaphor and its variants, synecdoche and metonymy.[37] And everyone knows Freud's claim that it was not he but the poets who discovered the unconscious. But what unconscious was it that "they" discovered? Not one that defines art as daydream, escape from reality, mild narcosis, or "substitute gratification" for "the oldest cultural renunciations."[38] Freud thinks it unfortunate that psychoanalysis must throw up its hands before "the problem" of art, but it is fortunate from the artist's point of view. Art is freedom of expression, health rather than sickness, genius rather than neurosis. Freud never grants to art the autonomy the artist gives it. He sees the imagination as a symptom of the unconscious. In this sense he values criticism over art. The interpretation of the subject is the key to art just as psychoanalysis is the key to the unconscious. As a novelist who values imagination, as a humanist whose art takes a particularly moral turn, as a human being who believes in the primacy of inspiration, Bellow could not agree with these formulations. "If I hold with Freud in anything," says Bellow, "I would hold with him in this one matter, that reality is a projection of something or other. Fictions are fascinating and relatively coherent projections."[39] He sees the novel, however, as a projection of "truth, or of reality," terms which do not correspond to Freud's idea of religion as a projection of revolt against the father or art as a projection of unconscious wish-fulfillment. To the term "truth" Freud prefers "fantasy."

Bellow's criticism of Freud does not break new ground as such. Rather it is a profound version of the familiar criticism Freud termed "unjust" in *The Ego and the Id*, when he said that "psycho-analysis has been reproached time after time with ignoring the higher, moral, supra-personal side of human nature." Freud claims that his critics ignore the nature of the ego and superego, "the representative of our relation to our parents."[40] But his ego-ideal or superego remains an outgrowth of Oedipal struggle. That is, Freud's moral world follows his limiting terminology, and it is a world which becomes increasingly claustral for Bellow. He is in essential agreement with Rieff's view of Freud as a modern thinker, as one who gives us a weak ego and an oppressive superego, with the nihilistic problematics this entails.

But Bellow is in radical disagreement with Rieff as to the consequences of seeing Freud this way. In Rieff's books on Freud and psychoanalytic theory, the author appears to accepts with open arms the diminished concept of the self which it has been Bellow's task to repudiate. Where the protagonist of a Bellow work is typically a citizen-hero, at least in fantasy, Rieff speaks of a "citizen-patient." Yet Rieff is wary of seeing "an admittedly sick society in terms of that subtlest . . . authoritarian image, the hospital."[41] If one can speak of a sociologist of mind having a controlling metaphor, however, this is Rieff's: "In the emergent democracy of the sick. . . . [the] hospital is succeeding the church and the parliament as the archetypal institution of Western culture."[42] Freud is "the first out-patient of the hospital culture in which we live."[43] In *The Triumph of the Therapeutic*, Rieff predicts that "modern society will mount psychodramas far more frequently than its ancestors mounted miracle plays, with patient-analysts acting out their inner lives, after which they could extemporize the final act as interpretation." Rieff calls this "hospital-theater."[44] What Rieff considers serious, Bellow considers farce in *The Last. Analysis*. The fruits of hospital culture may be strange. "We are, I fear, getting to know one another," says Rieff.[45] Freud saw ethics as a "therapeutic"[46] activity of the super-ego, assuming by this metaphor the sick person as the norm. Making the same assumption, Rieff sees any "system or moralizing demands" as "therapy," the "therapeutic" goal being "a manipulatable sense of well-being."[47]

It is precisely this view that Charlie Citrine attacks in *Humboldt's Gift* when Cantabile, looking through his library, asks about *The Triumph of the Therapeutic* (a phrase which first appears in Selma Fraiberg's negative review of Rieff's book on Freud). Citrine is quite clear about his dislike of the book: "It says that psychotherapists may become the new spiritual leaders of mankind. A disaster. Goethe was afraid the modern world might turn into a hospital. Every citizen unwell" (*HG*, 175). Rieff sees this new psychological man benignly as "the healthy hypochondriac."[48] But Citrine can only wonder whether "hypochondria" is "a creation of the medical profession," concluding with a flourish: "According to this author, when culture fails to deal with the feeling of emptiness and the panic to which man is disposed (and he does say 'disposed') other agents come forward to put us together with therapy, with glue, or slogans, or spit, or as that fellow Gumbein [Harold Rosenberg] the art critic says, poor wretches are recycled on the couch. This view is even more pessimistic than the one held by Dostoevsky's Grand Inquisitor. . . . A natural disposition to feelings of emptiness and panic is worse than that. Much worse. What it really means is that we human beings are insane. The last institution which controlled such insanity (on this view) was the Church" (*HG*, 175f). Rieff inverts Pangloss so as to say that the therapeutic is the best of all possible worlds.

It is true, as Rieff claims, that "the understanding of normal character through the neurotic character, of health through sickness, is Freud's master trope."[49] This method surely is at the heart of Freud's genius, but it may, finally, give us a greater insight into sickness than health. Moreover, it may impose a modernist norm where none exists. The matter of Freud's master trope could be put quite differently. "Freud could build a theory of human nature," says Irving Kristol, "on the basis of his experience with hysterics and neurotics, a unique and strange achievement which testifies to our modern psychic equilibrium, whose fulcrum is at the edge of an abyss."[50] A skeptical humanist balance resides in this perspective, with which Bellow would be sympathetic. Rieff acknowledges that "there is a fatal lack of commitment about Freud's ideal type. To be busy, spirited, and selfconfident is a goal that will inspire only those who have resigned the ghosts of older and nobler aspirations."[51] Yet Rieff willingly does so. (It is only in the later *Fellow Teachers* that Rieff clearly laments this state of affairs, claiming to have been describing but not approving it.) Unlike Freud, Bellow constructs a past that he can honor, and he is in frequent, perhaps too frequent, correspondence with its ghosts.

IV

Though Bellow rejects Freudian thought in these fundamental respects, he is nonetheless sympathetic to and sometimes indebted to it in others. An admirer of Montaigne, an observer of local mores, Bellow is, like Freud, very well aware of the cost of the civilization he defends. A character like Artur Sammler knows a good deal about renunciation. Yet Freud's attributing all civilization to renunciation seems to Bellow unnecessarily severe. "Take what you want," says the Spanish proverb, "and pay for it." Freud is the genius of this theme, one which Bellow fully understands. No one is so taken up with psychic costs as Freud, our economist of the self. Indeed, he knows as well the cost of many things you never even get to "take." But it may be that life has its unexpected rewards, its serendipitous moments, its joys unmixed with pain. Or at least if not that a possibility of accomplishment for which one need not go half-way to castration. It may be that, with Augie March, one can perceive the blessedness in the *amor fati*. Or that, with Herzog, one can be moved by the principle of creation.

To the extent that Freudian disillusion is a repudiation of utopian progressivism, Bellow endorses it. Both reject Marx, knowing the essentialist wisdom of *plus ca change plus c'est la meme chose* (though Herzog feels or hopes that there are good human qualities yet to be discovered). They are both conservative liberals (if Freud can be called liberal in any sense) who place personality above politics, knowing, stoically, that the self must be defined in the face of constant crisis. Both recognize the need to recover instinct. Though Bellow thinks Freud inflates the pleasure principle, both abide by some version of the reality principle, preferring reason to primal energy. Yet Bellow gives much more to intuition and inspiration, is more trusting of emotional response. *"Trouve avant de chercher,"* says Charlie Citrine (quoting Valéry). "This finding before seeking was my special gift. If I had any" (HG, 73). Citrine's is the very reverse of the Freudian procedure. Given the Freudian system, the chances are that one will find what one is looking for, and what one finds will not be very nice. "We may reject the existence of an original, as it were natural, capacity to distinguish good from bad," says Freud.[52] Bellow is not so disillusioned, holding with Sammler that "we know." With his metaphors of contract and obligation, Bellow is more Jewish. Jokes and family feeling, integrity and argumentativeness may not a Jew make. Though these are more indicative than pinochle and cabanas, or sleeping on Saturday afternoon, Freud's Jewish identity remains much more problematic than Bellow's. But they both have one.

As if in tacit homage, most of the Bellow protagonists have read Freud—even, in one manuscript, Eugene Henderson (B.6.22, 323). And there is frequent reference in Bellow to psychoanlytic terminology. There may even be a rare instance of an image Bellow has taken over from Freud in his fiction, consciously or unconsciously.[53]

As a novelist who pursues self-definition partly through a recapturing of childhood experience, Bellow's occupation parallels Freud's. Both Freud and Herzog have their "personal histories, old tales from old times that may not be worth remembering" (H, 149). Both literature and psychoanalysis posit the primacy of emotion. To complement Bellow's humanism, Freud is more of a thinker than a scientist. He thought of himself as a humanist rather than a physician. Some Bellow characters, perhaps too many, read like case histories—Tommy Wilhelm and Dr. Adler being the most prominent—but Henderson, Herzog, Mady and Humboldt may be so considered. Herzog does not seem to mind, thinking jauntily, "If I am out of my mind, it's all right with me" (H, 1). He is diagnosed as a reactive-depressive. A certain psychological disarray is essential to Bellow's comic sense. More than this, there are times when we seem to be eavesdropping on an analytic session, as in the following reflection from Herzog: "What I seem to do, thought Herzog, is to inflame myself voluptuously, esthetically, until I reach a sexual climax. And that climax looks like a resolution and an answer to many 'higher' problems" (H, 208). It is all the more significant that Herzog here is talking to himself, not to his analyst. Psychoanalysis has become part of personal style. In some of these "sessions," Herzog invokes the master, as when he records his guilt about being an apparition to Marco: "This particular sensitivity about meeting and parting had to be tamed. Such trembling sorrow—he tried to think what term Freud had for it: partial return of repressed traumatic material ultimately traceable to the death instinct?—should not be imparted to children, not that tremulous lifelong swoon of death. This same emotion, as Herzog the student was aware, was held to be the womb of cities, heavenly as well as earthly, mankind being unable to part with its beloved or its dead in this world or the next." But to Herzog, holding his daughter, the emotion is "tyranny" (*H*, 280). The first half of this idea comes largely from Freud's "Mourning and Melancholia," which is actually mentioned later in the novel when Herzog thinks that "the metabolic wastes of fatigue (he was fond of these physiological explanations; this one came from Freud's essay Mourning and Melancholia) made him temporarily light-hearted, even gay" (*H*, 302).

Though mentioned only in passing in *Herzog*, "Mourning and Melancholia" is more prominent in the manuscripts, elaborately pondered in a few versions (B.17.5; B.20.40; B.21.32). "*Dear Dr. Freud*," the depressive Herzog writes in a letter, "*I have recently in a dark hour studied your essay on Mourning and Melancholia, as well as the papers of your colleague Dr. Abraham. . . . As you might imagine I did not read your essay by accident. Man prays in our religion (or former religion) for a 'new heart.' Radical determinism like yours offers no place for new hearts. But why else would anyone pray or seek light?*" To seeking light through prayer Freud would hardly be responsive, so Herzog pursues the therapeutic line: "*The depressive character is narcissistic. It fears the disappearance of the beloved. Above all terrors it places the terror of abandonment and naked solitude. So with secret hate it cuts off the deserters. Who then reappears within—introjected as you say in your jargon. Then the voice of the love slain speaks continually within, and the depressive abuses and criticizes himself. You say then that the depressive is often able to state the truth about himself quite reliably and accurately, though he often overstates the case, and you add—it must have been irresistible—that it is odd to think that insights should be the result of disease. Or, truthfulness is a consequence of disease. But* my dear man, I am really very fond of that tart old man, *let us go back a bit. Is it possible that some people are born with a greater metaphysical terror than others, with less sheath or with [less] power to apprehend the inhuman and the void? William James makes room in his system for such types, whom he calls 'tender-minded.'. . . however I am grateful to you for certain information, such as that the melancholic is abnormal in stripping his libido so rapidly from the deserting lover. Suffering from love yet intolerably cruel. . . . Have however some singular power that prevents me from laying my head docilely under your sober shade. One of these Moseses of whom you wrote–called meek"* (B.21.32, 235f.). The prime clinical point is made briefly by Edvig in the novel (*H*, 53); in manuscript we see Herzog virtually savoring the Freudian wisdom. But with reservations, for Herzog rejects *a priori* Freud's "radical determinism" as he resists the illusion of total explanation in the diagnosis. He sees just how his reaction to his recent marital disaster has to do with "abandonment" (associated with fear of abandonment by the mother in the earlier versions, as in Freud). He concurs that sickness can be the blow that brings truth, but he attributes part of his depression to metaphysical causes, causes in the nature of things, preferring to include James's tendermindedness as a necessary element in the explanation, thereby converting sickness into a form of ordinary consciousness. Freud's tartness needs sweetening; even when Bellow is accepting him, it is only a partial acceptance. But if *Herzog* shows how seriously Bellow can take Freud, *The Last Analysis*, written at about the same time, shows that farcical reduction of the claims of psychoanalysis was not far away. Herzog's "singular power," his non-analyzable soul, will never let him rest comfortably with Freud. As if to underscore his tenderminded perception, one more amenable to humanistic comprehension, Herzog signs off, somewhat obscurely, as a meek Moses. The reference is to Freud's *Moses and Monotheism*, which posits two Moses figures who are made to become one: first, the masterful, violent Egyptian who worshipped Aton, and, second, the patient, "meek" Midianite who worshipped Jahve.[54] Freud's book is fascinating but atypical in the sense that, as Rieff puts it, "Freud acknowledges that civilization can be moved by spiritual as well as instinctual discontents."[55] The book is indeed ingenious but eccentric, for against virtually all canons of evidence, it imposes the Oedipal pattern as clearly as in *Totem and Taboo*. Our contemporary Moses does not make much of it.

Though Herzog tells Dr. Freud that he is *"immersed in your Collected Papers"* (B.18.18), though snatches of Freudian language appear in many places in Bellow, usually seriously (sometimes comically, e.g., Hoberly's unrequited love is now called "hysterical dependency," [*H*, 180]), though Bellow recognizes the reality of *an* unconscious, of repression, of the psychological importance of childhood, of filial ambivalence, of behaviour conceived as conflict, nevertheless he can accept Freudianism as at best a partial explanation. Yet he too wants man to be the masculine achiever, and he sees sensuality as a temptation along the way; he too defines woman too quickly in terms of sensuality, and he fears too readily that he will be weakened by her. He too is puzzled by what "they want," though he has a much more contemporary sense of how the intellectual and sensual actually do mix in women. And Bellow is taken by that most Freudian of fables, the ant and the grasshopper. "The ant was once the hero, but now the grasshopper is the whole show," laments Govinda Lal (*MSP* 216). Few people, it seems to Bellow, are willing to undergo the necessary renunciation which civilization demands. Immediate gratification has submerged higher purpose. For this perversion of his instinctual system, Freud is not responsible. Charlie Citrine is described by the post-Freudian analyst Ellenbogen as "an ant longing to be a grasshopper" (*HG*, 164). Not so, as a Freudian would understand. Perhaps the most enduring instance of Freud's influence on Bellow is the novelists's contempt for grasshopper culture. But, for Bellow, the Freudian instinctual system does not offer a strong enough moral counter to the demands of this culture. There is a lack of autonomy. Bellow sees that Freud wished to preserve human nature from cultural determinism, but he does not want to substitute for it a biological determinism. In a wise rabbinic commentary, it is suggested that God did not say "And it was good" after creating man because man's nature was not determined. The poets of *Genesis* knew what Freud did not, the pull of moral indeterminacy. Bellow possesses this knowledge.

Notes

1.   Saul Bellow, *Herzog* (New York: Viking, 1964), p. 13; further parenthetical page references will be preceded by *H*. References to other Bellow works, with their respective abbreviations, will be from the Viking Press editions: AM–*The Adventures of Augie March (1953)*; SD–*Seize the Day, with three short stories* (1956): LA–*The Last Analysis* (1965); MSP–*Mr. Sammler's Planet* (1970); HG–*Humboldt's Gift* (1975). The one exception to this Viking list is DD–*The Dean's December* (New York: Harper & Row, 1982).

2.   "Notebooks," *Herzog*, B. 19.36, 113. Used by permission of Saul Bellow. All subsequent "Notebooks" citations will be given in the text. For a systematic critical use of these materials, see my *Saul Bellow: Vision and Revision* (Durham, N. C.: Duke Univ. Press, 1984).

3.   Philip Rieff, *Freud: The Mind of the Moralist* (New York: Viking, 1959), p. 131.

4.   Clara Thompson, *Psychoanalysis: Evolution and Development* (New York: Grove Press, 1950), p. 43.

5.   Sigmund Freud, *Totem and Taboo*, trans. James Strachey (New York: Norton, 1962), p. 70.

6.   Robert Boyers et al., "Literature and Culture: An Interview with Saul Bellow," *Salmagundi*, 30 (Summer 1975), p. 19. Hereafter referred to as *Salmagundi*.

7.   Rieff, *Freud*, p. 43.

8. Philip Rieff, "Introduction" to D. H. Lawrence, *Psychoanalysis and the Unconscious, Fantasia of the Unconscious* (New York: Viking, 1960), p. viii.

9. One deep reader of a Freudian cast is John J. Clayton, in *Saul Bellow: In Defense of Man* (Bloomington: Indiana Univ. Press, 1977). For him Augie March's "darkness" is the Terrible Father. Never mind that Augie does not really have a father; Henderson's and Herzog's will do. What is so "terrible" about Henderson's father? Doesn't Henderson try to reach his dead father with his violin playing? (Return of the repressed?). Is poor, vulnerable, dignified Father Herzog "terrible"? (Herzog's perfectly resolved Oedipus complex?). Clayton says that Herzog is ridden by Oedipal guilt and the resultant fear of castration and death. Therefore, the murder scene in *Herzog* is more of the father's act of vengeance, mimed by the guilty party to relieve himself. Gersbach is like Herzog, so that by not killing him Herzog is saying, father won't kill me, I'm safe (Clayton, p. 222). And more: "Underneath Moses Herzog is Stephan Rojack" (Clayton, p. 195). If *this* were true, he would have killed Gersbach and Mady. Herzog's saying that Gersbach "sought me in her flesh" is interpreted as follows: Gersbach does so just as Allbee sought Asa Leventhal in the body of the whore. In other words, he is a sexual object for Gersbach, and feeling this, Herzog experiences guilt. His sense of being a male whore is projected into the court case of Aleck-Alice, an actual male prostitute (Clayton, p. 231). A sense of victimization is involved, but Herzog aware of being a male whore? Passionate about the dark motive, Clayton says that in *Mr. Sammler's Planet* "the black prince is acting out Sammler's buried self" (Clayton, p. 238). The proof of this is Sammler's getting upset at Eisen smashing the black man. Isn't the violence itself and all that it means in a richly developed moral context enough reason for being upset? Freud cannot be held accountable for every application of his ideas, but it was inevitable that his system would set this kind of response into motion. There have been more subtle applications.

10. Sigmund Freud, *Civilization and Its Discontents*, trans. James Strachey (New York: Norton, 1961), p. 13.

11. Freud, *Civilization and Its Discontents*, p. 24f.

12.   Bellow is hardly the first to question the Freudian unconscious in terms of motive. In Freud's Vienna, Karl Kraus, among others, made this criticism. He saw the unconscious as creative, healthy, fantastic, good. Jung saw the unconscious as something consciousness should strive for. D. H. Lawrence saw the unconscious or primitive motive as essentially good, though unlike Bellow, he saw this goodness as erotic.

13.   Rieff, *Freud*, p. 215.

14.   Freud, *Civilization and Its Discontents*, p. 65.

15.   *Salmagundi*, pp. 18f.

16.   Sigmund Freud, "A Religious Experience," trans. James Strachey, in *Character and Culture*, ed. Philip Rieff (New York: Collier, 1963), pp. 272f.

17.   Sigmund Freud, *The Future of an Illusion*, trans. W. D. Robson-Scott (Garden City: Doubleday Anchor, 1957), p. 85.

18.   Henry Lowenfeld, "Psychoanalysis Today," *Partisan Review*, 48 (Fall 1981), pp 446-455 *passim*.

19.   In Rieff, ed., D.H. Lawrence, *Fantasia of the Unconscious*, p. 4.

20.   Rieff, "Introduction" to D. H. Lawrence, p. ix.

21.   Erich Fromm, *Psychoanalysis and Religion* (New Haven: Yale Univ. Press, 1950), p. 37.

22.   Fromm, p. 88.

23.   Freud, *Civilization and Its Discontents, p. 101.*

24.   Freud, *Civilization and Its Discontents, p. 66.*

25.   Quoted by Rieff, *The Triumph of the Therapeutic* (New York: Harper Torchbooks, 1968), p. 34.

26.   Freud, *Totem and Taboo*, p. 39.

27.   Freud, *Future of an Illusion*, p. 22.

28.   Sigmund Freud, "Dostoevsky and Parricide," *Art and Psychoanalysis*, ed. Wiliam Philips (New York: Criterion, 1957), pp. 14f.

29.   Freud, *Totem and Taboo*, p. 156.

30.   *Salmagundi*, p. 16.

31.   Freud, "Dostoevsky and Parricide," p. 3.

32.   Rieff, *Freud*, p. 319.

33.   Freud, "Dostoevsky and Parricide," p. 4.

34.   Freud *Future of an Illusion*, pp. 67f.

35.   In Bellow's manuscript, Herzog praises Jaspers: "Recently went through 'The Future of Mankind'. . . . Excellent man, . . . When

good sense becomes sublime. Balanced faith based on reason"
(B.l7 .2). Jaspers' brand of existentialism does not offend him.

36. Freud, "Dostoevsky and Parricide," p. 3.
37. Lionel Trilling, *The Liberal Imagination* (New York: Doubleday
    Anchor, 1950), p. 61.
38. Freud, *Future of an Illusion*, p. 19.
39. *Salmagundi*, p. 18.
40. Sigmund Freud, *The Ego and the Id*, trans. Joan Riviere (New
    York: Norton, 1960), pp. 25f.
41. Rieff, *Freud*, p. 243.
42. Rieff, *Freud*, p. 355.
43. Rieff, *Freud*, p, xiii.
44. Rieff, *Triumph at the Therapeutic*, p. 26.
45. Rieff, *Triumph of the Therapeutic*, p. 22.
46. Freud, *Civilization and Its Discontents*, p. 101.
47. Rieff, *Triumph of the Therapeutic, p. 13.*
48. Rieff, *Triumph of the Therapeutic*, p. 20
49. Rieff, *Freud*, p. 45.
50. Irving Kristol, "God and the Psychoanalysts," *Commentary*
    (8 November 1949), p. 441.
51. Rieff, *Freud*, p. 55.
52. Freud, *Civilization and Its Discontents*, p. 79.
53. Compare Herzog, p. 232: "Sarah Herzog opened her hand and
    said, 'Look carefully, now, and you'll see what Adam was made
    of.' She rubbed the palm of her hand with a finger, rubbed
    until something dark appeared on the deep-lined skin, a particle
    of what certainly looked to him like earth." with Freud, *The
    Interpretation of Dreams*, trans. James Strachey (New York: Avon,
    1965), p. 238: "My mother thereupon rubbed the palms of
    her hands together . . . and showed me the blackish scales of
    epidermis produced by the friction as a proof that we were made
    of earth."
54. Sigmund Freud, *Moses and Monotheism*, trans. Katherine Jones
    (New York: Vintage, 1939), p. 49.
55. Rieff, *Freud*, p. 281.

5

Literature and Politics: The Bellow/Grass Confrontation

The Bellow/Grass confrontation at the PEN Congress of 1986 was like a conflagration set off by a spark; it did not take much to start because of the already existing explosiveness of the mix. Yet one might not have predicted an event. When I saw Bellow at the New York Public Library opening ceremonies, he made it clear that his talk was not a major effort; he had not even written it out but was going to "wing it" from notes, an expression he used again in his opening remarks at the St. Moritz.

The stated theme of the congress was "The Imagination of the Writer and the Imagination of the State." Bellow was on the "alienation" panel. His talk was casual but pointed, analyzing ways in which the term was both relevant and irrelevant. In his introduction, he agreed with the previous speaker, exiled Soviet novelist Vassily Aksyanov, that exile is not necessarily equated with alienation. "Language," said Bellow, "is a spiritual mansion in which you live and nobody has the right to evict you from it." He spoke personally of alienation in the language of divorce, recalled the fashionable

Marxist alienation which "I grew out of," noting portentously that "others didn't," and told of Robert Kennedy's naive question, "'What is alienation?' to which Arthur Schlesinger, swimming by in the pool, said, 'Alienation? Oh, that's a lot of crap. Forget it.'"

Bellow then gave a brief cultural history of alienation, in which he distinguished among five different meanings or resonances. First, he cited Rousseau's *amour propre* as the vanity which is the fast route to hypocrisy and self-distortion. Second, he cited Stendhal's Julien Sorel as an example of *amour propre* transcending itself to *amour passion.* Third, he listed the Marxist alienation, in which history is a nightmare from which only the proletariat can awaken us. Marx's dialectical materialism raised in Bellow's mind the question, alienation from what? This led him to his fourth category, spiritual alienation. The soul does not seem to count for much, the self people disagree about. Life has lost its sacredness.

At this point, Bellow's remarks took a subtle turn. This spiritual limitation derives from the very strengths of American democracy. State-of-nature philosophers founded democracies. "In America," Bellow says, "we didn't start very high, and we didn't rise very high, either. . . . We have shelter, health, protection, and a certain amount of security against injustice." In its founding, America was a political model; culture was never in the foreground, nor was there much rapport between the artist and the government. American democracy recognized no gods, no demons, and no philosophical idealisms; Romanticism was routinized and demystified. The absence of a vividly perceived above and below led to nihilism. Consequently, we do not believe in the existence of powers not guaranteed by the senses. We have, instead, the gratification of innumerable desires.

This was Bellow's main point—often brilliantly dramatized in his fiction. Clearly, he was not saying that alienation does not exist but rather that, despite the many benefits of American democracy, it also includes the hells of spiritual alienation. Yet alienation has been misunderstood and too broadly and glibly applied as a sociopolitical category. "We have a fatuous attachment to certain foolish words," Bellow said. "Alienation, creativity, imagination. These are part of the contemporary psychobabble we must endeavor to rid ourselves of." Alienation as nonsense brought him to his fifth and final meaning: a simple natural goodness that is vitiated by our government.

Of this fifth form, there was no shortage at the PEN Congress. Amos Oz spoke of it when he warned against the putative "Rousseauian assumption that governments and establishments are wicked—all of them—whereas 'common people' are born pure and sweet in heart. All of them. The 'state,'" Oz continued, "is a necessary evil simply because many individuals are very capable of being very deadly. Moreover, some states are almost fair, some are bad, some are lethal. . . . It is our job to differentiate."

When Gunther Grass challenged Saul Bellow, Grass was not interested in making such a differentiation. He did not speak to the central thrust of Bellow's argument—the spiritual deficiency of a generally benign, materialistic culture. Instead he argued, in effect, that materialism was not widespread enough and, therefore, unjust. Grass said: "I'm wondering when you're explaining that democracy gave people not only freedom but also shelter and food. I would like to hear the echo of your words in the South Bronx, where people don't have shelter, don't have food, and no possibility to live the freedom you have, or some have in this country." Grass added, not quite coherently, that certain dictatorships remained in power (Turkey, Pakistan) because of United

States support and said, "I'm thinking of the people in those other countries." What unified these two remarks was Grass's belief that America was reactionary because it was capitalistic.

The implication of Grass's comments—not actually questions—was that Bellow failed to take into account such realities of political economy as class struggle and imperialism. In other settings, Grass the SPD man has criticized traditional Marxism for its utopian beliefs in the dictatorship of the proletariat, the withering away of the state, and capitalism as moribund—even while he remains, in the eyes of some, a pseudo-Marxist.

Disturbed by the crudeness of Grass's remark about dictatorships, Bellow replied sardonically, "That's very commendable. I think of them too." But he then responded more seriously to Grass's assault: "I was talking about the majority situation in this country. I was not trying to include every exception one could think of. Of course there are exceptions. I was simply saying the philosophers of freedom of the seventeenth and eighteenth centuries provided a structure which created a society by and large free, by and large an example of prosperity. I did not say there are no pockets of poverty. I did not say this is a land full of justice. I didn't try to justify America as a superpower. I was simply saying there was no particular concern in the foundation of the country with the higher life of the country."

"No intelligent writer is devoid of political feelings," Bellow went on to say in that sense that, as he once put it, "the unavoidable immersion in the life of society [is] political" ("A World Too Much with Us"). Indeed, Grass's accusations seemed odd, applied to a writer who is centrally concerned with the citizen-hero and whose greatest character expresses a yearning for use, civility, politics in the Aristotelian sense. Like Grass, Bellow is bored with the artist as sensitive plant. He does not want to accept the opposition of public and private as irreconcilable, yet he sees that the public sphere threatens to swallow up the individual. The writer must speak for the individual, as Albert Corde realizes when he opposes the literature-denying political columnist Dewey Spangler.

In the impersonality of the communications age, Bellow holds, literature is the only thing that tells us we are human—assuming that we have to be told. "Communications," Bellow sees, "does [sic] not speak to persons. They speak to an average, a sort of lay person, not to an individual" ("Creative Edge"). Spangler is one of the influential communicators. He is also something of a fool and a charlatan, treacherously stabbing Corde in the back, as Bellow put it, out of *gaité de coeur* with no sense that he is doing harm. His life is part of the carnival of information, an adjunct to the news's diadem. Corde's political significance is the exposure of spiritual failure, as was Bellow's in his talk at the conference. "'Truth and beauty,'" Wyndham Lewis has said, "'are as much public concerns as the water supply'" (qtd. in Bellow, "A World Too Much with Us" 6). Bellow knows much more clearly than Grass the dangers of political seduction and warned the PEN Congress that "one must not get megalomaniacal notions of the powers of writers." What, he questioned, did the Feuchtwangers and the Rollands and the Brechts achieve "in containing the power of Hitler or Stalin? They were turned inside out and made to look like idiots."

At the mention of Brecht's name, Grace Paley and Toni Morrison, sitting in the row in front of me, gave one another a theatrical look of incredulity, as if to say, "Is nothing sacred? Now he's taking Brecht's name in vain." But was Bellow wrong about Brecht? Anyone reading Martin Esslin's account of Brecht and the Communists can see the validity of Bellow's judgment. Although Brecht made numerous accommodations to official criticisms of his work, he remained long unperformed in his own East Germany and, to this day, in the Soviet Union.

Hannah Arendt contends that Brecht lost his gift during his seven years of residence in East Berlin "where he could see, day after day, what it meant to the people to live under a Communist regime" ("Bertold Brecht" 216). He ran his theater, wrote an ode to Stalin, and, most spectacularly, was used by Walter Ulbricht in the uprising of 17 June 1953. Ulbricht had the newspaper print only the last sentence of Brecht's complicated three-paragraph statement: "I feel the need to express to you at this moment my attachment to the Socialist Unity Party" (Cunliffe 129). With his East Berlin theater, Austrian passport, and West German publisher, with his Stalin Peace Prize deposited mostly in a Swiss bank, Brecht knew all too well what his Galileo meant when he said, "'A man like me can get into a moderately dignified position only by crawling on his belly.'"

To Bellow's attack on Brecht, Grass responded with more fervor than coherence: "Sure, the German writers were not able to stop the war, but without them my generation would have been lost. Djilas wasn't able to change Stalinism, but his book was necessary for younger writers to know how to change things. I don't like this double thinking. If I criticize something in the Western world, I have to say I am not a Communist. If we speak nicely about aesthetic questions without speaking about the need around us, then I am in the wrong place."

Which German writers? Surely Grass sees Brecht negatively, as a Communist ideologue, while the Yugoslavian Djilas is clearly a hero of both Grass and Bellow. Bellow was warning against writers who politic, not politicians who write. As for Grass's necessary balancing of West and East—when the computerized study of Grass's political prose is done, it will show Grass almost always sniffing at both at the same

time. His final fillip, which transforms Bellow into an aes-
thete, makes one wonder how well—indeed whether—Grass
had read Bellow.

At the Temple of Dendur party, I could not resist asking
Grass whether he had read *The Dean's December*, surely a book
that addresses itself to "the need around us" in Grass's sense.
I suggested that the author of "Looking for Mr. Green," *Seize
the Day*, and *Mr. Sammler's Planet* was aware of these needs
and that Bellow was hardly oblivious to the negative effects
of capitalism. Grass seemed to agree but repeated that he
objected to Bellow's saying that people in America were not
alienated. (Is this what Bellow said?) He also resented Bellow's statement that writers should not be political; he failed
to grasp that Bellow was talking about everyday politics, not
awareness of the idea of society.

I also asked Grass whether he considered himself a
Marxist in any sense. He said that he did not, that he was a
democratic socialist. Indeed, Grass likes to think of himself
as a man in the political middle, one who wants snaillike
reformist progress and spurns revolution and reaction, as if
these were clear characterizations of the alternatives. Who, I
asked, were his political mentors? Eduard Bernstein and Rosa
Luxemburg, he replied. The former is understandable from
his political essays: Bernstein the revisionist, the reformer,
defender of trade unions, anti-Marxist, social democrat, who
knows that socialism and capitalism must co-exist. The latter
is not understandable, in that Luxemburg represents primarily the revolutionary left Grass affects to repudiate. Bernstein
thought that the middle class was not only economically but
morally healthy. Luxemburg thought revolution a moral
necessity. Grass, however, regards Luxemburg as a revisionist
because of her belief in individual and public freedom; he
sees her as an updated, adventurous John Stuart Mill. This
contradictory preference is ominous and it lends fuel to the

skeptical fire around Grass, to those who charge that he does not see the revolutionary for what it is and that he undermines only the West with his doctrine of moral equivalence, since his criticisms of the East have no effect.

At his press conference, Bellow acknowledged the difficult position of West German writers and intellectuals, caught as they were at the very center of the superpower struggle. But in typical anti-ideological fashion, he cautioned against "the stampeding of writers into political boxes." He expressed dismay at the anchorman jargon and "the jargon of militant radicalism going back to the thirties" with which the conference bristled and concluded that the language we use is "polluted" by politics, requiring us "to speak about life-and-death matters on these unfavorable terms."

At the heart of the Bellow/Grass confrontation is the vexed question of the relationship between truth and power, vision and action. It would be wrong, however, to say that the two writers represented poles. At the congress, people quoted Chekhov on this subject: "Great writers and artists ought to engage in politics only to the extent that it is necessary to defend themselves from politics." Chekhov thereby preserves art from compromise and the individual from the average. He thinks of art as the highest form of disinterested activity—as inspired play. When Salman Rushdie asked about the American writer's task in the context of America's international power, Bellow said, "We don't have any tasks, we just have inspirations." (In a later reading session, Rushdie denied that he had asked the question seriously.) As Richard Gilman once remarked, writers do not have to be *acknowledged* legislators. When Mario Vargas Llosa was nominated for prime minister in 1984 by the Peruvian president, he declined. "I don't think a writer should accept this possibility," said Vargas Llosa. "If he becomes an instrument of power he is not a writer any more" (47). Nadine Gordimer, addressing the issue squarely in terms posed by the congress, said, "The state has no imagination because the state sees imagination as something that can be put into service." It "projects a social vision . . . through planners, advisers." Its "product is social engineering." The imagination, Gordimer concludes, "must be private, not collective." Stalin, one recalls, called writers "literary engineers."

In his political essays, Grass has taken issue with the going view. "I know all the arguments against dual activity," he says. "A writer should keep his distance. Day-to-day politics with its insipid jargon is ruinous to a literary style. And, above all, intellect and power are incompatible. Here's my answer. A writer must face up to the test of reality; and that can't be done if he keeps his distance." Grass is correct if political reality is transformed into a private vision, as in the Danzig trilogy in which politics is subsumed by grotesque character. Indeed, both Bellow and Grass are notable for their integration of the lyrical and the socio-political. Grass's obsessive absorption in the Danzig milieu makes his work succeed to the extent that it does. He would never again capture this density of personal reference spinning off into fantasy. The more clearly ideational he becomes, the less energy his work possesses.

Grass's argument weakens as he proceeds. When he says that "a literary style cultivated like a hothouse plant may show a certain hothouse purity, but it won't really be pure," he is displaying his penchant for straw men. Grass adds, "As for the old cliché—intellect versus power—I call it a fiction, because power can be intelligent and intelligence can be powerful" (121). But power is not intelligent the way disinterested intelligence is, and intelligence is not powerful the way state power is.

One must consider that Grass is partly reacting to the Nazi appropriation of the cult of creativity, genius, and the demonic artist—in political terms, the *Fuhrerprinzip*. The genius was considered to be a law unto himself, isolated, beyond good and evil, messianic, *volk*-reviving, and visionary. Hitler and Mussolini were considered "poets of revolution." Never mind that real artists were exiled or imprisoned (or, as the case may be, won over), that real artists were used for propaganda purposes. This uniquely German situation is what T. W. Adorno responded to by saying that "after Auschwitz one can no longer write poetry." The Nazis were, in their own way, idealists. Grass reacts against the horrible Nazi distortion of the Romantics and Nietzsche, a distortion that to some extent Romanticism lent itself to. Hence, his homely comparisons—the artist as cook, for example, and his insistence on the ordinary, the nondemonic, on parody, and the grotesque. After Adrian Leverkuhn, Oscar Mazerath.

Yet Grass's bellicosity at the PEN Congress cannot be understood only as a function of such general and cultural considerations. It derives in good measure from a specific West German resentment of American power, which is clearly delineated in his political writings. Where you stand is where you sit, they say in Washington, and Grass sits in the middle of modern fragmentation. Coming from divided Danzig, born of a German father and a Kashubian mother, living in what he calls "the twofold Germany" (*On Writing* 60), Grass's prime impulse is to put Humpty Dumpty together again.

Grass resents America because Germany is not unified[1]— which he seems to regard as a Western or Capitalist plot. He also resents what he sees as a lack of German independence. "We're American epigones," he moans (*Speak Out* 121). "The Federal Republic is only on paper a sovereign state" (*NY Times* 5 Feb. 1986: A24). He blames Conrad Adenauer for undercutting social democracy and the possibility of reunification by establishing what Grass considers a Capitalist oligarchy, a condition worsened by Adenauer's rearming of West Germany. Grass's judgment of Adenauer is severe; and despite his political activism, Grass is notably short on practical proposals.

Grass thinks that the East and West are equally culpable. He equates the Stalinist suppression of Prague with the Paris and Berlin police actions against the student uprisings of 1968, thereby equating the destruction of democracy by foreign intervention with the keeping of civil order. In the panel on "utopianism," Grass once again got up to speak from the floor. He regretted that the attack on utopianism was so disproportionately anti-Soviet and went on to ask: "Is capitalism better than Gulag communism? I don't think so." There was a stunned silence. Grass later denied having made this remark, but knowing something of Grass's political preferences and something of the psychopathology of everyday life, we cannot consider it a meaningless slip. It was, after all, this particular slip and not so very different from his equating Prague and Paris 1968. Earlier in the session, Czeslaw Milosz told of a California student who asked him, "What is the difference between life in a concentration camp and life in Sacramento," a question from never-never land but one remarkably like Grass's, one which apparently reverberated in his mind. Though almost everyone in the hall took it as a joke, Grass, perhaps, did not. In *The Plebians Rehearse the Uprising*, Grass's most intriguing work dealing with the relationship of literature to politics, he gives us his version of Brecht's agony of 17 June 1953, the day the East Germans staged the abortive revolt against Ulbricht. Grass's view of Boss, his fictional Brecht, is more sympathetic than his view of the real Brecht, whom he regards as a Hegel-cum-Marx opportunist. In the play, Boss is rehearsing his version of Shakespeare's *Coriolanus*, *Coriolan*, which greatly reduces Coriolanus's stature and elevates that of the plebians. Yet when the rehearsal is interrupted by an actual uprising, Boss is irritated, interested only in his rehearsal. He is an artist; and besides, this does not appear to him to be a real revolution. But under pressure of the growing nobility of the workers' demands—first, fair work norms, next, free elections (which Brecht himself rejected, thinking that free elections would lead to World War III)—together with the parallel pressure brought on by the memory of the thwarted heroism of his own Katrin in a harrowing scene from *Mother Courage*, Boss senses the purity of the old revolutionary call. Just as he is about to join the uprising, martial law is declared. A melancholy, rather un-Brechtian Boss laments his fugitive opportunity and writes his three-paragraph letter to the authorities, the first two paragraphs critical and never quoted, only the last sentence of the accommodating third paragraph appearing in print.

Grass thus gives us a sympathetic view of the artist victimized by communism—for, in another sense, it is his own dilemma, the artist compromised by politics. Where art and politics can never be separated, art becomes the handmaiden of politics. Grass here saw the issue clearly but diminished his own artistic power for political polemics of the sort evident in his attack on Bellow.

Note

1.   This essay was written in 1987. Grass has often spoken of reunification. Now that Germany is unified, Grass speaks of confederation. He fears that the West will gobble up the East, assuming wrongly that the East wants to maintain a separate socialist identity. He does not seem to realize that many of the productive people of East Germany were leaving because they wanted the life of West Germany. He is out of touch with the East German electorate, which opted not only for the West but for the conservative party in power. Also, Grass prematurely had stated that the reunification bubble had burst on other grounds; namely that given twentieth-century history, no one should want a reunified Germany. This is another matter. (See NY Times 7 Jan.1990, sec. 4: 25.)

Works Cited

Arendt, Hannah. "Bertold Brecht." *Men in Dark Times*. New York: Harcourt, 1983.

Bellow, Saul. "The Creative Edge." BBC Interview, Channel 13. New York. 9 Nov., 1986.

——. "A World Too Much With Us." *Critical Inquiry* 2 (Autumn 1975): 1–9.

Cunliffe, W. Gordon. Gunter Grass. New York: Twayne, 1969.

Grass, Gunter. *On Writing and Politics: 1967–1983*. Trans. Ralph Manheim. San Diego: Harcourt, 1985.

——. *Speak Out*. Trans. Ralph Manheim. New York: Harcourt, 1969.

Vargas Llosa, Mario. *The Village Voice* 3 Feb. 1986: 47.

6

Malamud's *Dubin's Lives*: A Jewish Writer and the Sexual Ethic

In *Dubin's Lives* Malamud wanted to go all out, come closest to the bone of subjectivity. An interviewer informs us: "He said 'Dubin's Lives' was his attempt at bigness, at summing up what he has learned in the long haul. 'I was already approaching 60 when I began it and I had to be very severe with myself,' he said. 'What had my experience totalled up to? What did I know up to this point? I wanted to write a novel that was significant to me.'" (Malamud interview 31) To be sure, A *New Life* is an earlier break from the generally small, period pieces of a colorful and impoverished Jewish milieu, for which he is justly celebrated, already something assimilated and large, something in the nineteenth-century expansive manner. But it is *Dubin's Lives* which Malamud claims to be the big, personal book.

Dubin's Lives gives us a thorough and intimate portrait of a character in crisis, more so than anything Malamud has done. Formally speaking, it shows us most clearly how far Malamud has moved from being a writer of selection to a writer of saturation, a writer of exclusion to one of inclusion. The terms are from the Wells-James controversy about the nature of fiction and serve as a rough indication of Malamud's direction. Where Malamud was once strong on story he here excels at atmosphere; where he was once a master of dramatic lyricism, he now gives us a chronicle. No longer are we in the world of dramatic time but in a world where time brings things to ripeness or to rottenness, as the case may be.

Malamud has certainly changed and developed, but has he become better? Does more ambitious necessarily mean better; more subjective mean truer? It seems that *Dubin's Lives* is not the *summa* Malamud wanted it to be. Something has gone wrong in this novel and that something points as well to why the work he, so to speak, outgrew—*The Assistant, The Magic Barrel*—is superior to it.

It is a sign of the times that Malamud—often considered the most Jewish of the major Jewish-American writers—defines the parameters of what is truly significant in terms of his erotic life. Though hardly a stranger to this area of experience, Malamud here goes all out, makes an attempt, a fictional attempt, at full Rousseauian disclosure. The self cannot be understood without the erotic. But is the self to be understood primarily as a function of the erotic? D. H. Lawrence is one twentieth-century genius who answers yes. As he ponders this sort of question, Dubin is at work on a biography called *The Passion of* D. H. *Lawrence*. Dubin has about as much trouble with the biography as he does with his erotic life, which suggests that—dare it be said—the answer may be no.

The plot of *Dubin's Lives* resembles a Lawrencean triangle. A restless male, whose long marriage is winding down, is revived by an orgasmic young woman; the relationship in turn renders him impotent with his wife. This used to be called adultery. Adultery is a paradigmatic act in Lawrence, stemming from his own triumphant snatching away of Frieda (some fortuitous allegory here, the name suggesting peace, harmony) from (did it have to be?) Professor Weekley. *Lady Chatterley's Lover* is only the most conspicuous adultery in Lawrence. In the Lawrence triangle blood consciousness triumphs over mental consciousness, love over law. Dubin thinks in these terms up to a point. After finally succeeding with Fanny Bick (more allegory—Fanny is obvious; Bick is Yiddish, suggesting bovine), he believes that he "understood Lawrence more fully, his religion of sexuality: a belief in the blood, the flesh, as wiser than the intellect." Yet after thinking about "blood consciousness" for a while, Dubin remarks, "I can't say I fully believe in it" (*Dubin's Lives* 219). Dubin is, in fact, part of an uncompleted triangle. Rejecting his wife, he cannot accept Fanny as a body-and-Soulmate. Dubin—and Malamud—have reached an impasse, and Dubin does not so much triumph in adultery as flounder.

One may well wonder about the authenticity of Dubin's appropriation of Lawrence. Dubin immediately fantasizes about love with an as yet anonymous Fanny (*Dubin's Lives* 6). The aging Dubin, author of the rather lugubrious *Short Lives*, thinks of love as an antidote to death. Lawrence thought of it as an antidote to false consciousness, resurrection for him being a form of new identity. Dubin therefore muses, as Lawrence never did, about his being "an old billy goat—these feelings at fifty-six, disjunctions of an ordered life. We are all clowns" (*Dubin's Lives* 27). Lawrence, of course, died at forty-four but could never have thought in these terms had he lived to be fifty-six.

The mixture of Lawrence and Goldoni in the Venice bedroom fiasco is a strange one. Old, guilty Dubin gets his comeuppance. There is Fanny, "standing at the toilet bowl, retching, a blob of diarrhea dribbling down her leg"

(*Dubin's Lives* 64). Dubin is an avuncular sort and knows what to do. He cleans up. The scene is funny but the Lawrencean moral drawn from it (the Lawrence whose off mood is one of male isolation stemming, though, not from frustration but from avoidance of woman's sexual possessiveness) is malapropos. Dubin, in blue-balled isolation, thinks: "A man is an island in the only sense that matters, not an easy way to be. We live in a mystery, a cosmos of separable lonely bodies, men, insects, stars. It is all a loneliness and men know it best" (*Dubin's Lives* 66). The juxtaposition of bedroom farce and Lawrencean mysticism is jarring.

Dubin sees that Lawrence "was never an exponent of free sex . . . didn't like people aimlessly copulating" (*Dubin's Lives* 33). In this connection, the promiscuous Fanny seems an unlikely possibility for a Lawrencean. Dubin tries to guess how many lovers she has had. One thousand and three perhaps. Dubin can even think of her in totally non-Lawrencean terms as "one of those gifted people who give public pleasure" (*Dubin's Lives* 62), or "that little hooker" (*Dubin's Lives* 117). Of course, the comic point might have been that modernist high seriousness about sex has broken down, as in Nabokov's *Lolita* and Morris's *Love Among the Cannibals*. As things start out, this is Malamud's point: witness Fanny's obliging two Venetian nautical types as Dubin suffers. But this is not the main route Malamud wishes to go. There is Dubin's serious contemplation of the event. Furthermore, as the novel develops, Dubin thinks of Fanny as a project in moral reclamation. And the scenes with his wife are usually solemn.

People often tell Dubin, in effect, what's a nice Jewish boy like you doing with a wildman like Lawrence? Even when not questioned, Dubin wonders, "My God whatever brought me to him?" (*Dubin's Lives* 5) The local shrink (who gets in a few sessions with Dubin's frustrated wife) tells him, with some justification, "what a ball-breaking strain it must be to have to identify with someone whose nature is so radically different from yours. Isn't objectivity breached by his constant bilge" (*Dubin's Lives* 363). Even Dubin's remote daughter, who tells him almost nothing, tells him he is not much like D. H. Lawrence. Dubin equivocally responds, "He had genius. I doubt he loved mankind but he relished life, though he explained it insufficiently" (*Dubin's Lives* 171). The erotic, after all, can take you only so far in the realm of moral and spiritual explanation. Late in his adventures, frustrated with both Fanny and his wife, Dubin thinks that the Lawrence biography is a waste of time. Why, he wonders, doesn't he do something useful, like become an environmentalist. The strain is great. For the first time in his life Dubin passes out. Even worse, a vision of Lawrence appears to him in a nightmare, where a rather fierce, vituperatively anti-Semitic Lawrence (hardly a fictional extension here) curses him as a Jew antagonistic to the male principle. Great material for comedy here, but Malamud is dead serious.

There is, in fact, an antagonism between Dubin's Jewishness, such as it is, and Lawrencean doctrine, between the Jewish writer and the sexual ethic. As noble and life-giving as the sexual revolution has in many ways been, the constant emphasis on the primacy of sex, which identifies it as the wellspring of all being, grates against the Jewish sensibility. Few writers or intellectuals would, in the twentieth century, deny the importance of sex or belittle the work of reclamation done in its name, but to assert the cardinality of the erotic over the moral impulse is an object worthy of pagan Egypt—often so identified in Lawrence—rather than Israel.

The question then arises, how much of a Jew is Dubin? He is not observant, marries a non-Jew, does not maintain a Jewish household, and rarely talks to his children about things Jewish. His most explicit statement about Jewishness is negative. He defends his marrying a *shiksa* to his old father by writing, "Dear Papa, How can a man be a Jew if he isn't a man? How can he be a man if he gives up the woman he wants to marry!" (*Dubin's Lives* 64). The question of conversion never comes up for Dubin. He is an ethical Jew, whose ethics include discarding what is identifiably Jewish when it matters. In a sense Dubin's relation to Jewishness parallels Malamud's to his earlier "Jewish" writing—something he wanted to outgrow.

But there is a Jewish quality that persists; for better or worse Jewishness is defined by Dubin as a sense of obligation, a way of doing things characterized by the restraint of decency. As the Yiddish expression goes, *A Yid tit nicht azoi* (a Jew doesn't do that). Dubin, one recalls, turns down Fanny's first naked offer. "I'm a controlled type," he tells Fanny, thinking, by contrast and rather luridly, of Lawrence, who "used to go wild in the glow of the full moon" (*Dubin's Lives* 44). Dubin usually is nothing if not responsible, so much so that he meets his wife Kitty through a "personal" advertisement calling for a marriage-minded "man who is honest, responsible" (*Dubin's Lives* 46). Dubin's control carries to the point of brushing his teeth after meals so he won't be tempted by chocolate. It also comes to the point of his being very punctual. "The years I've wasted being on time," moans the *vecchio* waiting for the appearance of his young lover (*Dubin's Lives* 51). He even views adultery as a reward for being good. On the plane to Venice with Fanny he muses, "Enjoying myself. I have it coming to me" (*Dubin's Lives* 55). Dubin is so moral that he is faithful in adultery. "Don't consider her your equal," he thinks of saying about Kitty to Fanny (*Dubin's Lives* 57). And even when it becomes clear that Fanny is more than her equal, Dubin refuses to perform the sex act with her in the conjugal bed. So we have a definition of the Jew in America, circa 1979: a man who won't commit adultery in his wife's bed. (They do it on the nearby rug. *Dos meg min.* This is permissible!)

In this novel, the Star of David is a reminder of a former erotic attachment of his lover.

That Dubin feels some guilt about his incarnation as a swinger is evident in an occasional slip, as when he contemplates his newly acquired phallic heroism. He thinks of himself as "William the Bold, with upraised sword on a black charger" (*Dubin's Lives* 62). The charger might be white, but black has its subliminal appeal. Who is Dubin to say no when the randy Fanny proclaims, "I'm just as moral as you" (*Dubin's Lives* 83). Didn't the hairy-assed gondolier come to her out of need? Dubin's guilt may be fragile, but his general depressiveness seems God-given, a function of the fallen condition. People often urge him to cheer up, enjoy life. Even his straight-laced wife says, "Sometimes I think you've never felt young in your life; you almost always interpreted it as obligation or lost opportunity" (*Dubin's Lives* 145). It's hard to be a Jew, as the saying goes.

Dubin is too much the pagan to rest content in marriage and too much the Jew to enjoy adultery for long. Besides, like Flaubert's adulteress, he finds that adultery can be as boring as marriage. But he hangs in there. The novel goes on and on dramatizing a limbo of such tedium that one is left to wonder where the imitative fallacy begins and the drama of exquisite tedium ends. From time to time the writing becomes so limp that it breaks down into cliché: "He racked his brains thinking how not to fail her [Kitty] yet go on with Fanny" (*Dubin's Lives* 256). Or into banality: Dubin makes "an impassioned plea" to the no longer patient Fanny not to make "a hasty mistake" and end "what may have barely begun" (*Dubin's Lives* 276). But how impassioned can Dubin really be, and how hasty can Fanny be? It is already two-thirds of the way through the novel, and it is with good reason that Fanny tells him, "There are times I think all you want is a lay every couple of months or so, just to change the scenery" (*Dubin's Lives* 265). Nor can Fanny be refuted when she says, "You wouldn't have let me split that night if in your heart you weren't glad I was going" (*Dubin's Lives* 276). When his ignored wife asks, "Why don't you go back to her?", Dubin lamely replies, "She wasn't there to go back to" (*Dubin's Lives* 315).

Malamud is in a quandary here and does not seem to know how to break out of it. The narrative strains with melodramatic subplots concerning his stepson and daughter. Melodrama is even wrung out of Dubin's walks in the woods; the first disaster is a harrowing loss of direction in the winter, which parallels Dubin's spiritual confusion. Coincidence also reflects the narrative strain when Dubin is bailed out by Kitty in his first scary walk and by Fanny in his second. The greatest coincidence of all, though, is Fanny's moving in next door after receiving an inheritance. The now mature Fanny suggests divvying Dubin up with his wife—Monday through Wednesday for her; Thursday through Sunday for his wife. The ambivalent man's wish-fulfilment. We last see the sexually aroused Dubin leaving Fanny's house, as her young buck waits in the wings, and walking toward his own, "holding his half-stiffened phallus in his hand, for his wife with love" (*Dubin's Lives* 362), a half-cocked ending if there ever was one. We are led to believe, by a postscript listing works by Dubin, that this happy resolution unjams his writer's block on the Lawrence book and, further, that his hapless daughter comes around and writes a biography of Anna Freud with him. This tonal shift near the end from *les souffrances* to comic fantasy is the weakest part of the book. Malamud is trying to impose some of the earlier short story comic lyricism onto the intractable realism of a painful chronicle.

In Malamud's case it really seems that Jewish is better. *The Assistant*, *The Magic Barrel* and a few of the other early stories carry more aesthetic authority than his attempt at the big book on the current scene. Malamud's genius is lyrical and somewhat archaic at its best. Paradoxically, this lyricism is nurtured by a moral outlook. The author put it perfectly when he spoke of his "moral-esthetic." Not that his characters must be moral, or good, in a sense generally accepted to be consonant with religious principles, though they may be, as in "The Last Mohican," which dramatizes the meaning of giving. No, his "moral-esthetic" may bring forth a masterpiece like "The Magic Barrel" where, in a condition of stultified purity, a rabbinical student makes the fateful choice of a young prostitute to be his bride. Her appeal resides in the knowledge of good and evil her being exudes, a knowledge which does not preclude the innocence that can transfigure the fallen condition. The rabbinical student, Leo Finkle, is the Myshkin to her Nastasya Filipovna. Both men fall in love with a troubled picture which is nonetheless a divine image. Malamud's "moral-esthetic" easily transcends a simple didacticism but is no less moral for being here a marriage of heaven and hell.

Indeed, Malamud's "moral-esthetic" owes as much to romanticism as to his Jewish roots. The fateful female—not usually *femme fatale*—is a constant presence in Malamud, showing the pull of the passional life on an ordered existence. Included are such couplings as Roy Hobbs and Memo Paris in *The Natural,* Frank Alpine and Helen Bober in *The Assistant* (here the male/female pattern is reversed), Leo Finkle and Stella Salzman in "The Magic Barrel," Sy Levin and Pauline Gilley in *A New Life*, and William Dubin and Fanny Bick in *Dubin's Lives.* The woman is a passport to momentous experience, the breaking down of the forbidden. We are not so far from the Lawrence paradigm. But in Malamud the emphasis is not on the consequent Dionysian release of cosmic energies but on the moral burden passion entails. In Lawrence passion makes men, at least the male, powerful; in Malamud it makes one good, evil, or indifferent. This is why Dubin never feels a transcendent release through passion. He feels its weight.

Dubin is too Jewish to play a pagan game. Hence, his unwillingness to find a definitive transcendence in the erotic and his inability to break the bonds of matrimony. His broken relationship with Fanny recommences on moral grounds. She has become a better person because of him. This is a new version of the Malamud pattern of reverse assimilation, where the gentile world is made to see the light of Jewish values. However, where this pattern is convincing in *The Assistant*, it is not in *Dubin's Lives*. The young, promiscuous Fanny is more vivid than her mature incarnation. There is no sense of painful conversion as there is with Frank Alpine. The pattern does not convince because William Dubin is something of a blob, a deracinated, self-cancelling neuter, who is barely Jew or pagan. From this center of indifference we can see the appeal of an old-style Jew like Morris Bober of *The Assistant*. Though not an orthodox type himself, he is vivid in his moral being. He is an astonishing presence to Frank Alpine; Dubin, on the other hand, is typically shady and equivocal to Fanny, to Kitty, and to the reader.

For Malamud, the Jewish context provides a scene of significant suffering, decency struggling to maintain itself in a difficult world. Malamud's moral, as we have seen in "The Magic Barrel," is not necessarily Jewish, but all characters in that world breathe an air in which moral choice is considered to be momentous, where the constant, inner struggle known as conscience issues into dramatic illumination. Needless to say, these qualities are not exclusively Jewish, but they are typically so. Which is why Frank Alpine, having read *Crime and Punishment*, thought that Raskolnikov "must be a Jew and was surprised when he found out he wasn't" (*The Assistant* 86). Frank Alpine (again a quasi-allegorical name,

Frank suggesting the good St. Francis, and Alpine suggesting heights) is in this sense "Jewish" when he has "a terrifying insight: that all the while he was acting like he wasn't, he was really a man of stern morality" (*The Assistant* 139). He does not shirk his burden of suffering. Dubin, alas, does. He embodies the amorphous qualities of contemporary American life that drove Malamud to construct his Jewish milieu in the first place. For much of the novel we see Dubin weightless, gutless, feckless, and fuckless. True, Dubin suffers in the sense that every man must bare his crotch, in Joyce's pun, but there is no consequent moral illumination. *Dubin's Lives* gives us the theatrics of vacillation and a tacked-on ending. There is none of the simple, dramatic eloquence of, say, the marriage broker Salzman's repudiation of his daughter: "This is my baby, my Stella, she should burn in hell" (*The Magic Barrel* 212), or of Finkle's sense of his beloved: "From afar he saw that her eyes—clearly her father's—were filled with desperate innocence. He pictured, in her, his own redemption" (*The Magic Barrel* 214). Living in a morally opaque world, a world of which Malamud can make no definite sense, Dubin cannot seriously picture his own redemption. All of which is not to say that the Jewish writer had best stay with period or Jewish subjects. Saul Bellow is the first Jewish writer to come to mind to refute such a proposition. There are, of course, others. Malamud, however, does not succeed nearly so well in rendering the current world as he does the Jewish milieu of his own moral imagination.

Note

1.   There is a curious parallel to this scene in *The Fixer.* Yakov Bok's wife leaves him because he is impotent. In a rendezvous with Zina Lebedev, Bok notices a fine trickle of blood run down her leg as she washes. Bok is disgusted.

Works Cited

Malamud, Bernard. *The Assistant.* New York: Farrar, Straus and Giroux, 1958. 86.

——. *Dubin's Lives.* New York: Farrar, Straus and Giroux, 1979.

——. *The Magic Barrel.* New York: Farrar, Straus and Giroux, 1958. 212.

——. "Talk with the Novelist." Interview by Ralph Tyler. *The New York Times Book Review.* 18 Feb. 1979. 31.

7

More Die of Heartbreak: The Question of Later Bellow

More Die of Heartbreak came into focus, Bellow tells us, "when it struck me all at once that certain subjects, which in the past were treated very seriously, are now the subject of teasing and parody. . . . [A] lot of the things that used to mean so much to us—love, murder, family relations—have been emptied of meaning and feeling. Now they are toyed with purely as a mental game." This condition derives, in his view, from the nihilism resulting from World War I. Bellow says that in *More Die of Heartbreak* he "was really after how . . . serious people hold their own against this nihilism" (Sanoff 52). One may wonder why this perspective struck him "all at once," since, except for the toying, it is a familiar one in his work. He had earlier, for example, described *Humboldt's Gift* as "a presumptuous book which attempts to make a comedy of death" (Bragg 676) and had spoken eloquently some time before that of our special comedy in which introspection, so solemnly treated in earlier literature, is now differently seen, citing Nabokov's reworking of the *Death-in-Venice* theme in *Lolita* as an example. His own *Henderson the Rain King* and *Herzog* are equally relevant instances ("Literature" 173ff.).

Bellow's comedy reflects a muted idealism, even, it may be said, a reduced religious idealism. In explaining Charlie Citrine of *Humboldt's Gift*, he uses a favorite figure: "I think he is doing something that I have described as kidding his way to Jesus: seemingly frivolous and light, but actually quite serious, afraid to make a major statement about his intentions, but disguising himself comically" (Bragg 675). He adds that Humboldt does this, too. And we may add that it is an apt description of Bellow's moral comedy.

It certainly describes *More Die of Heartbreak*. Bellow is trying to read meaning into love and family relations and into death as well, but these are more often than not themes for parody. This becomes apparent to Kenneth Trachtenberg, the Bellovian narrator, an assistant professor of Russian literature, now in his thirties, who has left his Paris home to free himself from the orbit of an overbearingly successful sexual figure of a father by linking up with his idealist uncle in Midwestern America. For Ken, in any case, America is where the action is. A distinguished botanist and professor at the same university, Uncle Benn Crader is a widower who spends the better part of his middle years in search of, when it is not in flight from, an ideal love. His tergiversations are presented in all the awkward literalness of Gogolian farce.

Love is the first subject of Bellow's parodistic scrutiny. One of the qualities that draws Ken to his uncle is that Benn "was born with that increasingly rare capacity. He actually could fall in love" (23). Ken speaks with some incredulity, though he himself is a would-be lover. He notes that "except in a melancholy connection" love is a subject "you seldom hear about . . . any more" (44), a condition not changed by this novel. Penetrated willy-nilly by the eighties' language of money, he asserts that "the credit rating of love [is] now at an all-time low" (103). When a philosopher at the university tells the love-longing Ken that "your heart can also be a sophist," he is at first surprised but concedes that "everybody is more familiar with the absence of love than with its presence" and that, consequently, "the feeling of emptiness . . . becomes 'normal'" (24).

If love is here, can marriage be far behind? Ken is eloquent on the destructive quality of marriage, so likely to be a short-lived transcendence. He envisions "the wreckage of loves like Boeings that couldn't clear the peaks" (51). Benn concurs with Ken's grim assessment of the sexual scene: "All those mad men and mad women sharing beds. Two psychopaths under one quilt" (51). Ken likes this formulation so well that he repeats it later on in connection with Matilda and Benn (238), thereby qualifying his own shaky assent to marrying again. When the manipulated Benn applies the language of idealism to marriage and speaks of penetrating to the essence of a being, Ken is rightly skeptical.

Indeed, sex is far more prominent than love in this novel, and it is typically eccentric or degrading. The novel is vivified by an imagery of sexual fragmentation, a synecdoche for disintegration. Rudi's member; Matilda's shoulders, teeth, and the space between her breasts; Treckie's black and blue shins; Dita's facelift; gynecological ward privates; Kyoto's vulvas—these are the detritus of a failed view. Ken laments that "whether it's business, a career problem, character difficulties, doubts about one's body, even metaphysics, they turn to sex as the analgesic" (86). Sex is the opiate of the masses and the classes. Sounding somewhat like Mr. Sammler, Ken thinks, "Mere Nature [is] Hell, as Swedenborg wrote" (89)—and as his Russian mystics wrote, as well.

Ken's mistrust of sex has an oedipal animus. He says sardonically that his father "had spent years in the erotic wilderness looking for a sign" (35). Sex has been so pervasive in his father's life that he is oblivious to its significance. Ken holds that "it never dawned on my old man that he had lived for women primarily" (35). Profoundly, Ken sees that his "sex embrace was death-flavored" (69). There is surely a hint of extinction in his age. Though Ken recognizes that an old term like *libertine* does not apply to his father, he sees the hollowness of a sex-directed life. With the advantage of the Russian mystical perspective, Ken moans that even Western intellectuals do not see that the current sexual pleasuring is a form of corruption.

Something similar seems to be going on in the East, or in Japan at least, where the vulva display is one flower show for which our botanist is not prepared. Benn is shaken not because of prudery but because of the sexual sovereignty implied, reminiscent of the pickpocket's exposure in *Mr. Sammler's Planet*. Though Benn is in his fifties, he is still on the *qui vive*, unwilling, as Ken puts it, "to accept the stages of life as people did in antiquity or the Middle Ages" (325). Failing with Matilda Layamon in love, Benn succumbs to her "sexual enchantments" (155). Ken sees something masochistic in Uncle's dependence. He considers Benn a "sex-abused man . . . a woman-battered man . . . passive under abuse" (54–55) and later concludes that Benn "had *wanted* to come down . . . into the peculiar sexuality associated with such states" (166)—hence, the self-deception in his relation with Matilda.

Ken, too, is involved in sexual self-deception. Though he somehow thinks of himself and Treckie as ideally suited (63), this is one more ideal that bites the dust. Augie March believed that a woman wants a child by the man she loves. In a jaded version of such innocence, Ken believes that since Treckie bore his child, she loves him. But Ken's connection to Treckie mainly takes the form of child support. Ironically, it is Uncle who tells Ken that he is "[t]aking the usual beating from that dainty little woman" (60). Ken's father had discoursed on "domineering diminutives" (65). Ken, like Uncle, consciously finds himself "involved in the sadomasochistic question" (83). But mainly his tiny lover is indifferent to him sexually, speaks West-Coast style about incompatible auras, and falls for a mildly sadistic mesomorph. In this painful comedy, Ken's nice-guy quality is no turn-on.

In a fine stroke, Bellow sees that Poe is a cultural analogue to the going sexual eccentricity. Like Poe, Ken is fixated on a child-woman (63), though one with a degree in, appropriately enough, biology who has dividends from Granddad. And Benn, or part of Benn, sees Matilda as Helen in Poe's poem, an ideal projection with hyacinth hair and classic face. Ken is right to worry about "the marbled statue in the stained-glass niche," noting Poe's own strange sexual preference for Virginia Clemm. Helen, on the other hand, "was there to be contemplated, not embraced—Beauty in contemplation," Ken correctly judges, adding with earthly skepticism, "What are Jews doing, getting into all this Greek stuff, anyway?" (142–143). Ken sees as well that in Poe's prose women were glorified, and it is not long before Benn's Helen turns into Ligeia.

Poe is instructive as American *poète maudit*. Ken sees it this way: "[H]ere was a poet who had run straight into a world rolled flat as a pizza by the rational intellect (and at a primal, crude stage of capitalist development—let's not leave out capitalism), and he fought back with whisky and poetry, dreams, puzzles, perversions" (209). So he has, for Bellow, a special relevance to the computerized, leveraged, buyout 1980s, with their sexual legacy from the late sixties and seventies. But the high-trance lyricism of Poe has turned into comedy; the Gothic has diminished into Hitchcock. Matilda's shoulders remind Benn of *Psycho*, yet he persists in his forced idealization until panic sets in.

Poe is just another instance in a novel of nearly total sexual eccentricity. On the one hand, there is Ken's masochistic mother who tolerates tea-dates, according to Parisian convention, with Papa's girl friends. Her masochism finds a constructive outlet as a sort of Mrs. Schweitzer in ravaged Somalia. On the other hand, there is Matilda, vampire seductress and manipulator, who lines her husband up for sacrifice to Mammon, in a plot turn that strains credibility. A woman of her ilk would not so obviously pollute her own marriage for cash, not when so many lucrative alternatives exist.

Half of the women in the book are not quite victim or victimizer but fall into that wacky middle ground of love-farce of which Bellow is a master. Heiress Caroline Bunge, with her prenuptial agreement, her drugs, her fear of a von-Bülow-type love match, her preference for tufts of paper to the pill, her full makeup for lovemaking, is one such success—all a bit much for the beleaguered botanist, who leaves her stranded on the other side of the airport to fly to the other side of the world. If the excess of sexual indulgence seems too much, there is always Della Bedell, whose piercing, farcical question reminds us that the contrary may be worse. "What am I supposed to do with my sexuality?" (86), moans the middle-aged isolato. The apparent integrity of Dita Schwartz, a serene, older Ph.D. candidate, is undercut by her facelift, her need to wear a mask. Almost everyone wears one; take, for example, Mrs. Sterling, Treckie's mother, a one-time child-bride competing with her daughter in the maturity department by making a serious bid for her stranded lover.

Charges of misogyny against Bellow can usually be defused by countering that his men are just as vulnerable to comic deflation. The usual feminist criticism that, given the special subjectivity of the Bellow central character, women are rarely seen in their own terms—and even when the contrary is the case ("Leaving the Yellow House" and A Theft work with a woman as central intelligence) that they are defined exclusively by their relationships with men—can be deflected by considering the delight, even sometime tenderness, with which Bellow considers *la différence*. Then there is the fact that the lunatic variety he lovingly describes is often nothing less than sober realism.

Kenneth Trachtenberg certainly wants to believe in love. He knows something about it. He even teaches a seminar on "The Meaning of Love," but his knowledge remains largely theoretical. One of his lectures on the subject is given to Uncle Benn. Desperately confused about Matilda, Uncle tells Ken that he is opting for a Portuguese psychoanalyst to bail him out in Rio. Like other Bellow heroes, Ken launches an attack on Freud from the point of view of humanistic idealism. Ken holds that "Freud taught that love was over-valuation. . . . [I]f you saw the love object as it really was, you couldn't love it." He believes that "the clinical view of things" is underscored by Dr. Layamon in the gynecological ward: "This was what Dr. Layamon was illustrating when he showed you all those bald old privates" (265). The scientific view so grotesquely illustrated by the doctor's tour is countered by Ken's Russian religious thinkers, by Kojève's idea of the transfiguring lie, every lover his own artist. Ken wants Uncle to cling to this imaginative power. He wants him to avoid psychoanalysis so as not to spend his time fixated on infancy, exploring his weaknesses. As is often the case in Bellow, impassioned advice is undercut by structural irony. Uncle Benn is hurriedly scribbling notes on a gas company envelope in the dim light of a phone booth. And, of course, neither Ken nor Uncle will realize this idealism in the world of actuality.

As he often does, Bellow turns to William Blake as the truer alternative. Uncle, however, has by now hung up. For Ken, Blake's life "was governed by metaphysical and esthetic concerns. Put your strengths first and let the weaknesses catch up as they may" (267). He thinks of the first lines of

Blake's "The Crystal Cabinet." These lines suggest the entry into sexual experience of a passive, innocent youth who is "caught" by the Maiden. Bellow's quotation ends here but the whole poem is pertinent to his novel. There follows an impassioned sexual fulfillment. But when the youth attempts to derive ultimate truth, "the inmost Form," from erotic love, the cabinet shatters, and both youth and woman are left weeping. For Blake, as for Bellow, sexuality may be the first but can never be the last step in the individual's moral integration. It is a nearly fatal error to assume that it can be. But contemporary culture often makes just that assumption.

In *More Die of Heartbreak* sex is not the answer, and woman is equated with the erotic. The mistrust of woman exhibited, coupled with Bellow's increasing tendency to denigrate what he calls the fallen world of appearances, issues in a work which it is difficult not to call misogynistic.

Consider some of the narrator's views on woman. Ostensibly those of a man in his thirties, they speak of an exhausted disillusionment that may come only with aging. Ken speaks unfavorably of modern, educated woman and her fear of not being able to hold a man with a project: "So they dress, they talk, and they put their moves on you. They act light but they feel heavy" (93). Ken even invokes the Romans to confirm male platitudes: "Only the husband, the man that wears the shoe, can tell where it pinches" (137). Of course, women are connivers: Mrs. Sterling "was making a bid to take me over, just as Matilda had taken over Uncle. The very thing that Caroline Bunge had attempted. No way" (248). This last is more convincingly the worry of an aging, often-married literary celebrity than that of Ken Trachtenberg. The female vampire is really not a national emergency. But Ken thinks of his uncle's predicament and sees a representative bleakness: "[H]e could anticipate a zero life with Matilda. . . . Ten years in storage. . . . In Russia the government will send you to Siberia. Here you do it to yourself" (264–265). The big thaw has reached Russia, but not, apparently, the American bedroom.

Where Bellow's cries, plaints, and disputations are themselves often a form of desire, they have here a harsh, unredeeming edge. Giving us a variation on a theme from Proverbs, Ken thinks: "We human creatures should be at play before the Lord. . . . I doubt that it can interest Him much to watch the shits at their play . . . people of ordinary stunted imaginative powers. The work of psychology is to explain and excuse these shits" (116). There may be something, after all, to Ken's positing a "selfish, low-down age" (119); but when Benn tells Matilda that "[t]he model city for these days is probably Beirut" (125), we see cynicism out of control. When Ken says that "relationships . . . human entanglements, would be moody, fickle, capricious, daemonic, scheming, heartless" (128), or when he finds himself "knee-deep in the garbage of a personal life. The ordeal of the West" (312), or when he refers to "this era, described by an intelligent lady in a magazine as 'post-human'" (329), one is encountering Bellow's private version of the Great Depression.

The Reagan years thus have come to roost in Bellow's fiction, nowhere more so than in the Balzacian cynicism of the central plot complication. Uncle Vilitzer, an ancient wheeler-dealer real estate operator with political roots and the executor of Benn's mother's will, bought property from Benn's family through a phony company he himself owned. He parlayed this into a fifteen million dollar deal, knowing the corporate desirability of this centrally located property for which he paid his relatives little. A huge cyclops of a building goes up in place of the family homestead, corporate America lording it over a Midwestern city. Vilitzer is one of Bellow's terrible old men, like Rappaport in *Seize the Day*, a bag of bones with an imperious authority deriving from money and, in his case, connections. Death seems irrelevant to his power. But it is not, and Ken is struck by his collapse, in which the body seems less substantial than his pacemaker.

The real Balzacian twist occurs when Dr. Layamon engineers a plot to extort five million dollars (he will settle for three) for revealing that a judge had to be bought off by Vilitzer to make the deal. Benn's great virtue, it turns out, is his being otherworldly enough and at the same time respectable enough to serve as an ideal facade to these machinations. All is covered in a veneer of doublespeak. So is the botanist planted. The whole wild scheme reflects the tone established by the narrator, an apparent fantasy but typical of the decade of Charles Keating and Michael Milken — the decade of the bottom-line mentality, in which accounting gimmicks have temporarily replaced Judgement Day.

In all this greed and glitz, are we to believe in the usual Bellow scenario, in Ken as the voice of religious, humanistic truth, the still, small voice that will have its hearing? Perhaps not. Ken is concerned with the fate of "quality minds . . . the contempt in which they are held by the general public" (244). He has lived too long in Chicago. America, after all, respects its experts, some of whom are quality minds, to the extent that individual and family life are in danger of being undermined by them. It does, however, tend to define expertise in technocratic or scientific terms. We live in a quantified time in which individual significance has been relegated to the realm of the "anecdotal." A humanist in a think tank for the behavioral sciences felt momentarily at home on hearing one of his social science colleagues say, "I'm working on wisdom," only to hear another reply, "Really? What's your data base?" The humanist is the expert as individual, an endangered species. Ken thinks that people of his kind "were assigned to the humanities, to poetry, philosophy, painting—the nursery games of humankind, which had to be left behind when the age of science began" (247). This dehumanizing process has the Bellow protagonist sounding like one of the apocalyptic types the novelist used to ridicule. "The humanities," Ken continues, "would be called upon to choose a wallpaper for the crypt, as the end drew near. And if there is no turning point, it will soon be time for the 'esthetic' call" (247). So much for Bellow's onetime confident assault on the aesthetic ideology of modernism. The lapse, though authentic, seems only temporary, and Ken concludes that "[t]houghts like these are nearly as undermining as the problems they address" (247). Since they occur to him with some frequency, though, how temporary are they? Bellow's yearning for transcendence, present even in *The Adventures of Augie March* and becoming more explicitly religious in *Seize the Day*, *Henderson the Rain King*, and *Herzog*, takes a decisive turn in *Mr. Sammler's Planet*. It is not that the transcendent becomes much clearer but that the world of appearances, a phrase Bellow comes to favor, becomes less real. Ken's interest in the Russian mystics, Uncle Benn's Steinerian desire to get to the essence of the plant and to make the link to soul itself, are extensions of Citrine's encounter with anthroposophy and Sammler's with Meister Eckhardt. This mystic turn implies a shift from the world of Augie, Henderson, and Herzog, who are, despite their transcendental tendencies, inebriated with the actual. Bellow's world of actuality becomes less real as it becomes more illustrative of sex as salvation. Benn is so sexually disenchanted that the noted botanist cannot tell the false from the real—even in the case of azaleas.

The restlessness of the two central characters of *More Die of Heartbreak*, the quest for what Ken calls "a fresh mode of experience," derives from what he considers "the fallen state in which our species finds itself" (19). Bellow has assumed a stance of moral severity and loftiness akin to that of the biblical prophets and even uses that language from time to time. "Ye have eyes and see not," says Ken (305), a sentiment uttered as well by Alexander Corde in *The Dean's December* (224). The spiritual world, the reality flattened by science and capitalism, is the world with which the anachronistic soul must contend—hence Benn's retort to a newspaperman questioning him about the effects of radiation on plant life: "It's terribly serious, of course, but I think more people die of heartbreak than of radiation" (87). Moral pollution will always be the major part of the environmental crisis.

A spare, striking imagery of isolation does emerge from this predicament. Ken, full of self-doubt about dependence on his uncle, says to himself, "Why was Coleridge's albatross following that goddam ship anyway? It should have been satisfied with stormy solitude." He concludes, lugubriously, that "longing for human company can be a fatal mistake" (32). It can be, as the fate of the albatross shows, but this is a limited moral to be drawn from a poem which finally says the opposite. This from a man who thinks that "[i]nner communication with the great human reality was my true occupation," adding ironically, "few took it up" (188). But the inner communication is far more apparent than the great human reality. Indeed, the former becomes mystically attenuated and is mainly confined to one man, Uncle Benn, a man who admits how indifferent he can occasionally be to people and who is famous for his spectacular departures from ensnaring women. The centrality of isolation—and it is more often isolation than solitude in this novel—is underscored by Ken's recollection from Admiral Byrd's *Alone*, where Bellow draws a tacit parallel between the disillusionments of exploration and a bad marriage. Byrd says, "The time comes when one has nothing to reveal to the other, when even his unformed thoughts can be anticipated, his pet ideas become a meaningless drool" (20). Even when the isolation does become solitude, as in Ken's fantasized "modern-dress Eden," with aging, sensuous Uncle Benn in a Douanier Rousseau landscape of an arthritic old maple still putting forth millions of leaves, it is a case of two paradises 'twere in one to be in Paradise alone. With typical sadness Ken notes how "impulses from the fallen world surround this green seclusion" (27). For his uncle, Ken annihilates all that's made for a green thought in a green shade. Benn gives us a faraway, icy version of this ideal in his escape from marriage and flight to his faithful lichens, tiny green organisms that live five thousand years, growing an inch every twenty years in the hour or two they get of arctic sun. How's that for strength in solitude—or is it isolation? This brilliant image is an affirmation so minimal that it is indistinguishable from penance.

Still there is an aloneness beyond the power of greenery to vivify. For a man in his thirties, Ken is inordinately concerned with images of age and ends. The South Pole, besides being an arena for explorers, is to him "a foretaste of eternity" (163). And in the face of death, desire itself takes on a touching aspect as a form of reincarnation. "For after desire departs," Ken muses rather prematurely, "no man can be certain that it will *ever* return" (199). Yet Papa attracting women in his late sixties is not a figure of great sympathy. After Vilitzer's death, Ken thinks of the final bottom line, "the ninety cents' worth of chemicals we so often hear mentioned" (330). Death isn't useful or profitable to the man who dies unless, as Arthur Miller's Willy Loman thinks, he is worth more dead than alive. Death is the final estrangement, and Ken is all too familiar with it.

Since this is a Bellow novel, however, aging is also the subject of comedy. So Fishl comments on the overpsychoanalyzed aged: "I meet people of eighty who are still furious over their toilet training, or because their dad wouldn't take them to the ball game" (179). Memorably, there are Dr. Layamon's comforting words to the old folks with sex worries: "Look, as long as you have a knee, an elbow, your nose, your big toe, given an affectionate wife, as long as you did your duty by her in the days when you could get it up, she will take whatever you've got now, and you don't owe her any more than that" (159). The tone of the book, its fusion of cool contemplativeness with raucous comedy, is pure Bellow.

The reader of *More Die of Heartbreak* may have a sense of already having been there: the victimized idealist, the reality instructors, the women in their sexual politics variety, the comedy of the grotesque, the religious humanist narrator illuminating the threatening darkness. The most prominent dramatic echo is the mock revenge scene with Ken swooping down on the apartment of his beloved to concuss the head of her bruiser boyfriend with a hammer. But like Gersbach washing Junie, Ronald is engaged in an innocent activity: he has "gone to Mass" (309). The traditionally heroic posture is hopelessly obsolete in Bellow, the macho gesture laughed into the wind. Unlike Herzog who smashes nothing, Ken does smash up the toilet, Bellow saying, as it were, that that is where this kind of aggression belongs. The action does have a psychological justification in that, in one sense, Ken is enacting the aggression that Uncle Benn should have. But where Herzog is saved by the redemptive power of the ordinary, Ken does a fade-out. There is no ascent into meaning. Rather, "it was one of the commoner human experiences—neither to give a damn nor be given a damn about," what Bellow calls "the mutual quitclaim" (319). This tells us something about the lower energy level of late Bellow. Also, as in *Herzog*, there is a courtroom scene; this one relates in a grim way to the comedy of sexual intimacy but is otherwise not linked to Ken's brief life as a hero.

Among the more interesting echoes,[1] two—one of them really a strategy—relate to *Humboldt's Gift*. The negative fetishism about Matilda's shoulders derived from *Psycho* and the cry of surprise with which it is perceived, occurs a few times in the manuscript version of *Humboldt's Gift* (e.g., 1978 Deposit, 9.1), where it finishes Citrine's marriage with Denise. Perhaps it was too bizarre to have been included in the final version, Citrine being a more or less dignified character. But nothing is too bizarre for *More Die of Heartbreak*. The strategy, first employed by Bellow in *Humboldt's Gift*, is the narrative about somebody else, Charlie Citrine on Von Humboldt Fleisher and Kenneth Trachtenberg on Benn Crader. Of course, they tell their own stories as well.

In both novels, a Bellow surrogate weighs the fate of a partially failed idealist whose weaknesses are put in a generous perspective, a common use of this narrative arrangement. Both Humboldt and Benn fail in their striving for a sustained purity, for a lived clairvoyance. Citrine is the better narrator in that his complexity has a convincing subject—Humboldt. A major problem in *More Die of Heartbreak* is that Ken's seriousness is sometimes too deep for the primarily farcical events he records. Of all Bellow's novels, filled as they are with comic incongruity, this one comes closest to the outright farce of *The Last Analysis*, the wheeling and dealing, the fantastic gestures of imprisonment and escape. Ken is the least integrated Bellow voice, a somewhat boring voice because his insight is sometimes an appendage. Bellow seems aware of this and tries to defuse it by making Ken out to be an amateur at the job, full of awkward asides, like, "I will remember that I am here not to lecture on history but to relate the strange turns in the life of my uncle Benn" (210). He sometimes imposes a sophistication on him that Benn might not possess, explaining what perhaps could not be dramatized, as in the sex trial: "I really believe that I could make out his feeling, and roughly put, it went like this: that Crime, Punishment, Justice, Authority, were satirized in this hearing. Plus Penitence. Plus Truth. . . . Of course, that

happens every day and you've got to be a botanical clairvoy-
ant to have to wait till mid-life to find it out" (277). So we
will help him. "He was involved in all this by the sensations
he had had while watching *Psycho*, by the outrages his mind
had committed. . . . Eternity itself had warned him, using
Alfred Hitchcock as its medium, *not* to marry this woman"
(277). Ken is long on telling, short on showing.

Of this he is aware, most conspicuously so in the incoher-
ence of a rambling commentary deriving somehow from
Matilda, that includes reference to Marguerite Duras, the
Roanoke, Franz Joseph's royal residence, the Kremlin, Lenin
being shot. Dita rightly asks, "What's the connection?"
(253). Ken admits that wine, dinner, and the comfort of
the room make him "unusually—that is, emotionally—open
to suggestions. It was esthetically intoxicating to entertain
them all . . . the fantastic, the bizarre facts of contemporary
reality, making no particular effort to impose my cognitions
on them. I didn't especially want to make sense; I wanted
only to follow the intoxicating flow of these facts" (253). This
creates a problem in a novel. Literature is not free association. In *Herzog*, the intoxicating flow is brilliantly channeled
into letters, and the ideas and action are interlocked.

In *Humboldt's Gift*, Humboldt was complex enough for
continual, deep rumination. Not so here. There are times
when Uncle sounds incongruously like Ken.[2] It is hard to
believe that Uncle Benn, like Ken, reads Berdyaev and Ivanov.
He is a different kind of mystic. And it is impossible to believe
that the innocuous Benn is regarded as "an international
celebrity in the field—kind of a monument" (152), who would
attract a salon for his ambitious wife of Dobrynin, Kissinger,
Marilyn Horne, and Günter Grass. A Nobel Prize winning
novelist perhaps, but not a spaced-out botanist. Benn is too
much of a Bellow mannerism, the idealist putz caught up in
the double-dealer double whammy. His fate is sometimes too

weak a narrative link to support the pressure of Ken's whir-
ring intelligence. Indeed, Ken's voice is so dominant that the
thirty-year-old may patronize his fifty-year-old idol. After an
anti-woman diatribe, Ken can smugly say, "I was somewhat
disappointed in Benn. I had tried to tell him something most
fundamental and he hadn't followed me" (93). Will he follow
Kissinger? Yet even here there is a mitigating factor. For part
of the comedy of the book is that a youngish man is coming
to learn from an older relative who is in even greater need
of counsel.

Though *More Die of Heartbreak* has shortcomings, we
come back to its successes in the writing itself, the energy of
the sentence flow. Bellow is aware of this strength.[3] It is not
rare in our lyrical realist for the declarative to be more per-
suasive than the narrative, for sentences to outstrip plot, for
brilliant parts to outshine the whole sense that can be made
of them—and since Bellow is rather good at making sense,
this is saying much. *More Die of Heartbreak* takes us back, for
example, to the thumbnail-sketch virtuosity of *Augie March*.
The opening description of Ken's Papa in full sensual and
historical sail is an illustration:

> She gave him a big lunch—his favorite oysters, *fines Bélons*,
> with a good wine. Then we went to the couturiere for a
> fitting. It was here, behaving like an authority on women's
> fashions, *à. la* Proust, that he took charge. He mentioned
> the problem of Mama's *poitrine*, like a real Frenchman, and
> also made time with the girls. He was an *homme à femmes*,
> a chaser. A man of staggering charm, he was able to make
> good on his *là ci darem* promises. The lady who gave him
> her hand wouldn't be sorry. She wouldn't even regret going
> back to her husband, since a sensible person would under-
> stand that my father was a one-time event, like the Fall, or
> Noah's Ark. As a conversationalist he was limited, but his

repertory was terrific for his purposes. He had served as a Ninety Day Wonder on a destroyer and he had seen FDR, Harry Hopkins, Churchill and Montgomery close up. In the Red Sea, Ibn Saud and his court had come aboard and camped on the fantail under an awning, roasting their own sheep there and turning their cups over to spill coffee grounds on their fine carpets. Dad had once chatted with the Grand Mufti, who even hinted at a visit in disguise to Auschwitz, where he inspected the gas chambers. In Paris, Dad had met Malraux on many occasions. Sartre had accused my father of being an American spy because he spoke French *too* well. (34)

Here we see an English spiced with French, Italian, and the Bible, heightened by allusion to contemporary historical figures, Western and Eastern, sentences that contain stories and a paragraph that contains an encyclopedia, the nouns and verbs switching from the amatory to the political.

Despite the public references, in Rudi the political is eclipsed by the sexual. This is summed up in a Hegelian over-view, one of many instances in Bellow in which the private and the historical coalesce: "Now suppose that instead of Napoleonic armies you have women, instead of Jena you have bedrooms, instead of cannon you have you-know-what—then you begin to see Papa's life in a truer light" (36–37). The world historical reality of sexual style seems to elicit Bellow's most condensed verbal energy, one which is often comic in aim, for the ridiculous is near at hand. Telephone sex, for example, of which Ken thinks: "According to your special sexual need a voice will incite, talk sweet, talk dirty, and work you up until you get your rocks off. . . . You lie in bed with your instrument, your cordless phone, and it's like a retake of the State of Nature, a second return to beginnings" (22). So we have a witty juxtaposition of computerland and

Hobbes, raunchiness and American know-how, sex and farce. Bellow's sentences are motivated by the sharp perspective of an idealized intelligence.

The character of Fishl gives us another aspect of this intelligence. Good filial heart notwithstanding, Fishl shows us that Bellow is as good as ever at the Dostoevskian clown. "The general idea," Fishl says, "was to play the market from a spiritual base. Meditation, by reducing the oscillations of consciousness, made you a more capable investor" (172–173). Ken's foreignness is just what Bellow needs to absorb the incredibility of everyday American occurrence. Fishl, for example, also conceives of a (clearly faulty) borrowing scheme that will net one a million a month, sets up practice as an acupuncture abortionist, and so forth. All of this makes Ken think that originality as a mass phenomenon is uniquely American. In brief, the shortcomings of the book are glossed over by sheer intelligence and splendid wit, as Bellow's reader is usually mesmerized by a variegated voice.

Yet, like much of Bellow's later, spacey work, *More Die of Heartbreak* presents us with a conundrum. Bellow undercuts the actuality of the world he so vividly envisions by relegating it to the fallen world of appearances. His superb instinct for realistic representation is diffused by an ontological insistence. He holds that the novel is the greatest literary genre because of its resistance to the absolute. But Bellow has increasingly presented us with central characters who court—albeit often comically—just this ideal quality. Surely age has something to do with this distancing of himself, with his belief in something better than what people call reality, a view he once ridiculed. Confidence in the so-called ordinary world, never easily achieved, has waned. And the special pleasure of his work resides in the evocation of a vulgar facticity which he comes more and more to judge in sharp, satiric strokes. Many venerable writers, increasingly drawn to the transcendent, reach finally toward a theological or mythological summation. The question of later Bellow is: will he now do so, too? The elements of repetition and narrative strain we have noted indicate that this might be the case. But given the overall energy of *More Die of Heartbreak*, its comic balancing of ideal and actual, God and Mammon, the elegiac and the grotesque, given its realism that thrives on contraries, given Bellow's ultimate allegiance to the role of the novelist as historian of society and his continuing, self-validating distinction in this role—the answer would seem to be no.

Notes

1. In addition to those mentioned in the text, echoes abound. Like Herzog, Ken realizes that meekness is not successful with women and wonders whether he would have won his lover by roughing her up. But, of course, he is not the type. The bad relationship between Ken's father and mother is similar to that of Mady's parents; Mady resents them deeply, particularly her father. Treckie's interested mother sounds somewhat like Einhorn trying to elevate Augie. She tells Ken, "You may look mild, but you're a fighter" (213). Like Thea, she then attempts to appropriate. Somewhat like Augie and the Magnuses, Benn is distraught at being caught in the middle-class moneytrap, "Sick with repulsive gratitude to the Layamons for letting him be one of them, chocking on lies, accusing himself before God, crying out, 'What have I done! Why am I here!'" (245). Finally, like Augie, the younger ingénue who is taken over, he bolts. The Vilitzer-Fishl broken father-and-son bond echoes Dr. Adler and Tommy Wilhelm. As in Mr. Sammler's Planet, we get every woman's composite lover fantasy, which appears no less than three times in the new novel. A brief, almost exact echo from *The Last Analysis* occurs when the embattled Vilitzer says, "I've many a time been backed up to the cross, and my ass is full of splinters, but they haven't nailed me yet" (286), a sentiment first uttered by Bummidge.

2. This is part of a larger problem in the novel of voices not being sufficiently differentiated; there is an almost indiscriminate

spreading around of hip lingo by a writer who is usually a master of voice. Perhaps the book was written too quickly.

3.   In a recent conversation I asked him, an author who has not suffered from critical neglect, whether there was anything in his work about which more should be said. "My sentences," he responded. "It seems to me that I've invented a new kind of sentence and more should be said about it." I had to say, tentatively, that I did say something about it, particularly in my Augie March chapter (Fuchs 1984). "I know you did," he said with a positive resonance, but obviously it was a subject that would deserve more attention.

Works Cited

Below, Saul. *The Dean's December*. New York: Harper & Row, 1982.

———. "Literature." *The Great Ideas Today*. Ed. Mortimer Adler and Robert M. Hutchins. Chicago: Encyclopaedia Britannica, 1963. 135–179.

———. *More Die of Heartbreak*. New York: William Morrow, 1987.

Bragg, Melvyn. "Off the Couch by Christmas: Saul Bellow on His New Novel." *The Listener* 94 (20 Nov. 1975): 675–676.

Fuchs, Daniel. *Saul Bellow: Vision and Revision*. Durham, N.C.: Duke UP, 1984.

Sanoff, Alvin P. "The Reigning King of Literature." *US News and World Report* 7 Sep. 1987: 52–53.

8

Identity and the Postwar Temper in American Jewish Fiction

I have a vivid memory of a day in the spring of 1954 when a professor in the Columbia College English Department told me that the distinguished literary critic Lionel Trilling was Jewish. I could not tell what affected me more, surprise that this genteel and apparently gentile man was a Jew or exhilaration that if Trilling was Jewish then anything was possible. Trilling was the only professor to have asked me, "What is your Christian name?" And he wrote an impressive High Church critical prose that a teenage undergraduate from the Bronx contemplated with a sense of intimidated wonder. The author of the novel *The Middle of the Journey*, Trilling would not have been taken by my provincial emotionality. He had written in 1944, a time of particular Jewish vulnerability, that the American Jewish community is "sterile," partly because it reflects a history of "exclusion," which he thinks of as a willing parochialism. Though it was "a point of honor" to affirm his Jewishness as a "citizen," it had nothing to do with his being a writer. "I should resent it," he made clear, "if a critic of my work were to discover in it either faults or virtues which he called Jewish" (Trilling: vii, n. 1).

In saying so Trilling was expressing a sentiment that virtually any *Partisan Review* Jewish intellectual would have then echoed. In the Modernist, Marxist orbit, some had been resistant to engaging in the war against Hitler; few were especially involved in the fate of the Jews during World War II. On the home front, former Marxists and Trotskyites saw Judaism as a form of bourgeois smugness; Freudians considered it a form of bourgeois neurosis. Though Trilling's early fiction deals with Jewishness, it soon becomes a dead end. Yet Trilling's protestations to the contrary notwithstanding, *The Middle of the Journey* can be seen as a classic production of the secular Jew. But first it must be seen for what it primarily is, a dramatization of the conflict between liberalism and its enemies. The novel is didactic; its deepest emotion is ideational.

One of the main points about the postwar temper as manifested in Jewish writers is that it represented, in Leslie Fiedler's phrase, an end to innocence, an end to radical utopianism. In Trilling's novel John Laskell is the hero of disillusion, the Crooms are the illusioned radicals, and Gifford Maxim is the ex-communist turned Christian. The "middle" of the title refers to Laskell's liberal stance between left and right as well as to mid-life crisis—Laskell is 33, Dante's age at the beginning of his journey. Laskell's brush with death because of illness is endlessly elaborated but is important in that it shows the conditionality of life, which the Crooms prefer not to recognize. For them, there is nothing that cannot be changed. There is no marginal character who is not innocent, a victim of society. Therefore, they fail to see the negative qualities of Duck Caldwell, a ne'er-do-well whose vulgarity and aggression lead to the death of his heart-diseased daughter as she stumbles in the reading of a poem, a death by culture-envy. Other than that of class oppression, the Crooms recognize no guilt. Maxim recognizes only guilt; hence his view of Herman Melville's *Billy Budd* as a tragedy of theology rather than of justice. Between disbelief in conditionality (the Crooms) and belief only in conditionality (Maxim), Laskell opts for the liberal middle, responsibility. (The title of the French translation of the novel is *Les Responsibles.*) So the emotional highlight of the book, Laskell's final confrontation with the Crooms and Maxim, is didactic. If Laskell, in his wisdom, suffers from the liberal malady, passivity, he converts it into intellectual activity. And if his Keatsian rose shows him half in love with easeful death, he overcomes that temptation to forge an ego. Nothing is more typical of the postwar temper than this frame of mind, in which cultural Stalinism, the original political correctness, is denigrated and the individual elevated. (The scenario is rather Freudian: Laskell overcomes illness, a death-wish, and a brief neurotic episode, to arrive at a genital calm and a forceful ego.) What may be considered Jewish about Trilling as a writer is his focus on responsibility, the liberal virtue. Liberalism is not Judaism, yet most Jews are liberal. Such are the confusions of assimilation.

The most popular novel of the fifties was written by another assimilated Jew, J. D. Salinger. One might say that Salinger is Jewish American in that you can never tell he was. (He is half Jewish, half Irish.) Yet if there is one major contribution that American Jewish writers made it was the comedy of suffering. Here in affluent, affable America, suffering could be funny, especially in an age of self-regard. It is in this sense that Salinger's small masterpiece, *Catcher in the Rye*, can be considered a Jewish book. Of course, you do not have to be Jewish to be a comic sufferer. Vladimir Nabokov's *Lolita* and J. F. Powers's *Morte d'Urban* are notable illustrations from the period. But the frequency with which the literature of comic suffering occurs in Jewish fiction, including such masterworks as *Herzog* and *Portnoy's Complaint*—not to mention the films of Woody Allen, which show the popularity of pickled herring—would seem to indicate that it is an especially Jewish thing. Jews have been familiar with the role of suffering servant since biblical days. Golden America and the disintegration of the romantic ego brought the comedy. The main contour of Salinger's career, from psychological comedy to religion, might be seen as a Jewish one. Salinger is Jewish American in that he is Zen Buddhist! From *Catcher in the Rye* to *Franny and Zooey* to *Seymour*, Salinger's most notable fiction becomes increasingly otherworldly. But nowhere does Salinger become Jewish in any obvious sense. And Salinger is not at all Jewish in his characters' refusal to grow up, to take on the responsibility of full genital ego. He remains an instance of one kind of American Jewish writer at mid-century, assimilated to the point of Jewish exclusion.

Where Trilling and Salinger in their very different ways were deidentifying Jews in their fiction, Saul Bellow, Bernard Malamud, and Philip Roth, in their different ways, were identifying ones. Yet the latter three all say that they are American writers who happen to be Jewish. Although they mainly write about characters who are Jews, they want to be judged as novelists in the tradition of the novel. They aspire to artistic eminence. Like Trilling, like Salinger, they want to reach a general American audience, indeed an international one. Bellow, for one, resists being known as a Jewish writer to the degree that he is wary of being categorized as merely a Jewish writer. Like the great majority of Americans at mid-century they may best be characterized by individual rather than religious identity. Even when the element of self becomes soul, as it does in Bellow and Malamud, it is the reaching for individual awareness more than transcendent connection or belief that is dramatized. Would Shakespeare want to be known as "that Christian writer"?

During the discussion session after a lecture I had given at a University of Haifa symposium on Bellow, an Israeli asked me the inevitable question, "Is Bellow a Jew first or an American first?" I gave him the answer I have just given. But I could just as well have asked this kibbutznik—the kibbutz is generally known for its socialist rather than its religious identity, indeed the tension between secular and religious Jews in Israel well beyond the kibbutz can be substantial—"Are you a Jew first or an Israeli first?" In Israel the following joke came to mind. A woman is sitting on a bus talking to her son in Yiddish. The people in the bus look at her. She continues to talk to him in Yiddish. Finally, someone turns around and says, "Why are you talking to your son in Yiddish? You're in Israel now." She answers, "Because I don't want him to forget that he's a Jew." All nations, even the nation of priests, are witness to what Hegel called the secularization of spirituality. For Jews, who came late to the party, the Holocaust was a precipitating factor.

The Adventures of Augie March was Bellow's breakthrough novel from the point of view of reversing Modernist aestheticism and the sense of alienation and victimization that much twentieth-century literature embodied, including his own. It was a breakthrough into antiModernism, a real switch. Bellow found a style answerable to the energies of everyday life and an antiheroic hero who was amiable rather than alienated. This picaresque novel gives us a distinctly nonideological hero. The thirties is the time that comes after the twenties, tougher times, but not inhibiting much of the energetic immigrant rhythm. Augie is more concerned with female structure than class structure. And his one stint as a union organizer serves to expose union corruption.

A major contribution of the Jewish writers was the dramatization of a plausible positivity, often in the form of ethical comedy. *Augie March* was a popular success as well as, generally, a succès d'estime. The need to affirm—Herzog's middle name is Praise God, Elkanah—is a Jewish specialty. God's creation is good. The fifties were, amidst everything else, desperate for the myth of moral agency. The revival of an energetic realism satisfied an apparent craving for the affirmation of ordinary life. Bellow was resisting what he called the unearned pessimism of Modernism, but there were those who viewed Augie March as an illustration of unearned optimism. Because Augie undercuts his own optimism, beginning with even the first sentence of the novel, the buoyancy and level-headedness of the prose are one of the triumphs of the fifties.

In *Augie March* Bellow writes lyrically of America in his first and last sentences, a rarity in twentieth-century American fiction. More typically, America was a place to escape from, as in the expatriate twenties. *Augie March* ran parallel to the *Partisan Review* symposium on "Our Country and Our Culture" where, mainly, former Stalinists and Trotskyites said that America was not so bad a place. Compared to what? The Jewish writers and intellectuals were, then, politically as well as aesthetically affirmative, with endless modifications.

Yet, for many, the fifties were the worst thing that ever happened to us: McCarthy—Rosenbergs—conformity—gray-flannel-suit—counterfeit, raced the litany of complaint. What with Korea, the Soviet Union getting the bomb, the Cold War, there was a reactive hysteria, about which so much has been said. But other things happened in the fifties as well. GIs, who knew mainly the Depression and World War II, were given a new lease on life with the GI Bill, which many were still enjoying. The historic Marshall Plan (1947–52), as much generosity as self-interest, was reviving Europe. The momentous Montgomery bus boycott started the civil rights movement. The Ivy League schools, some more gradually than others, raised the quota bar to minorities (some had done so decades before), particularly, it seems, to Jews, who served as the vanguard of the movement in this respect. It is possible to argue that this democratization of the elites will be a more important and enduring legacy of the fifties than McCarthy and Rosenberg. The sense of possibility involved more than elites. For the first time, according to pollsters, most Americans identified themselves as middle-class. The prosperity of the period was not accidental. There were many full of talent, energy, and aspiration functioning within a workable society who rendered the negative cartoon suspect.

Was *Augie March* a travelogue for timid intellectuals, as the then radical Norman Mailer put it? Weren't Einhorn, Grandma Lausch, Augie's bumpy love-life justifications of the revival of realism? But if *Augie March* was a, triumph it was no reason to stand still. Bellow's works stand in a kind of dialectical relationship to each other. If he was positive in *Augie March* he was negative in *Seize the Day*. Yet both works are marked by a belief in what Augie calls the axial lines of life, often realized in the former, desperately but convincingly reached in the final scene of *Seize the Day*. Bellow's scathing portrait of capitalism as a spiritual category, Dostoyevsky-style, finds closure in the oldest of Jewish gestalts, transcendence through suffering. The juxtaposition of "oral" Tommy and "anal" Dr Adler, of naive Tommy and the petty bourgeois Tartuffe Dr Tamkin, of desperate Tommy and his financial-organizer estranged wife, make for painful comedy. The darkness is so real that it nearly eclipses the comedy.

Henderson the Rain King is a release from the near claustrophobia of *Seize the Day*. Like Augie's, Henderson's "I" expresses a personal lyricism. This time, though, the voice is middle-aged, funny and exasperated, desperately hopeful; Henderson is in search of experience adequate to his desire. A rich Wasp, even if an epigone, Henderson can afford to air out his miseries by traveling through Africa, where his American Faustian urge to do some technological good only backfires. What Africa can do for him, it seems, is give him the wisdom of nature, the pride of the lion. But Africa turns out to be another adventure in comic suffering. The lion's-den scene is at once a celebration and *reductio ad absurdum* of Romantic iconography. Vitalism gives way to Judeo-Christian moral abstraction as God is beseeched. Henderson's allegiance to Dahfu, the African wise man who sounds much like a post-Freudian analyst, is transcended by an allegiance to soul. Henderson considers himself mediumistic and is given to prayer, an archaic impulse perhaps but contemporary in that he pleads to be preserved from the unreal.

Herzog is another Bellow protagonist who finds himself beseeching God, and with his marital difficulties you can see why. *Herzog* gives us a deeper and funnier *de profundis* than even *Henderson the Rain King*. Those who say that Herzog is too much of a narcissist miss the point that Herzog is trying to find a way out of his narcissism. The lyrical, funny first person gives us a humorous perspective on the actual third person events. The present comments on the past and yearns for a future. In this epistolary novel, letters greatly intensify the "I" and connect in a crucial way to the comic climax of the book. The letters begin in gloom and end in release, always with a comic counterpoint complicating both. The climactic scene in the novel, a mock murder scene, supplies the pivotal tonal shift. The humanist Jew Herzog, of course, will not kill Gersbach, the man who cuckolds him. Not that he likes him or his wife, far from it, but as he sees Gersbach performing his child's ablutions with care, the patterns of civilization overtake the claims of barbarism. Gersbach may deserve death, but life is better than death, restraint better than murder. No, it is not Gersbach personally who makes Herzog relent, but the fact that any man subdued to benign custom is not killable. Herzog is renewed by a traditional moral restraint, once again a Jewish climax.

The other most vivid aspect of *Herzog* is Herzog's relation to Ramona. Here too the sensibility is Jewish in that Herzog resists, hard as it is to do, the sexual utopia promised by Ramona for some higher, axial sense of usefulness. Herzog is a comic idealist who must have moral seriousness. In this sense Herzog is the culminating American Jewish novel of the postwar era. For most Jewish writers the early to mid-sixties are far closer to the fifties than they are to the late sixties. *Mr Sammler's Planet* is a late sixties book, but also a Holocaust survivor book, in which the voice of traditional humanism is shaken if not shattered. In this world sexuality has evolved as the greatest force. Dionysus is prominent and what most people call morality is a still, small voice.

Before going on to Bernard Malamud and Philip Roth, for reasons both chronological and dialectical, the work of Norman Mailer in this period will be considered. Although Mailer spent his youth in one of the most securely Jewish neighborhoods in Brooklyn and even used to have his mother over for Friday night (I hesitate to say Sabbath) dinner well into his mature years, he is the most actively deidentifying of our Jewish writers. Trilling and Salinger pretty much ignored Jews as such in their mature work, but Mailer actively subverts them. He has said that the one thing not to call him is a nice Jewish boy from Brooklyn. Not much chance of that.

The well-known *The Naked and the Dead* is Mailer's first novel, naturalistic but with romantic undercurrents that undermine naturalism, which is a literature of conditionality. It is a political novel as much as it is a war novel set in the Pacific theater in World War II. The political dialogue between General Cummings and Lieutenant Hearn, dramatically focused in the pick-up-my-cigarette-butt scene, gives us a struggle between fascism and liberalism. Croft is the fascist or at least sadistic egomaniac on the enlisted level and Valsen is the liberal. Although an officer, Hearn resents the way the other officers treat the privates. In the narrative, Hearn and

Valsen are effectively destroyed in the power struggle. Since liberalism is powerless against fascism, a radical alternative is implied.

Because he is a liberal and because of his dark facial features, the Wasp Hearn at one point fancies himself a Jew. The real Jews in the novel, Goldstein and Roth, are two of the many victimized privates, but with a difference. Both feel the anti-Semitism of their compeers. But what Mailer is really interested in is their personal limitations. Roth is a college boy, a CCNY *klutz*, and a *kvetch* to boot, complaining about army this and army that even when it may not be justified. In the anti-climactic climax of the novel, the meaningless and failed ascent of Mount Anaka, his physical incompetence is a contributing factor to his death. In Private Roth, the Jew is a half-educated geek who cannot get it up. Goldstein is a very different case. Competent, married, in love with his children, patriotic, he is, in Mailer's view, insufferably square. He is a good man for a physical emergency and performs heroically in this regard, but he is unaware of his victimization by the system. In short, he is middle-class, or even worse, aspires to be. Goldstein and Roth do what Mailer thinks Jews do—both sublimate. Mailer wants something more.

What does he want? He has said that the character in the novel for whom he had the most secret admiration was Croft—sadistic, sonofabitching Croft. Sergeant Croft has aggression, which includes sexual aggression. In this respect he transcends General Cummings, whose sexually aggressive impulses merely mask homosexuality. Croft presages Mailer's hipster, the white Negro, who acts on the morality of impulse. Mailer is moving toward the sexual politics that will, before too many years, replace Marxism. Where in *The Middle of the Journey* Trilling shows part of the general repudiation of radicalism in the postwar period, Mailer's *Barbary Shore* gives us a sympathetic if agonized

account. Mailer posits a moral equivalence between Stalinism and capitalism through the fallen radical McLoed and
the intimidating, sadistic Hollingsworth, a McCarthy era
FBI agent. Though there is blood on McLoed's hands, he
tries to redeem himself through Trotskyite faith. Sexuality
in this novel is a reflection of political hysteria, violent
and desiccated. There is nothing Jewish in this Brooklyn
boarding-house novel, except, perhaps, Mailer's apparently
ineradicable sympathy for the failing left.

The Deer Park was Mailer's next novel and it meant much to
him. He reportedly was very pleased when, at a White House
gathering, JFK asked him about it and not The Naked and the
Dead. His war novel was somewhat derivative and exhibited
a flat style. The Deer Park was original and attempted a more
ambitious style, though it was not until An American Dream
that Mailer went for baroque. The Naked and the Dead and
The Deer Park are similar in strategy in that they both attempt
an indictment of fascist America through delineation of one
of its segments, the army and Hollywood. Mailer cheats a bit
using the army in this way in that it is an institution inherently
authoritarian; his Hollywood is a more plausible account of
the authoritarian, in this case, McCarthyism. Teppis, the stu-
dio's big brother, plays the role that Cummings played in the
earlier novel, the fascist who wins. Eitel (I-tell) is the confused,
cowardly liberal, a victim of HUAC (the House Un-American
Activities Committee). In Teppis and Eitel, Mailer presents
the Jew as villain. The rebel psychopath, Marion Faye, is the
novel's Croft. He is the hipster, Mailer's first white Negro,
though far more self-conscious in his romantic Satanism.
Considering the desiccated relationships of everyone else,
Mailer creates a certain sympathy for him. Eitel's former lady
friend Elena says that the one way Marion is like him is that
when Marion is engaging in dirty sex he thinks it is going to
blow up the world. This is the first mention of Mailer's idea

of the apocalyptic orgasm. Mailer, in short, has switched from a political to a sexual radicalism.

Of all of Mailer's deidentifying strategies this is the most prominent. Its clearest exposition occurs in his essay "The White Negro," a glorification of the morality of impulse, however destructive that impulse may be. An age of apocalypse—Mailer lists the concentration camps, the bomb, and "slow death by conformity" (Mailer: 312)—justifies apocalyptic orgasm, the sexual aggression necessary, indeed appropriate, to survival. Political justifies personal violence. In a notorious passage Mailer justifies the murder of a storekeeper by violent hipsters on the grounds that they are destroying the institution of private property and "daring the unknown" (321). So Mailer has decided to settle for revolution as gesture. As Jean Malaquais has said in the discussion appended to the essay, his hipster is an attempt to resurrect the myth of the proletariat. In his glorification of impulse Mailer becomes the anti-Jew. He could not see that the next major wave of American conformity would be the infantile. And he did not see that his lurid revolutionary bore little resemblance to the rather passive, stoned ethic of the hipster.

During the fifties Mailer engaged in an all-out assault on the middle, which he sees as a deadly conformity rather than an accommodating civility. *Advertisements for Myself* is one of his most important books, largely because it contains three vivid short works, "The White Negro" and the stories "The Man Who Studied Yoga" and "The Time of Her Time," addressed to this point. "The Man Who Studied Yoga" is a satiric account of bourgeois conformity, with its nostalgia for radicalism and its current attachment to psychoanalysis or at least psychobabble. A four-room flat in Queens, a ten-year marriage, children, a hack writer hiding a wish to be a novelist—can anything be more expressive of the dead center of dullness? Can a porno movie save them, elicit the liberating orgy? Let us hope not.

Denise Gondelman is the female lead of one of Mailer's best fictions, "The Time of Her Time." She is attractive, educated, in analysis, haughty, engaged to a Jewish pre-law at Columbia College, and virginal. Clearly, this girl needs help. Enter Village stud of working-class origins Sergius O'Shaughnessy, the "I" narrator, as he was as a character in *The Deer Park*, where his sexual escapades with the capricious movie star Lulu lead him a merry chase. The self-styled "Messiah of the one-night stand" (447) breaks the ice with Denise with a sadistic flourish—"you dirty little Jew" (464), slap—as he turns her every which way. Apocalyptic orgasm indeed! Bourgeois smugness and totalitarian psychoanalysis exploded in one swell foop. Well, at least for a minute.

In this last story Mailer finds a voice adequate to his aggression. The voice becomes more elaborate in *An American Dream*. Rojack is another portrait of the hipster. He too acts on immediate impulse in this case to the point of criminal psychopathology. He strangles his wife and throws her out of the window. After all, she crudely questioned his manhood and literally went for his sexual jugular. We are somewhat distanced from the white Negro. In no way can Rojack be considered an extension of the proletariat. And Mailer the sexalogue has moved from the rebel without a cause to the rebel with one. Moreover, Rojack has worked within the system, has even been elected to Congress, and is a professor of psychology. And, most conventional of all, he is much married. His current wife was a castrator and, given her social background, a representative of the corrupt power structure itself.

Marriage for Rojack is not just a form of alienation but a form of war. As it is for wife Deborah whose incestuous victimization brings with it a revenge against men. Drawn by the magic at the top and its contempt for the mediocre middle, Rojack soon enough discovers the depravity of her powerhouse father. A pop *Crime and Punishment, An American Dream* reverses Dostoyevsky's moralism by giving us crime without punishment. Mailer presumably is really interested in certain states of mind and not murder, but these states of mind come somehow only after murder. Mailer's hero is one-eighth Jewish. This is an irrelevance. Mailer can rest assured that no one will confuse Rojack or any of his other heroes with a nice Jewish boy.

Herzog came out in 1964, *An American Dream* in 1964 and 1965 (serialized). Their appearance generated an excitement that, with the exception of Philip Roth's *Portnoy's Complaint* and Thomas Pynchon's *Gravity's Rainbow*, has not appeared in the literary community since. Bellow and Mailer showed that the culture of the postwar period contained its own contradiction. The humanist and the sexalogue are opposed. This can be vividly seen in comparing the murder scenes of these novels. Mailer's murder scene is a dramatization of negative transcendence, an antinomian ascent by descent, romantic immoralism writ large. It is lurid, bloody, final, and rewarding to the murderer, even sexually rewarding, since after killing his wife, he has sex with her maid! It is a scene that begins and ends in eroticism. Bellow's murder scene begins in revenge and ends in restraint. The mesmerizing benignity of ordinary custom holds sway. Murder is not an option but a joke. Herzog comes to a moral not a sexual exhilaration, a positive if modest transcendence. Bellow shows what is most typical of American Jewish fiction of the postwar period, the sway of the ordinary. In this sense he is thematically of the postwar period. Mailer illustrates the power of rebellion and is thus more attuned to the late sixties, another period. Mailer was lauded for a while but became disillusioned by what he called left hard-ons.

Most of Bernard Malamud's best fiction comes out in the fifties and is as representative of that decade as it is of Jewish qualities. *The Assistant* appears in 1957 but is an attempt to capture the thirties immigrant milieu, to recapture qualities of Jewishness that no longer clearly existed. This attempt to seize the evanescent past is a result of the increasingly secularized, increasingly assimilated fifties. It is why in *The Assistant* and in *The Magic Barrel*, whose characters live in a similar time-warp, Malamud's Jewishness has a precious quality. So, in *The Assistant*, Morris Bober, in explaining to the inquiring Frank Alpine what suffering means to a Jew, answers, "I suffer for you . . . you suffer for me" (98). If it is extremely unlikely that any Jewish storekeeper ever said that to a gentile employee, it is nonetheless memorable as a poetic formulation of moral life. As has often been said, Malamud at his best presents us not with realism but with a sort of moral mythology. His best effects are those of an intense lyricism. For the big, open, contemporaneous world, the world of social fiction, one reads Bellow or Roth (who do other things as well). Not that *The Fixer* and *Dubin's Lives* do not have these qualities, but Malamud rarely achieves the distinction of his postwar period work. So if these works seem precious in the sense of curiously affected, they are equally precious as value.

In *The Assistant*, the economic pressures on Morris are such that he finally yields to the temptation of burning his store for the insurance money. Luckily, he is too much the *schlimazel* to handle the fiery celluloid and is saved. Even Morris yields to temptation but, mainly, Morris and Frank Alpine take life from their moral avatars, Moses and St Francis. Morris lives by the law, humanely, the law being synonymous with the good heart, as the rabbi says at his funeral. Frank, miscast as a burglar and confused rapist of Morris's daughter Helen, is fascinated by suffering. Becoming a Jew is his redemption. He bears the pain of circumcision, which may be seen as a triumph of superego over id. Frank becomes a Son of the

Covenant, a man of stern morality. He takes on Morris's burden. And Morris's daughter, Helen, is still there.

In most of the stories of *The Magic Barrel* Malamud stays old-fashioned ethnic, paradoxically appealing to the outside world by avoiding it. Ethnicity serves as a stay against fifties homogeneity, the all-consuming and all-consumering present. Moreover, World War II revived the reality of categories like good and evil. Belief was taken seriously by many, including Heschel, Maritain, and Niebuhr. The appeal of the Jewish writers in America was, in part, the need for roots, even if the need was sometimes more apparent than the roots. Still, there was far more rootedness to T. S. Eliot's rootless Jew than he perceived.

"The First Seven Years" is another story about a no-longer-young man trying to win a shopkeeper's daughter. This time the man is Jewish, the daughter loves him, but the father, Feld, has better hopes for his girl than the bald, bookish refugee Sobel. He wants a college boy. Despite her love of reading, he could not provide that sort of education for her. Miriam isn't impressed with the young man he has introduced to her. It turns out educated means accountant and Miriam rejects his materialism. When he finds out Sobel's intentions, the astonished Feld rejects him, only to be taken by the assistant's grief at being rejected. In a variation on the biblical story, Sobel has been working for five years for the girl of his dreams and almost does not get her. Feld relents. For reasons of modesty—she is only 19—Feld will have him work for two years and then she will be his. The heavy-hearted Feld need not have bothered to come to the store early the next day. Sobel was already there "pounding leather for his love" (16). Eros, builder of arch supports!

Malamud's immigrant Jews evoke an idea of community through redemptive suffering, wry though this may be. In "The Mourners," Kessler, a miserable and dirty old man, is chucked out on the street with his belongings when the smell from his apartment becomes too much. He is brought back upstairs by his Italian neighbor and her two sons, who take pity. "What did I did to you," weeps Kessler to landlord Gruber (23). Gruber, who is, after all, Jewish, thinks of offering to put the old man in a nursing home. But Kessler's mourning is so rending that it occurs to Gruber that the man is mourning for him—"it was he who was dead" (25). Such is Gruber's perception of the event. There is a moment in these stories that involves a transcendent giving. Gruber makes a *talis*, a prayer shawl, of Kessler's sheet and becomes a mourner. I mourn for you, you mourn for me in the community of suffering.

"The Last Mohican" is a variation on the giving theme. Fidelman, failed painter and present art student, is plagued by the ever-needy, ever-demanding *schnorrer* Susskind. The not exactly wealthy art student can never seem to give him enough. There is the Joint Distribution Committee, there is repatriation to Israel, but no, Susskind (the name, ironically, means sweet child) insists on salvation through Fidelman. Denied Fidelman's suit, Susskind steals his briefcase, including the Giotto chapter he has been working on. In a dream Fidelman sees a Giotto painting in which a saint is handing a knight "in a thin robe his old gold cloak" (181). Fidelman has the answer to his previous question, "Am I responsible for you then, Susskind?," to which the latter had answered that he was, "Because you are a man. Because you are a Jew" (166). So he runs to give Susskind his suit and receives back his briefcase. But the Giotto chapter has been burned. "The words were there but the spirit was missing," says the somehow knowledgeable Susskind as he flees. "All is forgiven," Fidelman shouts and we are supposed to believe in this climactic goodness (182). There is never enough of giving, a moral for an increasingly acquisitive culture grown subtle in the morality of self-interest.

Malamud's moral aesthetic rests on a stylized Jewish identity. But suffering is a mess, Jewish history a mixed blessing. Henry Levin of "The Lady of the Lake" would like to forget the whole thing and takes to calling himself Henry R. Freeman. He is an American, not a Jew. Alas, he falls for a young woman whose Holocaust experience means everything to her, whose pride is her Jewish identity. This former resident of Buchenwald will not marry someone who cannot share her meaningful past. "I treasure what I suffered for," she says, a true Malamud heroine (132). She is not a son but a daughter of the Covenant.

Marriage made or broken is often the moment of truth in Malamud's fiction of the fifties. In his world it is, ideally, responsibility made flesh. In this respect Malamud spoke to a wide fifties audience, which believed in the accessible ideal of married normalcy. As the divorce courts of the seventies attest, this is one more ideal buffeted by reality. Yet people remarry, so even here maybe it was not the ideal but the particular enactment. Given his stylized milieu, Malamud is still dealing with marriage brokers in his fifties fiction. Appearing in passing in "The First Seven Years," the marriage broker takes center stage in "The Magic Barrel." Sex in Judaism is not inhibited in a Puritan way, but it is, traditionally, holy, involving marriage and leading to reproduction. Marriage brokers in the fifties were a rarity, except in Orthodox communities. Hence Leo Finkle and Salzman.

A rabbinical student at Yeshiva University, Leo Finkle does not love God, because, except for his parents, he does not love man. When he does fall in love he does so with a picture of someone who has deeply suffered, who gives him an impression of "evil." He finds this "good: good for Leo Finkle" (209). She is Salzman the matchmaker's daughter, whom the father considers "an animal. Like a dog" (212). Could Leo convert her to goodness, himself to God? "The idea alternately nauseated and exalted him" (213). For, in embracing her, he is embracing life, a reality of innocence and experience, as her white dress and red shoes indicate. Leo momentarily thinks of the colors in reverse, as she waits like a fallen woman under the street lamp. He notices, however, the "desperate innocence" of her eyes and pictures, in her, "his own redemption" (214). Leo's Jewishness, then, is a romantic appropriation of the traditional. Yet once again insight into suffering brings redemption. Suffering crystallizes identity in Malamud's best work.

This variation of the more traditional religious theme is an indication that Malamud may be feeling too much the heroism of giving and selflessness. Frank Alpine may be, finally, too painful a case. And Fidelman may be involved in a parody of solicitude. Should one continually give to an egregious *schnorrer* like Susskind? There is something hokey about such goodness (and something implausible about setting Susskind up as a critic of Giotto).

The radical break between the first Fidelman story and the rest may indicate Malamud's unease with it. The erotic replaces the altruistic in his character as it does to some degree in Malamud's imagination. In "Still Life," a ravenously sex-hungry, uxorious Fidelman falls into sex almost fortuitously as he happens to dress as a priest in a self-portrait. This elicits penitential guilt in his elusive Italian lover, whose story includes incest and murder. She can function as an artist and a love only under the aegis of Christian guilt. Eroticized, Fidelman surprises himself with a moral though not a Jewish world as he pumps his difficult *inamorata* to her penitential cross. By the next Fidelman story, the picaresque takes over. The Jew becomes, of all things, pickpocket, art thief, immoralist. Judging from the frequency of these stories Malamud seems to have found them liberating. We get an idea of Fidelman's predicament when, involved in a copy-and-switch scheme, he kisses the hands, thighs, and breasts on Titian's *Venus of Urbino*, murmuring, "I love you." Fidelman is given to a tawdry eroticism, a tumble with an unattractive model, a memory of his sister stepping into the tub. Trapped in a criminal element, he is victimized by an art theft gone awry. The later Fidelman stories, though not without flashes of moral earnestness on the part of the would-be artist, are even more strained examples of comic eroticism taking over the life of a failed artist. Fidelman is a dead end.

But his pursuit of the erotic is not. *Dubin's Lives*, which Malamud intended to be something like a summa, is its ultimate expression. Malamud in the fifties may be considered the most Jewish of the Jewish writers. He now defines the truly significant in terms of erotic life. This is a sign of the times and a difference between the fifties and the seventies. Though even "The Magic Barrel" was seen as a way out of oppressive moral restraint, classic Malamud is more typically given to heroes who can creatively repress, heroes of conscience. That the self cannot be understood without the erotic is not exactly news in fifties Malamud. But is the self to be understood primarily as a function of the erotic? The 56-year-old Dubin seriously entertains this idea. D. H. Lawrence, in Dubin's view, answers yes. And Lawrence is his culture hero. But since Dubin has as much trouble with his biography of Lawrence as with his erotic life, the answer may be no. In a nightmare, Dubin is confronted by a vituperative, anti-Semitic Lawrence who curses him as a Jew antagonistic to the male principle. Dubin thinks of Jewishness as a sense of obligation and met his gentile wife through a "personal" in which she expressed the desire for a marriage-minded man who is "responsible" (46). He even sees his subsequent adultery as a reward for being good. He remains responsible to his wife in his own way. He defines the Jew in America, circa 1979—Dubin is a man who will not commit adultery in his wife's bed! Dubin is what

Lawrence is not, ambivalent. That his young lover, Fanny of course, thinks of sharing Dubin with his wife is a wish fulfillment. Displaced by Fanny's young man, Dubin leaves her house for his, "holding his half-stiffened phallus in his hand, for his wife with love," a halfcocked ending if there ever was one (362). Dubin is too much the Jew for a pagan game. No erotic transcendence for him. And he never breaks the matrimonial bonds. Suffering amorphously, Dubin is through much of the novel weightless, gutless, feckless, and fuckless. He embodies the lack of moral clarity that inspired Malamud to create his fifties period milieu in the first place. This is Malamud's brilliant world, where characters can picture their own redemption.

The period we are mainly dealing with, about 1946 to 1964, coincides with Philip Roth's bar mitzvah and his turning 31, one might say his symbolic and real manhood. Roth is of the next generation, the one to come of age after the war, not during the Crash, the Depression, and World War II. For this reason Roth deals with affluence rather than poverty. Nor does he deal with the American immigrant experience, his parents having been born in America. Irving Howe, whose best-selling *World of Our Fathers* defined the immigrant Jewish heritage for a multitude of American readers, has considered Roth cut off from the roots of Jewish feeling, but it would seem that Howe is making that contingent upon intensity of contact with the immigrant experience. With Roth's emphasis on family, even on the extended family of Israel, with his unique grasp of Jewish Newark and his close grasp of Jewish suburbia, with his self-lacerating comedy of suffering, one would be hard pressed to think of a writer who more Jewishly expresses the reality of the post-Howe generation of assimilated American Jews. Howe is like the Jewish lady in the Israel joke who will not stop talking Yiddish to her son because she does not want him to forget that he is a Jew.

Surely Roth's development as a writer undermines Howe's contention that Roth is "never a writer deeply absorbed by experience for its own sake," that he is after some of his early stories reduced to *kvetching*, which Irving Howe, writing in *World of Our Fathers*, defines as "a sterile humor" (596f).

But *kvetching*, in my understanding, is more accurately rendered as "unjustifiable complaint." Roth's complaints are generally justified, not only in their social and moral ambience, but by their frequent transformation into brilliant comedy. In art, as Howe has said in conversation, performance may be its own justification. Howe recognizes that what he considers Roth's deficiency regarding traditional Jewish values need not be fatal if American values are put in their place. Without even considering the first, can anyone doubt at this point in Roth's career his American values? You cannot, for example, make people laugh unless you share their values. And even if Roth reverses the classical Molièrean pattern by flaying the typical and sympathizing with the eccentric, he does so in a community of self-regard.

Howe's distinction between Jewish and American values has little currency for a writer who insists that he is an American writer who happens to be Jewish. So though Roth often writes about Jewish characters, the context is American. This is true from the beginning. "Goodbye, Columbus," in the volume of the same name, is a social portrait of suburban Jewish America as seen through the eyes of a young man from urban Jewish America. Judaism as religion is given only satiric treatment. Neil Klugman finds himself praying or at least making a little speech to himself in St Patrick's Cathedral as his love gets a new diaphragm. "If we meet You at all, God, it's that we're carnal, and acquisitive, and thereby partake of You," he reflects, in what is not a particularly Jewish moral or locale. A confused Klugman wonders if God can provide Patimkin heaven. Impossible. Brenda's parents discover the diaphragm, which she subconsciously wished them to find. Having to choose between her lover and her parents, she chooses the parents, little though they mean to her. "Goodbye, Columbus" is a sort of domesticated, fifties, Jewish *Gatsby*. Poor boy, rich girl, dreaming, heartbreak. Daisy Buchanan too chooses respectability, but she chooses between lovers. Both heroines wilt, but the triumph of family piety, empty in this case, is Jewish. The story ends with Klugman going back to work on the Jewish New Year, a holy day. So Roth's hero breaks with Jewish tradition, defined here as bourgeois provincialism. Klugman is a stick, the satire a bit obvious, but particularly in its evocation of social surfaces and an athletic America, it will do nicely.

Another story in the volume equally evocative of the fifties, and the only one to have become a household word, at least in Jewish households, is "Eli, the Fanatic." Whether or not the level of satire meets with Howe's approval, Roth has touched on an ambivalence in the character of Eli Peck, as his name indicates. Eli is short for Eliyahu or Elijah, Peck is his changed, assimilated name, Wasp-sounding. Roth prepares us for his conversion *to* the Jews by making him a sensitive man who has had two nervous breakdowns. The Protestant and Jewish calm of Woodenton is pierced by Eli's heartfelt affinity with Jewish suffering. The assimilated lawyer out to keep the Yeshiva in line becomes the penitential Jew, and the assimilated lawyer is what he is doing penance for. "You are us. We are you," he says, suggesting the traditional community of Jewish concern (Morris Bober was, shall we say, more catholic). This takes precedence over Eli's lightweight suburban friends, of whom he nonetheless thinks, "I am them. They are me" (265). Roth here gives us sympathetic, quixotic, hilarious comedy, siding with the eccentric. Roth is in this story a master of the socially incongruous.

In *Letting Go*, his novel about the fifties, Roth is the realist rather than the satirist. It is the literary rather than the
vernacular tradition that Roth favored in his first book.
Vaguely Jamesian, with a focus on consciousness, it is a work
of psychological realism. James's characters are alluded to a
number of times in the text, particularly Isabel Archer. She
seems to be a symbol of failed marriage, as she is, toward the
end of *Letting Go*, an exemplar of obligation. Early marriage
was part of fifties mores and, in Paul and Libby Hertz, Roth
gives us one of the most painful marriages in literature. Even
so, Roth is capable of superb, excruciating dialogue reflecting,
for example, the breakdown of belief as it mirrors personal
breakdown. Libby's hysteria is one of the best things in the
book. In this novel of lost illusions, Paul is to duty what
Gabe is to feeling. But Gabe, the Roth surrogate, is, like Neil
Klugman, a tepid conception. His amorphousness helps to
transform the novel into a beached whale. His last-minute
selflessness, in the style of James's Lambert Strether of *The
Ambassadors*, is a desperate attempt to act on feeling. The best
flat portrait in the novel is that of Bigonness, the conniving
unionist. In his utter lack of sentimentality about labor,
Roth reflects another fifties quality. That Roth could have
sustained himself through so dreary a tome was an indication
that here is a writer who can do anything.

In Roth's writing up to *Portnoy's Complaint* libido is generally a form of imprisonment. His small masterpiece was
published in 1969 and has a freedom and wildness Roth
possesses to some degree thus far in only some of the comic
stories of *Goodbye, Columbus*. Portnoy's desire is to put the id
back in Yid, a sentiment more typical of the late sixties than
of the postwar period. Portnoy is a child of the fifties, the
1950 valedictorian of Weequahic High and an editor later
in that decade of the *Columbia Law Review*. He remembers
Pumpkin, the psychologically sound all-American girl, with

her naturally streaming early fifties hair, one of a number of indications in Roth that the fifties might be an embodiment of normalcy when it was not its inversion. Portnoy is what is not nice about the nice Jewish boy, with his parents, his guilt, his furtive sexuality, issuing eventually into a rebellious troilism where he cannot quite navigate through such pagan traffic. *Portnoy* is a landmark in the Jewish comedy of self-exposure.

The comic agony of erotic salvation is mined eight years later in the underrated *The Professor of Desire*. It shows again that, with the possible exception of some of the late social novels, Roth is at his best in the wild mode, though here that mode is tempered by an almost Chekhovian bittersweetness. Like Byron, David Kepesh is studious by day, dissolute by night. Unlike Byron, Kepesh has an analyst. A problem is that he is Jewish so that where id should be there ego is. Although he thinks of the fifties as "that woebegone era in the history of pleasure" (92), our sexual gourmet also thinks about "the libidinous fallacy" (94). The professor critic is taunted by his swinging, megalomaniac, Jewish friend Baumgarten— "Virtue, virtue, who's got the virtue? Biggest Jewish racket since Meyer Lansky in his prime" (131). But after a number of women, including ex-wife Helen, an energetic and cantankerous sexual athlete, Kepesh seems to find calm as well as voluptuousness in Claire, Clarissa as he sometimes calls her, her name invoking light, clarity. "My obstructed days are behind me—along with the unobstructed ones," he declares harmoniously (169). But as fate? love? Kafka? would have it, Kepesh soon becomes impotent. His analysis proves to be interminable. Kepesh remains a Jewish Dionysus, one part Priapus, one part depression.

Zuckerman takes over from Kepesh when Roth realizes that the persona of artist rather than scholar gets closer to the bone, even the funny bone. The coincidence of comedy and subjectivity is Roth's métier, showing superbly in the Zuckerman trilogy masterwork, *The Anatomy Lesson*.

In *The Ghost Writer*, the first volume of the trilogy published as *Zuckerman Bound*, Roth gives us, centrally, a portrait of Malamud (Lonoff) and, tangentially, one of Bellow (Abravanel). He emphasizes Malamud's residually Jewish qualities and thinks of him as the most famous literary ascetic in America. Lonoff grants authority to the prohibitive and thereby gives young Zuckerman "visions of terminal restraint" (14). Lonoff represents "Sanity, Responsibility, and Self-Respect" (15), the capital letters paying due deference to moral abstraction, a Jewish, anti-Modernist trope. Yet Lonoff's troubled marriage and his open flirtation with, of all people, the still living Anne Frank shake the abstractions. The audacious story line almost succeeds. What does succeed is this further step in the literature of the bachelor impatient to assume the world.

By *Zuckerman Unbound* he has assumed it. The novel is post-*Carnovsky* (*Portnoy's Complaint*). Zuckerman is a celebrity living in the paradoxical glare of hermetic luxury. As if to set some critics straight, he lucidly describes his motivation for writing *Carnovsky*: "You set out to sabotage your own moralizing nature" (305). The book was not an apology for Dionysus. Zuckerman's life seems always to involve contradiction. Like Thomas Wolfe, he left home for Art only to find that he had taken home with him. Has his celebrity cost him his heart? He feels no grief at his father's death. He does feel guilt. Did his father actually call him "bastard" on his deathbed, his final word? Or is it, Zuckerman sardonically notes, a writer's wishful thinking, "If not quite the son's" (380)? His rivalrous brother is there to assure him of patricide—"You killed him, Nathan" (397). Loyalty, responsibility, restraint, the brother inveighs, "Jewish morality, Jewish endurance, Jewish wisdom, Jewish families—everything is grist for your fun machine" (397). In the eyes of this solid bourgeois the artist's cannibalizing life is essentially guilt and sterility. His brother is not man enough to see that Zuckerman, himself a conscience-ridden Jew, is in partial agreement. Rather, his brother goes on about how he knows what it is to have a child and, he tells Zuckerman, "You don't, you selfish bastard, and you never will" (399). No family—this is the ultimate Jewish curse. Neither son, husband, nor brother, Zuckerman finds himself unbound. Will he bring the Promethean fire of art?

The final novel of the trilogy, *The Anatomy Lesson*, shows us that Zuckerman is far from indifferent to his brother's accusations. He is, in fact, decimated by guilt, not having completed a page since his father's presumptive dying rebuke. He is in a writer's depression: "he had nothing left to write, and with nothing to write, no reason to be" (416). He finds himself, literally, in traction. Not that he does not manage intercourse, fellatio, and cunnilingus from a supine position with the help of a thesaurus under his head. Zuckerman's static position is balanced in the narrative by the speedy movement of obsessive rage. When it is not directed at himself it is directed at the critic Milton Appel (Howe), to whose generation Zuckerman owes much of his aggressive marginality and independence—the style of literary Jews like himself, who came of age in the fifties. Zuckerman reflects that "to be raised a post-immigrant Jew in America was to be given a ticket out of the ghetto into a wholly unconstrained world of thought . . . Alienated? Just another way to say 'set free'!" Does this imply a severance from Jewish consciousness? No. There is a "thrillingly paradoxical kicker," for Zuckerman: "A Jew set free from Jews—yet only by steadily maintaining self-consciousness as a Jew" (480). In his own mind Zuckerman is not an affective apostate but a Jew.

What Zuckerman finds most disturbing is that Appel does not see this. Moreover, Zuckerman thinks that Appel loathes the bourgeois Jews he seems to be defending "now that the

Weathermen are around, and me and my friends Jerry Rubin and Herbert Marcuse and H. Rap Brown" (505). Zuckerman assures us that as an undergraduate at the University of Chicago in the fifties he "savagely reviewed beat novels in *The Maroon*" (585). Though Appel does not do this, Zuckerman feels down deep that the critic obtusely classifies him with the crazies and the morality of impulse people. Yet it is not much of a leap to Zuckerman's cogent criticism of the critic. He shrewdly objects that Appel seems to have read *Carnovsky* "as a manifesto of the instinctual life. As if he'd never heard of repressed, obsessive Jews" (505f). This position does not prevent Zuckerman from experiencing the hospital ministrations of sex priestess Gloria Galanter, who visits him with vibrating dildo, K-Y Jelly, a length of braided rope, and a talented and adventurous finger. After all, goes her maternal wisdom, "A child is sick . . . you bring toys" (526). That Gloria is married is no obstacle to anyone. Zuckerman, against his will, almost, speculates on Dionysian rites and the physically afflicted in ancient days. Gloria and the wise and disillusioned Jaga are the most memorable sketches from his harem. Jaga touches a nerve in describing writers as "warm ice" (538), interested in women primarily as material. Zuckerman ruefully admits as much but can only plead being possessed and the therapeutic out that "the only patient being treated by the writer is himself" (540). With answers like these, maybe Appel has something.

The irony of Zuckerman's life is that perfecting the writer's iron will "began to feel like the evasion of experience . . . like the sternest form of incarceration" (586). Zuckerman is bound by his art. "Once one's writing," he contends, "it's all limits. Bound to a subject. Bound to make sense of it. Bound to make a book of it" (609). Roth circles the square here in that the life of aesthetic impulse is inseparable from the life of obligation. He becomes totally absorbed in the life of art in a Jewish way. He may have fooled Appel, but he does not quite fool the students who submit a questionnaire to the patient whose mouth is literally if not metaphysically shut by a fall. They ask, "Do you feel yourself part of a rearguard action, in the service of a declining tradition?" This apropos of postmodernists like Barth and Pynchon. Even with his mouth wired shut Zuckerman is the liberal Jewish humanist. If it were not perhaps he would have bitten them.

The Anatomy Lesson crystallizes the trilogy into formidable stature and, in its debt to *Herzog*, brings us back to 1964. In tempo, in tone to some degree, in its epistolary style, in its first person/third person narrative making at once for sympathy and intensity and for comic and social distancing, in its lovable, reflective, lunatic protagonist who remembers his erotic life as he seeks to transcend it for a higher wisdom, in its beleaguered Jewish quality, Roth's novel owes much to Bellow's masterwork. Stretching chronology, one might say that in these two works a good measure of postwar Jewish sensibility is contained.

In *Zuckerman Bound* Roth carries the comedy of self-regard to an exhausting end (only to reach comic heights again in *Operation Shylock*). At first, as in *Portnoy*, this comedy was a way of breaking out of the postwar bourgeois doldrums, and to a degree it remains so in *Zuckerman Bound*. In a totally different vein, however, the postwar period engages Roth in some of his most striking recent fiction. In this fiction, ironically, the postwar period bails him out of the narcissistic doldrums. "I've had my story," says Zuckerman in *I Married a Communist*. We now get a Balzacean narrative which seeks to examine character through segments of social history. *I Married a Communist* presents the depredations of the McCarthy era through the eyes of young Nathan Zuckerman (class of 1954) and, decades later, his great high school English teacher, who narrates the story of his flamboyant brother

Ira, a communist who rises from the Party to a disastrous marriage to a one-time movie star now settling for daytime radio. Her book, entitled *I Married a Communist* (a turn on Claire Bloom's name-naming account of her marriage to Roth), decimates an already shaky relationship and assures election of a right-winger to Congress. Young Zuckerman is something of a left-winger who is eager to shed his bourgeois Jewish identity. Religion, for him, is the opiate of the masses. He "didn't care to partake of the Jewish character . . . [he] wanted to partake of the national character" (39). In the end he inevitably partakes of both, assuming, as does his Jewish teacher, the postwar style, an anti-utopian, ethical cast of mind. His nonagenarian teacher warns the already old, now ascetic, artist against "the utopia of isolation" as well (317). For Zuckerman adulthood has meant orphanage and he shares his teacher's stoicism as he admires his endurance. His teacher once paid the price of refusing to cooperate with HUAC and later pays the price of his liberal inclinations by staying on in Newark—his wife was murdered in a mugging. The teacher laments "the myth of your own goodness—the final delusion" (318). Zuckerman bleakly concludes, "There's the heart of the world. Nobody finds his life. That is life" (319). One wonders at this point about the reality of identity, Jewish or otherwise.

American Pastoral, which came out in 1997 a year before *I Married a Communist* but deals with the late sixties as well as the postwar period, is a novel which would seem to counter this bleakness. It is highlighted by one of Roth's finest character portraits, Swede Lvov, a former star high school athlete who carries on his family's lucrative glove business. Roth shows compassion for what he once ridiculed in Ron Patimkin, for example. In Swede, Roth succeeds in portraying a good ordinary man, a difficult task. Swede embodies responsibility, rectitude, superego, chastity even. And he loves America.

(Zuckerman appears to be particularly elated at his marrying out.) As social novelist Roth develops a sense of figures of masculine virtue: Murray Ringold, the wise, sympathetic high school teacher, if not Ira Ringold, the once idealized, spectacular, unstable, radical brother, and Swede Lvov. In *American Pastoral* Roth presents a bourgeois family lovingly perceived. "What on earth," this hard book concludes, "is less reprehensible than the life of the Lvovs" (423). That life is devastated by their daughter, Merry, who is radicalized by social unrest and, even more, by the hypocrisy of the American administration during the Vietnam War (which also disturbed many middle-class protesters). She is moved to blow up a post office, killing an innocent man in doing so. "Inspired" (258), she plants two other bombs, killing three more people. She has expressed her violent hatred of America. She eventually becomes an Eastern religious ascetic, living in dire poverty, guilty about taking the life of plants by eating them.

American Pastoral, one of Roth's finest achievements, does not sit well with some critics on the left, who remember the energy of the late sixties without remembering its dangers, without, in some cases, ever having considered them. They fault Roth for short-changing the period, as if it were the novelist's obligation to be sociologically exhaustive. It is quite enough to brilliantly record the savage impact of one late-sixties revolutionary on one family. It is true that Zuckerman, dreaming his realistic chronicle, equates this radicalism with infantilism, that he denigrates Merry's reading of Marx, Marcuse, Malraux, Frantz Fanon, that he loathes the radical literary critic wife of an old friend for playing "the old French game of beating up on the bourgeoisie," as a guest puts it (383). These are, to say the least, plausible positions, not to mention the basic political (not artistic) immunity in such matters that a novelist has. Indeed, some of Zuckerman's most brilliant perceptions are anti-radical perceptions, the description of Rita Cohen's Isro (Jewish Afro) hairdo, for example; it says "I go wherever I want, as far as I want—all that matters is what I want!" (134). Perception like this transcends politics.

Some of the deepest emotion in Roth occurs when he reconciles himself with the middle-class world he is no longer a part of, in *American Pastoral* and in *Patrimony*, for example. Rarely in fiction does fact rise to such a loving eloquence as Roth's description of the manufacturing of gloves. Roth is describing the process of civilization. His superego nostalgia, a nostalgia for the fifties, cannot be simply attributed to his own narcissism. Swede is an alter ego. Moreover, he and his family are faulted for living by "the utopia of a rational existence" (123). The Lvovs are in the end subject to Roth's late pessimism, dramatizing as they do a disintegrated innocence, a deracinated sense of obligation. Yet the dominant tone is elegy, just as it was rage in *I Married a Communist*. Such is Roth's late encounter with the era that gave him mature consciousness.

American Jewish fiction, then, shows us deidentifying writers (Trilling, civilly; Salinger, indifferently; Mailer, aggressively) and identifying writers (Bellow, Malamud, Roth). Yet with the exception of much of early Malamud, all of these writers dream American dreams, anxiety as well as wish fulfillment. Cynthia Ozick wishes to dream Jewish dreams. Doing so involves a journey into normative Judaism far longer than any of these writers is willing to take. Quoting *The Ethics of the Fathers*, writing about Rabbi Akiva and the destruction of the Temple, writing fiction with titles like "The Pagan Rabbi" and "Levitation," and essays entitled "America: Toward Yavneh" and "Toward a New Yiddish," attacking Harold Bloom for idolatry and Lillian Hellman for Holocaust denial in the case of Anne Frank, Ozick represents a significant zeitgeist shift. She admires Bellow, Malamud, and Roth as writers, even Jewish writers, but feels a lack. So, probably, do they, but normative Judaism is not a direction they care to pursue. Of course, Ozick herself can be a traditional writer only at a remove. But if she is the first (or one of the first; Hugh Nissenson and Arthur Cohen got there at about the same time) to be a writer of Judaism, she will not be the last.

The rise of ethnicity, the turn to religion, the reflection of history (for example, the Holocaust, Israel), individual temperament— these all give rise to a new generation of fiction writers whose variations on tradition or the lack of it is reflected even in the titles: Steve Stern's *Lazar Malkin Enters Heaven*, Rebecca Goldstein's *Mazel*, Thane Rosenbaum's *Elijah Visible*, Melvin Jules Bukiet's *While the Messiah Tarries*. Ironically, this turn occurs at a time when Jewish assimilation has been so much of a success that, for many, particularly "minorities," Jews are regarded as part of the Wasp establishment— to the extent that such a thing exists. As the marriage statistics show, Jews being in bed with Wasps is not just a metaphor. Of course, this may itself be a major reason for the turn. In any case, with the exception of some of Ozick's stories, it remains to be seen whether a more intense concentration on Jewishness can produce the level of art attained by Bellow, Malamud, and Roth.

I recall browsing in shops of the Mea Shearim or Orthodox section of Jerusalem to no avail. I finally asked a Chassid in black caftan and sidelocks where I could pick up some objets d'art or artifacts. He had trouble understanding what I was looking for. Between his English and my Yiddish we were in some difficulty. Finally, I got through. He knew what I meant. *"Tchatchkis,"* he said, the Yiddish word conveying a bemused contempt for the merely aesthetic, for art and artifacts. This incident made me think that if the moderate swing to religious themes in contemporary American Jewish fiction were to become an extreme shift to the totally religious it would undo itself. One would dispense with mere literature and focus only on the revealed word of God. It is neither probable nor desirable that the breakthroughs of the Enlightenment be reversed.

References and further reading

Howe, Irving. *World of Our Fathers*. New York: Simon and Schuster, 1976.

Mailer, Norman. *Advertisements for Myself*. New York: Berkley Medallion, 1966.

Malamud, Bernard. *The Assistant*. New York: Signet, 1957.

——. *The Magic Barrel*. New York: Farrar, Straus and Cudahy, 1958.

——. *Dubin's Lives*. New York: Farrar, Straus and Giroux, 1979.

Roth, Philip. *Goodbye, Columbus*. New York: Meridian, 1960.

——. *The Professor of Desire*. New York: Bantam, 1978.

——. *Zuckerman Bound*. New York: Farrar, Straus and Giroux, 1985.

——. *American Pastoral*. New York: Vintage, 1997.

——. *I Married a Communist*. New York: Vintage, 1998.

Trilling, Lionel. Comments in "Under Forty." Symposium. *Contemporary Jewish Record* (vii. 1) (February 1944): 16f.

9

The Holocaust and History in Bellow and Malamud

In *Zakhor: Jewish History and Jewish Memory*, Josef Hayim Yerushalmi points out that the fathers of transcendent meaning in history were the Jews, that "human history revealed God's will and purpose" (*Zakhor* 8). This set up a pattern of "divine challenge and human response . . . a tense dialectic of obedience and rebellion." Thus there was a profound sense in which traditional Jews considered the destruction of the first and second Temples a result of their sins. The Holocaust has shaken this mentality to near oblivion. Few contemporary Jews would consider the Holocaust their fault. Yet many consider the Holocaust.

In the tradition, God reveals himself historically. Moses speaks of "God of our fathers" who says, "I have surely remembered you," (Ex 3:16) and "I am the Lord . . . who brought you out of the Land of Egypt" (Ex 20:2). Memory, therefore, becomes crucial to faith and its very existence. "Only in Israel and nowhere else is the injunction to remember felt as a religious imperative to an entire people," as Passover remembers the exodus. As the tradition develops into long-lived rabbinic Jewry, a Jewry of exile in its inception, the meaning of history is derived more from the prophets than from the historical narratives of the Bible, "as collective memory is transmitted more actively through ritual than through chronicle" (21). Memory is sanctified through mythic time. There was no Jewish historian for fifteen centuries. Maimonides, so attuned to the universalizing of philosophy, considered the reading of history "a waste of time" (qtd. 33).

Modernity radically changes this, particularly The Enlightenment, where the Haskalah movement, a secularizing vanguard of German Jewry, scientifically, nonapologetically, considers the nature and viability of Judaism. Judaism becomes historicized, no longer a sacred text; it is something defined rather than revealed. "Jewish historiography," Yerushalmi says, is "divorced from Jewish collective memory" (93). History, he says laconically, "is the faith of fallen Jews" (86). The Holocaust, like the Spanish Inquisition before it, led to historical involvement but in a historicizing time. Yerushalmi feels a part of this modernity, part of this disintegration which brings such great gains in consciousness. He feels the losses as well. And, for him, there is something intrinsic to the nature of history that can never recapture the deeply affective context of the prophetic tradition.

Enter literature. For even though "the Holocaust has engendered more historical research than any single event in Jewish history," Yerushalmi has "no doubt whatever that its image is being shaped, not at the historian's anvil, but in the novelist's crucible. Much has changed since the sixteenth century; one thing, curiously, remains. Now, as then, it would appear that even where Jews do not reject history out of hand, they are not prepared to confront it directly, but seem to await a new metahistorical myth, for which the novel provides at least a temporary modern surrogate" (98). Presumably the Jewish fiction writer would have a special purchase on this subject. Yerushalmi believes that "those who are alienated from the past cannot be drawn to it by explanation alone; they require evocation as well" (100). Bellow and Malamud are American exemplars. They help to define Yerushalmi's desired affective context. The few works of fiction considered here may seem small in the tremendousness of the event. But there is a literary brilliance to be observed, and the longest journey begins with a few steps. Surely these writers are representative of the contemporary consciousness Yerushalmi describes and exemplifies.

"The Holocaust haunted him always as a writer," according to Malamud's friend Nicholas Delbanco (*Talking Horse* 162). Malamud wrote about it at a remove, never directly but through the refugee experience, in some of his most memorable stories, including a few from his best book of stories, *The Magic Barrel.* In "The Last Mohican," Fidelman, a failed painter turned would-be-critic, is the central intelligence. His soul is tested by the enigmatic refugee Susskind. Serious though it is, in its sense of accelerated importunity the story is almost an extended Jewish joke, with Susskind a variation on the classic *schnorrer* or shameless hanger-on. (In one version of the joke, a *schnorrer*, after endless, humiliating pleading, is invited to a party where he does not belong—and brings a guest!) The *schnorrer* is an emblem of an East European Jewry that was often on the borderline between respectability and desperation. At first blush, Susskind fits the typology, an illustration of folk memory. But the joke, as Malamud has it, is on Fidelman, whose unexpected new awareness is the epiphanic center of the tale. The exquisiteness of the story lies in Malamud's making the necessary moral object so nearly impossible to like, let alone save.

In his oxblood shoes and tweed suit, Fidelman is an American type, a relatively well off innocent (even though a poor student) suddenly confronted with the impressive monuments of experience. He sees the Baths of Diocletian, thinks of Michelangelo's role in converting them to a church and convent, and then, of the museum it ultimately became. From the politically autocratic to the religious to the aesthetic—or the course of European consciousness in a nutshell. "Imagine," thinks Fidelman, "imagine all that history . . . It was an inspiring business, he, Arthur Fidelman, after all, born a Bronx boy" (*Magic Barrel* 156, 162). Fidelman experiences the standard reverence and stupefaction. But there is a complication. For Fidelman, "history was mysterious, the remembrance of things unknown, in a way burdensome, in a way a sensuous experience" (162). Like Henry James in the Louvre, Fidelman experiences a confusion that signifies both love and fear. And well he might. For the aspect of history that the story involves him in is one that he seems not strong enough to assimilate.

The Holocaust is European history as well, history with a capital H at that. Fidelman feels the burden of history in the form of skinny Susskind, whose lack of weight suggests another Jewish folk figure, the *luftmensch* or impoverished soul who apparently lives on air. He is the test of Fidelman's humanity, and Fidelman almost fails it. "Am I responsible for you then, Susskind?" says Fidelman. "'Who else?' Susskind loudly replied . . . 'Because you are a man. Because you are a Jew'" (165). Again Malamud relates to Jewish typology—am I my brother's keeper? But if he almost fails the test it is with good reason. The crowning indignity from Susskind is the theft of his manuscript. Poor Fidelman, a "tightly organized" (162) anal-retentive obsessive-compulsive, who records his research expenditures in a notebook and who is disoriented without a work schedule, runs head-on into this whirlwind of need, unexpectedness, and slovenly disproportion named Susskind. Comedy is indeed about the juxtaposition of opposites. And there is a Kafkaesque comedy in this crisis in the life of a well-ordered existence.

Looking for the elusive Susskind in a cemetery, Fidelman comes across a gravestone that screams, "My beloved father/ Betrayed by the damn Fascists/Murdered at Auschwitz by the barbarous Nazis/O *Crime Orrible*" (176). Some resistance in Fidelman breaks. That night he dreams he is in a cemetery, with Virgilio Susskind rising up out of an empty grave, asking "Have you read Tolstoy?" and "Why is art?" Tolstoy's *What is Art?* makes a strong, an excessive, argument for morality in art. But it is nonetheless the right direction for Malamud. The switch from "What" to "Why" presents art as a moral imperative. Art must be moral says this Virgil to his willing Dante. Fidelman is then in a synagogue apparently converted from a church with a Giotto fresco that shows St. Francis "handing an old knight in a thin robe his gold cloak" (181). This is a perfect venue for the ecumenical Malamud. The dream galvanizes Fidelman's moral sense. Susskind will get his suit, which he offers to him with the particularly Yiddish wish, "Wear it in good health." This is Fidelman's only Yiddish expression in the story. But when he discovers that Susskind has burnt his chapter, using it apparently for candle lighting page by page, he wants only to complete what the Holocaust failed to do—annihilate Susskind. The refugee says, "The words were there but the spirit was missing" (182). Fidelman is violently struck by the rightness of this judgment and forgives everything. How Susskind is suddenly set up as a critic of a critic of Giotto, the story does not explain. But Malamud is impelled by two logics: the proud logic of narrative, which takes the story to its fantastic end whether it is believable or not, and the logic of morality, which insists that the spirit is higher than the letter. Two of Malamud's obsessions, writing stories and "giving," come to a glaring conversion and we are left to wonder whether Malamud's self-described moral aesthetic is too didactically stylized.

"Giving" is so intense in "Take Pity" that it transcends the bounds of realism into fantasy. Malamud is creating a fable, the old Jewish habit of transforming history into myth. Giving is not only a primary obligation in the tradition, but a heightened obligation in cases of suffering engendered by the Holocaust. So it is to Rosen. This is a story about a man who offers everything, including, finally, his life (he commits suicide so that a widow can collect his insurance). Rosen is trying to preserve her from a second "graveyard" as well: a Malamudian grocery store. Despite the somberness, the story once again has the elements of a Jewish joke, with Eva and Rosen as accelerators in terms of her ever-mounting refusals of anything from the more and more giving Rosen. In a line that could have come only from Malamud, Rosen notes, "Here . . . is a very strange thing . . . a person that you can never give her anything.—*But I will give*" (94). The reader isn't quite sure whether to laugh or cry. He makes out his will and takes gas: "Let her say now no," (94) he says in Malamud's impeccable immigrant Jewish syntax. But Eva has come to his perch in limbo, beseeching him now, but too late.

What Malamud's fiction often shows is the power of fantasy even to the extent of going all the way to symbolism, as in "The Jewbird," itself perhaps an example of Holocaust fiction in its chilling, final image of the decimated bird. In holding fantasy so high, Malamud gives us a secular version of an essentially religious sensibility. "One effect of fantasy," he says, "is to give a feeling of timelessness, another of universality" (*Talking Horse* 51). In his discussion of "Take Pity" Malamud cites the classic Yiddish writers in their folk fantasy showing "ordinary people in time of stress" being saved by "unreal or supernatural beings" (59). As if expanding on Yerushalmi's distinction between myth and history, Malamud says that the classic Yiddish texts "show how God tries the Jews and are clearly derived from certain books of the Bible," adding that his works deal "not so much with the miraculous element but the trials and sufferings of poor people." Malamud tells us that "Rosen is being judged for his suicide, perhaps even paying for" it (58), in his super realistic purgatory, complete with an anaesthetized angel who has seen it all and then some. "Perhaps he is being punished for his pride, for giving when it isn't wanted," Malamud says. As for Eva, "perhaps because of an embittered quality, stubbornness, pride or simple incapacity, through lack of generosity, [she] can't accept his generosity and compassion" (61). However intricate the plot, Malamud wants to suspend it in the realm of moral fable. "Fantastic, symbolic, myth, timeless, universal, poetic, or anything else that fantasy may be, the truth it tells is true."

Malamud's Holocaust stories are not all in the fabulist mold. "The Lady of the Lake" is realistic and Jamesian, juxtaposing new world and old in a tale of intrigue and duplicity, all in an exotic European setting. Though even here plot hangs so heavily in the air that we are only a few steps from fable. Malamud has said that in writing a book, "usually I have the ending in mind, usually the last paragraph almost verbatim . . . The destination is already defined" (*Conversations* 64). If this is true of his novels it is that much more true of his stories. So of "The Magic Barrel" he has said, "the story was almost all thought out before it was written, usual with me" (*Talking Horse* 85). "The Lady of the Lake" is so preconceived that, effective though it is as dramatic irony, the characters are basically a function of plot. The story of Henry R. Freeman, née Henry Levin, is one of Jewish deidentification. As he emotes over the romantic Italian lake district he thinks, "who ever got emotional over Welfare Island?"(106). (He means Ellis Island.) The answer is millions, most of them the children of immigrants, like himself. He wants to radically transform his "unlived life" (109). This Jamesian desire is in itself commendable, and the name Freeman indicates an American expansiveness, but his embarrassment about his own history, in contrast to his fascination with "thees 'eestorical palatz" of the family del Dongo and the attraction of the Lady's "dark, sharp Italian face [that] had the quality of beauty which holds the mark of history" (113), is something Malamud does not forgive. Freeman's present is saturated in her imagined past: "Her past he could see boiling in her all the way back to the knights of old and then some, his own history was something else again" (115). His own Jewish past had brought him nothing but "headaches, inferiorities, unhappy memories" (126). Well, perhaps, but it is a shame that it has brought him nothing else. His Lady is not Isabella del Dongo, and she is Jewish and a Holocaust survivor (the only one in Malamud to have actually been in a concentration camp), who must reject his proposal of marriage because, as she says, "My past is meaningful to me. I treasure what I suffered for."

In Malamud's Holocaust fiction, not all pasts have meaning in her sense, and not all suffering is a treasure. Far from it. In "The German Refugee" Oskar Gassner is an assimilated German Jew whose main connection with Judaism is the hatred it inspired in his native countrymen. A well known Berlin critic and journalist, he is lucky enough to have gotten out of there before and, again, after *Kristallnacht*, leaving his wife and appallingly anti-Semitic mother-in-law behind. He is quite different from his East European fellow Jews in that he must leave a country he was very much a part of. He feels lost in the United States. Depressed, he cannot learn English, though any possibility of employment makes it necessary to do so. His speech has none of the nervous, witty, ironic vigor of Yiddish, the language of East European Jewish immigrants, but is rather a forlorn patchwork that falls between the stools of German and English, usually with a loud plop. The history he lives is the history we all know from the newspapers. His private life mirrors public life, his past is the present. The only fantasy element of his life is the world of fact. His story is in the realistic, heartbreak manner of Chekhov and early Joyce, a subtle psychological narrative culminating in a personal insight, an illumination of a missed connection. Malamud takes the story from his own experience as a tutor of German refugees at just this historical and biographical moment. But because Gassner is so deeply depressed—he had attempted suicide during his first week in America—Malamud converts his own depression of the period into the balanced sunnyness of his narrator, whom we trust to give an objective account of this extremely painful case.

Malamud gives us fine images of Gassner as a fish out of water—his dressing in full regalia (coat, tie), even in the oppressive New York heat, his sitting in the New York Public Library unable to read. The narrator thinks of him "always suspended between two floors," neither here nor there. His *Kristallnacht* of the soul keeps him from writing. It is, he says, "as though someone has thrown a stone at a window and the whole house—the whole idea, zmashes" (*Idiots First* 206). He cannot get over his feeling that his wife too is an anti-Semite, that she too is complicit. Gassner becomes unblocked, though, and gives a lecture on German poets in German when the tutor points to their connection with Whitman, particularly his feeling of Brudermensch. This breakthrough occurs as the Nazis invade Poland in 1939. The reader is all too aware that "'all men ever born are also my brothers/and the women my sisters and lovers,/And that the kelson of creation is love'" is but another window waiting to be smashed. Gassner's wife, he discovers, was shot by the Nazis after she had converted to Judaism and is left in an open ditch "with the naked Jewish men, their wives and children, some Polish soldiers, and a handful of gypsies," (212) a tableaux that is a ghastly inversion of Whitmanesque brotherhood.

"People say I write so much about misery, but you write about what you know best," said Malamud to an interviewer. He elaborates significantly: "As you are grooved, so you are grieved . . . the grieving is that no matter how much happiness or success you collect, you cannot obliterate your early experience" (*Conversations* 93). Malamud makes a key link between the grocery store and the tomb. His best books—*The Assistant, The Magic Barrel*—relate to this link. Malamud's work is a product of the two Great Depressions, economic and psychological. Janna Malamud Smith, his daughter, sheds light on his psychological makeup in her absorbing memoir, *My Father is a Book*. As a psychiatric social worker, she is particularly sensitive to the sorrows stemming from youth. "I was gypped," said Malamud of his nonexistent youth (6). She says that in Oregon, on good days, he would say, "some day I'm going to win" (20). Well, he did, through the transformation of suffering. His boyhood friend Ben Loeb notes that in 1939, the time the narrator of "The German Refugee" met his tutor, "He is badly depressed. He once allowed to me that he'd felt enough despair at some moments during these years to at least glance at suicide" (51). The winter of 1939 into 1940 was "the lowest, loneliest ebb" (52). And Janna says that a favorite poem of his was Keats's "When I have fears that I may cease to be." It did not help that his psychotic mother attempted suicide. She died when he was fifteen.

Depression links to his work in another way. His brother was very seriously depressed. Smith tells us that when Malamud left New York for Oregon his father felt abandoned and brother Eugene, "who after many years of struggle had ventured out into the world and was working, fell apart when Dad moved away" (95). In a wrenching letter of January 7, 1952, Malamud's father writes to him, "he told me that he received writing paper and a Pen [sic] from you. But he through [sic] everything out the window. . . Maybe you will find the Pen" (101). As Smith writes, "the Pen carries conno-tations of Dad's writing, Max's illiteracy, Eugene's inevitable recognition that his older brother had escaped and he had not" (102). She adds, thunderously, "I have always believed that Dad had to leave Brooklyn and his family before he could write freely. What I didn't understand until I read these letters was the price he paid. Neither his father nor his brother really survived his departure" (103). *The Magic Barrel* is dedicated to Eugene, and the story "Idiots First," which, as Robert Solotaroff puts it, involves "a heightened commitment to otherness—for Malamud the glue that holds together the moral world," (69), might have been. He lived twenty years beyond father Max's death, dying at age fifty-five. Despairing, he "sometimes wished to end his life. My father knew this, and it haunted him" (104). Malamud felt a certain guilt about his freedom, felt that in some sense he was not "giving" enough, that a major suffering was due to him. This is one of the reasons—the Jewish ethical tradition is the other—that he writes deeply about Holocaust survi-vors and the necessity to "give." They are the very image of need. One must give the coat (or suit) off one's back, as Fidelman does to Susskind. Yet giving may be a compulsion amounting to a kind of life-destroying sickness, as it is to the fatally masochistic Rosen of "Take Pity." Gassner of "The German Refugee" could not give his love, his trust, and that too proves fatal. And Freeman of "The Lady of the Lake" is a personification of a respectability so constipated that he will not recognize his own historical vulnerabilities. For Malamud, the Holocaust proves to be an opportunity to redeem the nongiving self. Some take it and some do not. Either possibility comes with difficulties, but Malamud's preference is obvious.

"The German Refugee" is a rarity in Malamud for being a narrative concurrent with contemporary public events. What in Malamud is the exception in Bellow is the rule. Bellow's *oeuvre* is, by and large, *in history*, tales of private lives synchronous with public events. Bellow writes centrifugally, Malamud centripetally. In *The Bellarosa Connection* Bellow employs his typical procedure of starting with a real character or two in mind. Unlike Malamud, he generally does not know how his story will end; he is not nearly as dependent on plot. There is a gain in energy which may be offset by a loss in unity. Bellow is involved in a process of discovery—in this case self-discovery. Malamud is involved in a process of invention. (The categories overlap somewhat in any writer but remain valid). Bellow's method is expansive, Malamud's selective. In an exchange between them about *The Adventures of Augie March*, Malamud says that the freedom of the book made him realize how much he himself had "been so entirely conditioned by the constructivist approach" (*SBJ* 8). Bellow's response is that his novel "declared against what you call the constructivist approach. A novel, like a letter, should be loose, cover much ground, run swiftly, take the risk of mortality and decay" (9). He might as well have been speaking about his holocaust novella. That Malamud's short stories are his highest achievement is an indication of how deeply connected to the constructivist approach Malamud is. Malamud has said of Bellow, "I can never write as he does. His books are idea-centered, mine are people centered," (*Conversations* 70) a weak judgment on so prominent a novelist of character. Bellow has said "the main reason for rewriting . . . is to discover the inner truth of your characters" (*Enck* 157). That his narrators may be capable of deep reflection does not diminish their stature as human beings. In *The Bellarosa Connection* Bellow discovers the inner truth of his surrogate. This truth uncovers his true connection to Jewish history.

The Bellarosa Connection presents the reader with a double narrative, that of Harry Fonstein, who flees Nazi Lemberg (Lvov), and that of the "I" narrator, who wrestles with the meaning of the event. Fonstein's father, a jeweler, did not survive the confiscation of his valuable property in the Vienna of 1938. Most of Fonstein's family were killed by the Germans. He himself is an American success story. After the war, he arrives in the United States from Cuba via Milan, where he did kitchen work, and Turin, where he was a hall porter and shined shoes. He eventually makes good in the heating business in New Jersey. All this despite his being hampered by an orthopedic boot. He lives, he thrives. In his refusal of victimization, in his resurrection as a forceful character, Fonstein's fate reminds us of a crippled Einhorn and Grandma Lausch of *Augie March*, characters notable for their self-overcoming.

Bellow's rendering of event is saturated in history. The narrator contemplates Fonstein's fate: "In Auschwitz he would have been gassed immediately, because of the orthopedic boot. Some Dr. Mengele would have pointed his swagger stick to the left, and Fonstein's boot might by now have been on view in the camps exhibition hall—they have a hill of cripple boots there, and a hill of crutches and of back-braces and of human hair and one of eyeglasses" (4). The conflation of the particular and the historic is almost breathless for Bellow in this case, a writer not used to backing up his coordinating conjunctions as if he were an incredulous child. The Roman Jews, the narrator reports, "were being trucked to caves outside the city and shot" (9) in the Adreatine Caves, the same mentioned in "The Last Mohican," an allusion not picked up by Fidelman in his ignorance.

Historical particularity consistently animates the prose. The narrator's parental retirement home in Lakewood is "near Lakehurst, where in the thirties the Graf Zeppelin had gone up in flames" (5). In Poland, the "Nazi paratroopers dressed as nuns spilling from planes" (6). Bellow reaches his apogee in the description of Billy Rose, the show biz entrepreneur who is Fonstein's skittish savior. The narrator can hardly believe it: "Billy Rose? You mean Damon Runyon's pal, the guy who married Fanny Brice?" (9). Yes, Billy was running an Italian underground operation in Rome to free Jews. "The late Billy, the business partner of Prohibition hoodlums, the sidekick of Arnold Rothstein; multimillionaire Billy, the protégé of Bernard Baruch, the young shorthand prodigy whom Woodrow Wilson, mad for shorthand, invited to the White House for a discussion of Pitman and Gregg; Billy the producer, the consort of Eleanor Holm, the mermaid queen of New York's World's Fair; Billy the collector of Matisse, Seurat, and so forth . . . nationally syndicated Billy, the gossip columnist. A Village pal of mine was a member of his ghostwriting team" (12). Bellow is the master of the portrait that is at the same time an epitome of social history. When the narrator adds, "I assume that Mafia people from Brooklyn had put together Billy's Italian operation. After the war, Sicilian gangsters were decorated by the British for their work in the Resistance," we have the typical Bellovian juxtaposition of respectability to crime. This too is part of social history. We see, then, that where Malamud tends toward fable, Bellow tends toward realism in the nineteenth century sense; the novelist presents society as its own historian.

Billy Rose is a beautifully rendered character partly because he is given in full ambiguity. He saves Fonstein but does not want to acknowledge him or any saved refugee personally. He wants no emotional scenes. The narrator seems to make a balanced judgment of him. Sorella, Fonstein's wife, is Billy's nemesis and accuser.

The narrator points out that Billy's benign and successful scheme "was Billy acting alone on a spurt of feeling for his

fellow Jews and squaring himself to outwit Hitler and Him-
mler and cheat them of their victims." He recognizes that "on
another day he'd set his heart on a baked potato, a hotdog,
a cruise around Manhattan on the Circle Line." He insists,
though, that "there were, however, spots of deep feeling in
flimsy Billy. The God of his father still mattered" (13). Proof
of this is that despite his "buglike tropism for publicity . . . his
rescue operation in Europe remained secret." So his turning
away from Fonstein at Sardi's in New York and, a few years
later, at the King David Hotel in Jerusalem, is something
that he feels needs no defense. Billy tells the pressuring, well-
dressed Sorella, "I did what I could . . . Now what do you
want from me—that I didn't receive your husband! What's
the matter? I see you did all right. Now you have to have
special recognition?" (54). Billy holds firm: "What I did, I
did. I have to keep down the number of relationships and
contacts" (56). The narrator, who is neutral, tells Sorella "I
can understand that."

Adding to Billy's stature as a giving Jew, it seems, is his
desire to donate a sculpture garden designed by Noguchi
consisting of many masterpieces he owns to the city of Jerusalem. Again, the narrator describes his motives favorably:
"His calculation in Jerusalem was to make a major gesture,
to enter Jewish history, attaining a level far above show business" (60). He tells Sorella, "You were asking too much. You
could not have gotten very far with him" (61).

Billy certainly has his personal weaknesses. He apparently
underpays and intimidates his workers. He has a shady and
depressing sex life. Yet even here Billy has a disillusioned
clairvoyance. When Sorella wants to tell him more about Fonstein's story, he says that he does not care for stories, adding,
"I don't care for my own story" (58–59). Luckily, Bellow does.
Not admirable but remarkable, Billy's character is probed
in the narrator's attempt to calm Sorella. First, the narrator

attempts to reduce it to show biz, but even Sorella rejects this as inadequate. Next comes a deeper explanation: "Maybe the most interesting thing about Billy is that he wouldn't meet with Harry. . . . He wasn't able to be the counter example in a case like Harry's. Couldn't begin to measure up" (65).

Sorella is a competent, intelligent woman, whose practical watchfulness is instrumental in Fonstein's business success. She is also a high-school teacher of French who understands the Nazi Ubuist style. She too overcomes obstacles, principally her own weight problem, and, after a lifelong drought, marries the club-footed Fonstein. She is insistent on Billy's personal recognition of Fonstein, but, seeing that he will not do it, gives it up. The moral of the story for her: "The Jews could survive everything that Europe threw at them. I mean the lucky remnant. But now comes the next test—America. Can they hold their ground, or will the U.S.A. be too much for them?" (65). The implication is that Billy's moral failure, as she sees it, derives in part from an American inability to comprehend the deepest suffering. It is this idea that has a lasting impact on the narrator.

So who is right, Billy or Sorella? The narrator is the deciding presence. He is a totally assimilated Jew complete with Main Line Philadelphia wife named Deirdre, an antebellum house with twenty-foot ceilings, eighteenth-century furniture selected by her, a closed garden, and an 1817 staircase photographed in *American Heritage*. How goodly are thy tents, O Jacob! Will success spoil Rock Hunter? "I force myself to remember," he says, "that I was not born in a Philadelphia house with twenty-foot ceilings but began life as the child of Russian Jews from New Jersey. A walking memory file like me can't trash his beginnings or distort his early history" (3). Still, he has to force himself. Like Billy, like almost all Americans, he has two identities. And the American identity is not, he says, "inclined to discuss Jewish history," but "damn it," after

Nazi Germany "you had to listen" (27–28). Yet the narrator's total assimilation leaves him squeamish from time to time about things Jewish. So he thinks of having the long lost Fonsteins "for Thanksgiving, for Xmas" rather than Passover because Passover "never comes to pass" (67)—a monumentally false judgment but in character. The conversation with the Jerusalem rabbi about Fonstein's impoverished relative is described as "a Jewish conversation" (67). And when the rabbi mentions the word *mitzvah* (moral obligation) his silent reaction is "Christ, spare me the mitzvahs" (69). Vaguely optimistic, scientifically oriented contemporary American that he is, he says, "I didn't want to think of the history and psychology of these abominations, death chambers and furnaces. Stars are nuclear furnaces too" (29). He is nonetheless absorbed in Fonstein's case and thinks that the holocaust refugee "saw me, probably, as an immature unstable Jewish American, humanly ignorant and loosely kind: in the history of civilization something new in the way of human types, perhaps not so bad as it looked at first" (7).

The novella is divided into two parts: the first full of wonderful character description and dramatic complication that culminates in the Billy/Sorella shootout; the second revolves around the narrator's nightmare. The narrator finds himself in a pit at night. He tries to get out but cannot. His legs are tangled in "ropes or roots," implying the context of part one. "What made the dream terrible," he tells us, "was my complete conviction of error . . . I had made a mistake, a lifelong mistake: something wrong, false now fully manifest" (87). His American innocence—"in the New World . . . you could not be put to death, as Jews there had been"—has been deeply shaken by darkest experience. "It wasn't death that scared me, it was disclosure," he thinks. "I wasn't what I thought I was. I really didn't understand merciless brutality" (88). It seems that the price one pays for being this benign entity, an American, is an inability to deal with radical evil. He has apparently read Whitman but not Melville. That the lamp in the room then suggests Abraham, Isaac, and the ram, brings him to a moment when Jewish belief was so intense that one would sacrifice everything for it. He relates for the first time to one of a number of "illuminated particles of Jewish history" (89). Having gone definitively from innocence to experience by virtue of his momentous dream, he can conclude, "I had discovered for how long I had shielded myself from unbearable imaginations—no, not imaginations, but recognitions—of murder, of relish in torture, of the ground bass of brutality, without which no human music ever is performed" (90). This may be more than he has actually discovered, since he seems to be confusing Nazi barbarism with the tragic sense of life.

The second part of the story, which includes the pivotal dream, takes place thirty years after the first part. The narrator makes the connection: Sorella's Douglas Fairbanks remarks were "meant for me . . . There was no way, therefore, in which I could grasp the real facts in the case of Fonstein. I hadn't understood *Fonstein v. Rose*, and I badly wanted to say this to Sorella. You pay a price for being a child of the New World" (89). But it seems to me that the two parts of the story remain somewhat disjunctive. After all, the narrator's modulated judgments of Billy are not wrong in that the first part was about a question of behavior, of style. Billy's heart is, in its idiosyncratic, even distorted way, in the right place. Not even Sorella wants a change of heart from Billy. He may not have a profound relationship to Jewish history and to Holocaust history in particular—or to anything else—but he does have a relationship. His actions are not mere vanity but even if they are they have a positive outcome. Billy's lack of personal sympathy does not preclude an *active* cultural sympathy, however spectacular, with his fellow Jews. It is different from the narrator's frozen-over *passivity*, a form of self-denying and meretricious respectability and exclusivity characteristic of the overassimilated Jew. True, Billy might well have shaken hands with Fonstein, spoken to Fonstein, even adored Fonstein, but how much does this have to do with the metaphysics of evil the narrator considers in part two?

It is possible to consider *The Bellarosa Connection* as an act of self-exorcism, with the narrator an extension of Bellow. "I came late to the Holocaust," he told his son Gregory (another psychiatric social worker) ("Talk" n.p.), adding that it was only after 1970 that he no longer objected to being called a Jewish writer. In any case, it was the Trotskyite and rather Jewish *Partisan Review*, with its view of World War II as an imperialist standoff, that delayed Bellow from seeing Hitler "for what he was. I was horrified by the position they—we— had taken" (*Conversations* 273). But it was not only *Partisan Review*. In another interview, he says that prior to writing *The Adventures of Augie March*: "Things got away from me. The Holocaust for one. I was really very incompletely informed. I may even have been partly sealed off from it because I had certainly met lots of people in Paris who had been through it. I understood what had happened. Somehow I couldn't tear myself away from American life" (276). (Could it be, in part at least, because America was key in decimating the Nazi colossus?). He later (in 1991) sees that in writing *Augie March* he "was still focused on the American portion of my life. Jewish criticism has been harsh on this score. People charged me with being an assimilationist in that book. They say I was still showing how the Jews might make it and that I saved my best colors to paint America. As if I were arguing that what happened in Europe happened because Europe was corrupt and faulty. Thus clearing the U.S.A. of all blame." The interviewer says, "For a Jew to say that is like saying to be a Jew is to be condemned." Bellow answers: "That's right. That's as much as to say the West has nothing to offer Jews."

Of course, Bellow knows that America and the West generally have much to offer—the freedom to write, for example. As for the Holocaust, it was not until Bellow "went to Auschwitz in 1959 that the Holocaust landed its full weight on me. I never considered it a duty to write about the fate of the Jews. I didn't need to make that my obligation. I felt no obligation except to write—what I was really moved to write. It is nevertheless quite extraordinary that I was so absorbed by my American life that I couldn't turn away from it. I wasn't ready to think about Jewish history . . . Not until *The Bellarosa Connection* (276–277). (Bellow is not forgetting *Mr. Sammler's Planet*, which precedes the novella by two decades. Sammler is Bellow's only character to have escaped from a mass grave during the Holocaust, the only one to have killed a Nazi. The novel, though, is mainly about a survivor's view of late sixties America.)

This work, then, is charged with great personal significance. The gap in Bellow's consciousness accounts for the thirty-year hiatus in the story, the guilt of omission for the narrator's nightmare. It is also the reason why the two parts of the story are somewhat discontinuous. Bellow's story reveals a literary love of Billy that works against a simple judgment of him. Bellow is harder on his narrator-surrogate. Truth comes in blows, says Bellow's Henderson, and the blow here takes the form of the nightmare, a welling up from the unconscious, like Fidelman's dream. The commercial specialist in memory neglected to remember one of the profound things. The novelist too, or Bellow in particular as he has said in a number of places, is a specialist in memory. *The Bellarosa Connection* transcends the commercial and scientific application to present memory (as it is in *Zakhor*) as the essence of Jewish being. This is why the narrator's generally successful Mnemosyne Institute fails in Tel Aviv. The narrator recalls the Jewish Yizkor service, where God is asked to remember a particular soul who is gone. This may give a religious dimension to what happens to the secular narrator of *The Bellarosa Connection.*

With the advent of postmodernism, the reputation of American Jewish writers generally has diminished. Their humanism is seen to be inadequate in the face of the absurdity that is us. Many, not buying into postmodern assumptions, still read them with intensity. Bellow's reputation among this part of the reading audience remains high among novelists and critics and a fairly broad reading public. There has been some recent discussion, though, as to why Malamud has "faded." Perhaps this essay can shed some light. Three of the four Malamud stories here are among his best. The Bellow selection is very fine Bellow. Malamud's characters are so intense that they transcend the charges of narrowness or parochialism brought against them. Their alienation is more real than the conformity which was a salient part of the fifties in which they were written. Yet the note of depression and loss misses something. Malamud is writing about failure in a time when America is moving toward "success." (Of course, success brings failures of its own and failure may be a form of redemption.). Bellow's great virtue as a writer lies in his ability to construct fictions to view this new fat America while Malamud remains devoted to pursuing his skinny Susskinds as avidly as Fidelman does. It is as if Malamud missed the boat, missed the great American Jewish turn to affluence for better or worse that Bellow's vibrant prose records so brilliantly. Too often Malamud sings in the *veynedich* (tearful) cantorial style. It is moving but somewhat outdated. Bellow moves on to the wider energetics of contemporary American harmonics, thriving in the dialectical air between assonance and dissonance. The *Bellarosa Connection* is a case in point. For Malamud the Holocaust evokes the tearful past. Bellow brings the Holocaust into the pleasure-ridden present.

Works Cited

Bellow, Gregory. Informal Talk on Saul Bellow, American Literature Association Conference on Jewish American and Holocaust Literature. Salt Lake City, Utah, 2008.

Bellow, Saul. *The Bellarosa Connection*. Hammondsworth: Penguin, 1989.

Cronin, Gloria L. and Ben Siegel, eds. *Conversations with Saul Bellow*. Jackson: University of Mississippi Press, 1994.

Enck, John J., int. *Wisconsin Studies in Contemporary Literature* 6, 1965.

Lascher, Lawrence M., ed. *Conversations with Bernard Malamud*. Jackson: University of Mississippi Press, 1991.

Malamud, Bernard. *The Magic Barrel*. New York: Farrar, Straus and Cudahy, 1958.

——. *Idiots First*. New York: Farrar, Straus, 1963.

——. *Talking Horse*. Ed. Alan Cheuse and Nicholas Delbanco. New York: Columbia University Press, 1996.

Salzberg, Joel, ed. "Malamud on Bellow, Bellow on Malamud: A Correspondence and Friendship". *Saul Bellow Journal* 14, 1996.

Smith, Janna Malamud. *My Father is a Book*. Boston: Houghton Mifflin, 2006.

Solotaroff, Robert. *Bernard Malamud: A Study of Short Fiction*. Boston: Twayne, 1989.

Yerushalmi, Yosef Hayim. *Zakhor: Jewish History and Jewish Memory*. Seattle: University of Washington Press, 1982.

Index